LANGUAGE AND STYLE SERIES

General Editor: STEPHEN ULLMANN

14

MEANING
AND STYLE

COLLECTED PAPERS

STEPHEN ULLMANN

BARNES & NOBLE
BOOKS
10 East 53d St., New York 10022
(a division of Harper & Row Publishers, Inc.)

Published in the U.S.A. 1973 by HARPER & ROW PUBLISHERS, INC. BARNES & NOBLE IMPORT DIVISION

ISBN: 06-497075-2

This volume incorporates the substance of the Sir D. Owen Evans Memorial Lectures delivered at the University College of Wales, Aberystwyth, during the Session 1971 to 1972.

Printed in Great Britain

TO MY WIFE

CONTENTS

PREFACE

In recent years there has been considerable activity both in the study of meaning and in that of style, and some promising new lines of enquiry have been opened up in both areas. The present volume is concerned with both disciplines as well as with their interrelations. It begins with a survey of current trends in semantics, paying particular attention to the definition of the word, the concept of meaning, relations between the form and meaning of words, ambiguity, and the structure of the vocabulary. Next, three crucial problems of stylistics are explored: its relations with semantics; the possibility of studying a writer's personality through his language; the existence of two approaches to style, one centred on linguistic devices, the other on the effects which these devices help to produce. The book then moves from the general to the particular and examines two aspects of Proust's attitude to language: the similes and metaphors which he evolved at an early stage in order to describe the workings of time and memory, and his absorbing interest in linguistic and stylistic problems, as reflected in part of his correspondence.

The survey of semantics, which is published for the first time, incorporates the substance of the three Sir D. Owen Evans Memorial Lectures which I delivered at the University College of Wales, Aberystwyth, in January 1972. I am very grateful to the Senate of the College, and in particular to the Principal, Sir Goronwy Daniel, and to my old friend, Professor E. R. Briggs, for inviting me to give these lectures. The remainder of the volume is based on articles printed during the last few years, all of which have been revised, brought up to date and integrated into the general structure of the book. Chapter VI amalgamates two articles published in *The French Language. Studies Presented to Lewis Charles Harmer*, edited by T. G. S. Combe and P. Rickard (London etc., Harrap and Co. Ltd., 1970), and *History and Structure of French. Essays in the Honour of Professor T. B. W. Reid* (Oxford, Blackwell, 1972). The other chapters are based on articles which appeared in the following volumes:

Chapter II: *Literary Style: A Symposium*, edited by Seymour Chatman (London and New York, Oxford University Press, 1971), © 1971, Oxford University Press.

Chapter III: *New Attitudes to Style*, in *A Review of English Literature*, edited by A. Norman Jeffares, vol. VI, no. 2 (London, Longmans, Green and Co. Ltd., 1965).

Chapter IV: *Patterns of Literary Style*, edited by Joseph Strelka (*Yearbook of Comparative Criticism*, vol. III; University Park, Pennsylvania, and London, The Pennsylvania State University Press, 1971).

Chapter V: *Currents of Thought in French Literature. Essays in Memory of G. T. Clapton* (Oxford, Blackwell, 1965).

My sincere thanks are due to the editors of the above publications, to the editorial secretary of the Clapton Memorial Volume (Professor J. C. Ireson), and to my fellow-editors of the Reid Festschrift, for authorizing me to use this material.

Trinity College,
Oxford, 1973   STEPHEN ULLMANN

CHAPTER I

SOME RECENT DEVELOPMENTS IN SEMANTICS

'When all things began, the Word already was. The Word dwelt with God, and what God was, the Word was.' This famous passage which opens the Gospel according to Saint John, and which is quoted here from the New English Bible, marks the culminating point in the cult of the word; it is indeed tantamount to an apotheosis of this linguistic unit. From this point of view it is immaterial that the Greek term λόγος, translated as *verbum* in the Vulgate, was ambiguous: it could mean either 'the word or that by which the inward thought is expressed, Latin *oratio*', or 'the inward thought itself, Latin *ratio*'.[1] When Goethe's Faust tried to translate the Gospel into German, he was disturbed by this ambiguity and reluctant to 'rate the word so high': he experimented with some alternatives: 'sense', 'force', and eventually opted for 'deed'.[2] Characteristically, Victor Hugo had no such qualms when he proclaimed: 'Car le mot, c'est le Verbe, et le Verbe, c'est Dieu.'[3]

The influence of words on human behaviour was already fully realized in Classical Antiquity. Speaking of the lowering of moral

---

[1] See Liddell and Scott, *s.v.* λόγος. Cf. my book, *Language and Style*, Oxford, 1964, p. 236.

[2] Ibid., pp. 236f.

[3] 'For the name is the Word, and the Word is God'. For the context, see ibid., pp. 183f.

standards during the Peloponnesian War, Thucydides wrote, in a passage reminiscent of Orwell:

The ordinary acceptation of words in their relation to things was changed as men thought fit. Reckless audacity came to be regarded as courageous loyalty to party, prudent hesitation as specious cowardice, moderation as a cloak for unmanly weakness, and to be clever in everything was to do nought in anything (Book III, lxxxii),

This passage is echoed in Sallust's *War with Catiline* where Marcus Porcius Cato declares:

But in very truth we have long since lost the true names for things. It is precisely because squandering the goods of others is called generosity, and recklessness in wrong doing is called courage, that the republic is reduced to extremities (ch. lii).[1]

Belief in the power of words lies at the root of countless taboos and superstitions in the most diverse civilizations; to mention but one striking example, in mediaeval Hungarian some babies were given names like 'You are not', 'He is not alive', or 'Little Death', in order to divert the attention of evil spirits.[2]

In the rapid and highly selective survey which follows, an attempt will be made to show how the word and its meaning—or meanings—are viewed in modern linguistics. Two other problems will also be examined: relations between the form and the meaning of words, and relations between words within the general structure of the vocabulary. It will be noted that the survey will be confined to word-meanings; other, equally important areas of semantic study will have to be disregarded.

A. THE WORD AND ITS MEANING

Although modern man is extremely word-conscious, it is not easy to define the word as a linguistic unit. Various attempts have been

---

[1] Cf. H. Kronasser, *Handbuch der Semasiologie*, Heidelberg, 1952, pp. 70f.

[2] Z. Gombocz, *Jelentéstan* (Semantics), Pécs, 1926, p. 48.

made to arrive at definitions based on phonological, grammatical or semantic criteria.[1] Three approaches to the problem are particularly prominent in contemporary linguistics:

(1) According to a famous definition put forward by Leonard Bloomfield, a word is a 'minimum free form'.[2] In Bloomfield's terminology, 'free forms' are linguistic elements which occur as sentences, as opposed to 'bound forms' which are never used in this role. Bloomfield's formula thus means that the word is the smallest linguistic unit capable of standing by itself and acting as a complete utterance. This would account for one-word exclamations like 'Fire!', answers like 'Yes' or 'Definitely', and questions like 'Where?' or 'Sure?'. Such elliptical utterances are supplemented by the verbal context or the 'context of situation',[3] but occasionally a single word can be entirely isolated and yet convey some information, as it does in certain titles, headlines and advertisements. On the other hand, Bloomfield's definition has two weaknesses. Firstly, compounds seem to lie astride the border-line between words and phrases:[4] a compound like *washbasin* is a word but it is not a minimum free form since its two constituents, *wash* and *basin*, are themselves words and thus have the status of free forms. The other difficulty concerns certain minor parts of speech like conjunctions and articles which hardly ever stand on their own in ordinary speech.

[1] For details, see my books, *The Principles of Semantics*, 2nd ed., Oxford, 1963 impr. ch. 2, section 1, and *Semantics. An Introduction to the Science of Meaning*, Oxford, 1962, pp. 27ff. and ch. 2.

[2] L. Bloomfield, *Language*, New York, 1933, p. 178.

[3] On this concept see my *Semantics*, pp. 32 and 50f. On relations between meaning and context, see recently G. Nickel, 'Sprachlicher Kontext und Wortbedeutung im Englischen', *Germanisch-Romanische Monatsschrift*, xlvi (1965), pp. 84–96; J. Ellis, 'On Contextual Meaning', in the volume *In Memory of J. R. Firth*, London, 1966, pp. 79–95; A. Rudskoger, '*Plain.*' *A Study in Co-text and Context*, Stockholm 1970; G. Kjellmer, *Context and Meaning. A Study of Distributional and Semantic Relations in a Group of Middle English Words*, Gothenburg, 1971; T. Schippan, *Einführung in die Semasiologie*, Leipzig, 1972, pp. 96ff.

[4] Cf. Bloomfield, op. cit., p. 180.

(2) Another criterion is based on the internal cohesion of the word, on what a British linguist recently called its 'uninterrupt-ability'.[1] Thus it has often been suggested that one of the differences between so-called 'analytical' languages and 'synthetic', highly inflected ones, is that the former use 'prefixes' rather than endings to mark person and number in the verb: in the English phrase *you do*, the personal pronoun plays exactly the same role as the ending *-tis* in Latin *facitis*. The criterion of cohesion shows, however, that this is not so and that the English *you* is a word in its own right whereas the Latin *-tis* is a bound form: we can say: 'you *always* do', but not '[x]faci-*semper*-tis'. This criterion even confers word status on the article: 'a *naughty* boy', 'the *clever* girl'.

(3) A third criterion evolved by modern linguists in their attempts to define the word is that of 'positional mobility'.[2] Thus, to take the same example as before, the two elements in the English phrase *you do* can be inverted in interrogation: *do you?*, but no such possibility exists in Latin: *facitis* cannot be trans-formed into [x]*tis-faci?*

The elaboration of these and similar criteria[3] represents an important step forward since they are more objective and more precise than impressions based on meaning. The same is true of another fundamental problem connected with words: the distinc-tion between 'form-words' and 'full words' or between minor and major parts of speech. This distinction, which goes back to Aristotle and has reappeared under various names, was also founded on semantic arguments: nouns, verbs, adjectives, adverbs of manner, it was alleged, have a more independent meaning and convey more information than pronouns, conjunctions, articles,

---

[1] J. Lyons, *Introduction to Theoretical Linguistics*, Cambridge, 1968, pp. 202ff.

[2] Ibid., pp. 203f.

[3] See R. Harris, 'Words and Word Criteria in French', in *History and Structure of French. Essays in the Honour of Professor T. B. W. Reid*, Oxford, 1972, pp. 117–33, and J. Krámský, *The Word as a Linguistic Unit*, The Hague–Paris, 1969.

prepositions and other 'minor' parts of speech. Modern linguistics has tried to put the distinction on a more formal basis by identifying certain phonetic and grammatical features in which the two types of words differ from each other in a given language.[1] To mention but one of these, in English words starting with a *th-* followed by a vowel, the *th-* will be voiceless in full words (*thing, think, thick, thinly*) but voiced in form-words (*the, this, their, than*). Recent research has added another valuable criterion to the argument: that of the wider distinction between 'closed' and 'open sets'. To quote a recent text-book, 'a closed set of items is one of fixed, and usually small, membership: e.g. the set of personal pronouns, tenses, genders, etc. An open set is one of unrestricted, indeterminately large, membership; e.g. the class of nouns or verbs in a language. In terms of this distinction we can say that grammatical items belong to closed sets, and lexical items to open sets.'[2] The distinction is clearly applicable to that between major and minor parts of speech; it also shows that the latter belong to grammar and not to lexical semantics which is the subject of the present chapter.

The other fundamental term of word-semantics, *meaning*, is even more ambiguous and more difficult to define. Half a century ago, Ogden and Richards devoted to this problem their famous book, *The Meaning of Meaning*, which H. G. Wells described, in *The Shape of Things to Come*, as 'one of the earliest attempts to improve the language mechanism'. Here they listed no less than sixteen definitions of the term—or twenty-three, if each subdivision is counted separately. Since then, the ambiguity has escalated; nevertheless, a pattern is clearly discernible in the maze of alternative approaches. Definitions of meaning seem to fall into two main types, and in recent decades there has been an interesting oscillation, a to-and-fro movement, between the two. The two types may be described as 'analytical' and 'operational': the former seeks to break down meaning into its components whereas the latter is less concerned with what meaning is than with how it actually works.

[1] Cf. my *Semantics*, pp. 44ff.   [2] Lyons, op. cit., p. 436.

(1) '*Analytical*' definitions of meaning are also known as 'referential' or 'denotational'. An early model of such an approach, which has been very influential in semantic research, is the 'basic triangle' devised by Ogden and Richards, in the book which has just been mentioned. A modified form of this model, replacing the somewhat cumbersome terminology by a set of simpler terms which I have used elsewhere, has the following shape:

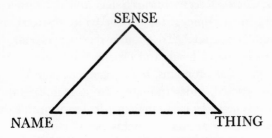

In this diagram, the *name* denotes the phonetic and graphic form of the word; the *sense* is the information conveyed by the name; the *thing* is the non-linguistic phenomenon to which the word refers.[1] Since the 'thing' is non-linguistic, it has no place in a purely linguistic analysis.[2] The linguist can confine his attention to one side of the triangle: the line connecting the name with the sense. Between the two terms, there exists a reciprocal and reversible relationship: the name calls up the sense and vice versa, the sense makes us think of the name. It is this reversible and

[1] Cf. my *Semantics*, pp. 55ff., and L. Rosiello, 'La Semantica: Note terminologiche ed epistemologiche', *Archivio Glottologico Italiano*, xlvii (1962), pp. 32–53. For a slightly different model, see now L. R. Palmer, *Descriptive and Comparative Linguistics. A Critical Introduction*, London, 1972, pp. 175f.

[2] Except when we are speaking about language itself or some aspect or element of it. On this problem, see J. Rey-Debove, *Étude linguistique et sémiotique des dictionnaires français contemporains*, The Hague–Paris, 1971, pp. 43ff. The author distinguishes between 'metalanguage' (statements about language) and 'metametalanguage' (statements about a metalanguage). 'The word *permissive* is fashionable' would be an example of metalanguage, whereas metametalanguage could be illustrated by the statement: 'a *monosyllable* is a word with one syllable' (ibid., pp. 50f.).

reciprocal relationship between name and sense—or between *signifiant* and *signifié*, in Saussure's terminology—that I have called elsewhere the *meaning* of the word.

The heel of Achilles of the analysis of meaning just outlined is what we have called the 'sense'. There is an obvious need to distinguish between the sense and the 'referent', the extra-linguistic phenomenon to which the word refers. Our words—except proper names—stand for classes, not individual items; as Bloomfield put it, 'we must discriminate between *non-distinctive* features of the situation, such as the size, shape, colour, and so on of any one particular apple, and the *distinctive*, or *linguistic meaning* (the *semantic* features) which are common to all the situations that call forth the utterance of the linguistic form.'[1] It is precisely these distinctive features which make up the sense, the information communicated by the name. The trouble is that the sense thus conceived is an abstract, intangible mental entity, accessible only through introspection. As a critic of the theory has pointed out, 'an empirical science cannot be content to rely on a procedure of people looking into their minds, each into his own'.[2] Various attempts have been made to get round this difficulty, including a recent experiment to 'measure' meaning, or more precisely to quantify people's reactions to the emotive overtones of certain concepts. Another way out is Bloomfield's suggestion that the meaning of a linguistic form is 'the situation in which the speaker utters it and the response which it calls forth in the hearer'.[3] I have discussed these alternative solutions in an earlier book.[4]

A less serious objection to analytical theories of meaning is that the duality of name and sense, *signifiant* and *signifié*, imports into linguistics a kind of 'psycho-physical parallelism',[5] the metaphysics of body and soul. However, to describe the name as the 'body' of the word and the sense as its 'soul' is obviously a mere

[1] Op. cit., p. 141.

[2] W. Haas, 'On Defining Linguistic Units', *Transactions of the Philological Society*, 1954, pp. 54–84: p. 74.

[3] Op. cit., p. 139.   [4] *Semantics*, pp. 58ff. and 68ff.

[5] Cf. Haas, loc. cit., p. 71.

figure of speech; nor is it a particularly appropriate metaphor, as Saussure had already pointed out.[1] The duality in question is of quite another kind: it is based on the difference between a sign and what that sign refers to. The distinction between *signifiant* and *signifié* has proved extremely fruitful not only in the study of language but in the wider field of 'semiotics', the general theory of signs, linguistic as well as non-linguistic. In the words of a linguist not particularly sympathetic to analytical theories of meaning, 'what is wrong with traditional "conceptual" semantics is not the dualist principle itself, but its extension beyond the limits within which it is empirically applicable, and of course the unnecessary postulation of intermediate concepts'.[2]

(2) Because of these and other difficulties inherent in the analytical approach, there was at one time a strong reaction against this concept of meaning, and attempts were made to replace it by an *operational* theory. The roots of operational semantics go back to P. W. Bridgman's book, *The Logic of Modern Physics*,[3] but the most famous definition of this kind is found in Wittgenstein's *Philosophical Investigations*, published posthumously in 1953: 'For a *large* class of cases—though not for all—in which we employ the word "meaning" it can be defined thus: the meaning of a word is its use in the language.'[4] Other scholars have put the same idea in different terms; according to one formula, for example, 'the meaning of an expression is not an entity denoted by it, but a style of operation performed with it, not a nominee but a rôle'.[5]

This theory is undoubtedly attractive since it makes meaning amenable to observation and objective analysis. On the other

[1] F. de Saussure, *Cours de linguistique générale*, 4th ed., Paris, 1949, p. 145.

[2] J. Lyons, 'Firth's Theory of "Meaning"', *In Memory of J. R. Firth*, pp. 288–302: p. 293.   [3] New York, 1927, esp. p. 5.

[4] Oxford, 1953, p. 20. On Wittgenstein's semantic ideas, see T. De Mauro, *Introduzione alla semantica*, Bari, 1965.

[5] G. Ryle, 'The Theory of Meaning', in C. A. Mace (ed.), *British Philosophy in the Mid-Century*, London, 1957, pp. 239–64: p. 262. See also by the same author, 'Use, Usage and Meaning', in G. H. R. Parkinson (ed.), *The*

hand, the equating of meaning with use raises certain difficulties. It has been plausibly argued, for example, that 'the use of a word depends on many factors many of which have nothing to do with questions of meaning': it is part of the use, though not of the meaning, of the Latin verb *ūtor* 'employ' that it is a deponent and is accompanied by the ablative;[1] and there are also other weaknesses. It should also be pointed out that analytical and operational approaches to meaning are not incompatible with each other: they merely represent two successive phases in the same enquiry. A lexicographer, for instance, will start by collecting a number of representative contexts in which a particular word appears. When further collections of examples cease to yield any fresh information, the operational phase comes to an end and the analytical phase begins: he will extract from his contexts the meaning—or meanings—of the word. To quote Bertrand Russell: 'A word has a meaning, more or less vague; but the meaning is only to be discovered by observing its use; the use comes first, and the meaning is distilled out of it.'[2] The duality is but a special aspect of the more fundamental opposition between *langue* and *parole* or, in Chomskyite terms, between 'competence' and 'performance'.

An interesting development of the operational concept of meaning is the study of '*collocations*'. This was strongly emphasized by the late J. R. Firth and British linguists influenced by his ideas.[3]

Theory of Meaning, Oxford University Press, 1968, pp. 109–16. Different formulations of the operational theory will be found, for example, in N. E. Christensen, *On the Nature of Meanings. A Philosophical Analysis*, Copenhagen, 1961, and L. Antal, *Questions of Meaning*, The Hague, 1963.

[1] P. Ziff, *Semantic Analysis*, Ithaca, N.Y., 1960, p. 158. Cf. also L. J. Cohen, *The Diversity of Meaning*, London, 1962, pp. 53 and 123ff., and the articles by J. N. Findlay and W. P. Alston in the volume edited by Parkinson and referred to in the preceding note.

[2] Quoted from *Logic and Knowledge* in A. Schaff, *Introduction to Semantics*, English translation, Oxford etc., 1962, p. 255.

[3] See now T. F. Mitchell, 'Linguistic "Goings On": Collocations and Other Lexical Matters Arising on the Syntagmatic Record', *Archivum Linguisticum*, New Series, ii (1971), pp. 35–69.

A collocation has been defined as 'the habitual association of a word in a language with other particular words in sentences'.[1] Firth himself has given a very simple example of such associations: 'One of the meanings of *night* is its collocability with *dark*, and of *dark*, of course, collocation with *night*.'[2] Another linguist has analysed the meaning of *cat* in slightly different terms: 'substitutions for *cat*, in more comprehensive units such as *The — caught the mouse, I bought fish for my —*, etc., display its meaning; its privilege of occurring in those contexts, with a certain distribution of frequencies among the occurrences, *is* the linguistic meaning of *cat*'.[3] In recent years the collocations into which English words enter have been systematically explored in an ambitious research project, and a new terminology and methodology has been evolved to handle these problems.[4] Collocations, like other operational concepts, have the great advantage of precision and objectivity: as a text-book conceived on 'neo-Firthian' lines declares, 'the formal criterion of collocation is taken as crucial because it is more objective, accurate and susceptible to observation than the contextual criterion of referential or conceptual similarity'.[5] This is no doubt true, but it should not be forgotten that the use of a word and the collocations in which it appears are consequences and manifestations of its meaning, and that it is misleading to equate them with meaning itself—though it could of course be argued that these consequences and manifestations represent the most profitable avenue of approach to the elusive phenomenon of meaning.[6]

(3) During the last decade or so, a remarkable revolution has

[1] R. H. Robins, *General Linguistics. An Introductory Survey*, London, 1964, p. 67. Cf. M. Joos, 'Semology: A Linguistic Theory of Meaning', *Studies in Linguistics*, xiii (1958), pp. 53–70: pp. 62ff.

[2] Quoted by Robins, ibid., p. 68.   [3] Haas, loc. cit., p. 80.

[4] J. McH. Sinclair, 'Beginning the Study of Lexis', *In Memory of J. R. Firth*, pp. 410–30.

[5] M. A. K. Halliday, A. McIntosh, P. Strevens, *The Linguistic Sciences and Language Teaching*, London, 1964, p. 34.

[6] Cf. L. Antal, *Content, Meaning, and Understanding*, The Hague, 1964, p. 37, and H. E. Brekle, *Semantik*, Munich, 1972, p. 62.

taken place in semantics. One of the features of this revolution
was that the pendulum swung back from operational to analytical
concepts of meaning. In America, this was mainly due to the
advent of transformational-generative grammar which is strongly
mentalistic in orientation[1] and deeply interested in the semantic
side of language. European semantics has been less directly
affected by the generative movement, but even here a similar
change has been noticeable in approaches to meaning. What
these various tendencies have in common is an attempt to reduce
meaning to its smallest components. Hence the term *componential
analysis* which is sometimes applied to these theories. The new
analytical methods are a great deal more elaborate than the
traditional type, and it is symptomatic of the changed climate in
semantics that a group of European linguists has replaced the
Ogden-Richards triangle (see above, p. 6) by a more differentiated model: a trapeze connecting not three, but six different
elements of meaning in a certain order.[2] Since componential
analysis is of direct relevance to the structure of the vocabulary,
it will be discussed in the last section of this chapter. First, however, we shall have to consider investigations concerned with the
semantic structure of single words, and in particular with relations
between form and meaning.

B. FORM AND MEANING: THE SEMANTIC STRUCTURE OF INDIVIDUAL WORDS

In this area of semantic study, two crucial problems arise: relations between name and sense in 'simple semantic situations'
where only one *signifiant* and one *signifié* is involved, and the

[1] On this problem see J. J. Katz, 'Mentalism in Linguistics', *Language*,
xl (1964), pp. 124–37, and E. A. Esper, *Mentalism and Objectivism in
Linguistics*, New York, 1968. Cf. also N. Chomsky, *Language and Mind*,
New York, etc., 1968, especially pp. 24 and 81.

[2] See for example K. Heger, 'Les Bases méthodologiques de l'onomasiologie et du classement par concepts', *Travaux de Linguistique et de Littérature Publiés par le Centre de Philologie et de Littératures Romanes de
l'Université de Strasbourg*, iii, 1 (1965), pp. 7–32: p. 31; Id., 'Die Semantik
und die Dichotomie von *Langue* und *Parole*', *Zeitschrift für Romanische*

analysis of more complex structures where one name is connected with several senses.

I. SIMPLE SEMANTIC SITUATIONS: TRANSPARENT AND OPAQUE WORDS

Relations between name and sense are among the oldest and perennially recurring problems of linguistics and the philosophy of language. As readers of Plato's *Cratylus* will remember, Greek philosophers were already divided on this issue: some believed that there was a natural and intrinsic (φύσει) connexion between name and sense whereas others argued that the link was purely conventional (θέσει). The same division between 'naturalists' and 'conventionalists' reappears among writers and thinkers in modern times. Locke, Berkeley, Hegel and others regarded the connexion between form and meaning as a matter of convention; Locke, for example, asserted that words signify 'by a perfectly arbitrary imposition'.[1] Among writers, Rabelais and Shakespeare held similar views; everyone knows Juliet's words:

> What's in a name? That which we call a rose
> By any other name would smell as sweet.

The naturalist theory also had some distinguished representatives such as Herder and Humboldt,[2] and in his *Essay on Criticism* Pope gave this prescription for sound effects in poetry:

> 'Tis not enough no harshness gives offence,
> The sound must seem an echo to the sense.

Philologie, lxxxv (1969), pp. 144–215: p. 168; K. Baldinger, *Teoría semántica*, Madrid, 1970, Part II, section 2; H. Henne–H. E. Wiegand, 'Geometrische Modelle und das Problem der Bedeutung', *Zeitschrift für Dialektologie und Linguistik*, 1969/2, pp. 129–73: pp. 149ff.; G. Hilty, 'Bedeutung als Semstruktur', *Vox Romanica*, xxx (1971), pp. 242–63.

[1] See E. Coseriu, '*L'Arbitraire du signe*. Zur Spätgeschichte eines aristotelischen Begriffes', *Archiv für des Studium der neueren Sprachen und Literaturen*, cciv (1967), pp. 81–112: pp. 91ff.

[2] For Rabelais, cf. J. Vendryes, 'Sur la dénomination', *Bulletin de la Société de Linguistique de Paris*, xlviii (1952), pp. 1–13: p. 9. On Herder

Among the pioneers of modern linguistics, W. D. Whitney declared more than a century ago: 'Inner and essential connexion between idea and word . . . there is none, in any language upon earth.[1] This had a direct influence on Saussure who regarded 'l'arbitraire du signe' as one of the two fundamental characteristics of linguistic signs—the other one being the 'linear nature' of the *signifiant*.[2] The debate flared up again in 1939,[3] and in the course of the discussion which followed, the whole issue was clarified so that we can now see the various factors in their proper perspective. It is clear that all vocabularies have two kinds of words: some are 'motivated', transparent, others 'unmotivated', opaque. An example of the latter type would be the series: English *oak*, German *Eiche*, French *chêne*, Italian *quercia*, Spanish *roble*, Hungarian *tölgy*, where six totally different forms are used to denote the same object. As regards the transparent type, words may be motivated in three different ways: phonetically, morphologically and semantically.

(a) *Phonetic motivation (onomatopoeia).*—This form of motivation has two varieties. If the word denotes some sound or noise which is imitated by the phonetic structure of the name, we have 'primary onomatopoeia': *bump, clink, crack, hiss* (cf. 'the hiss of

and Humboldt, cf. I. Fónagy, 'Le Signe conventionnel motivé. Un débat millénaire', *La Linguistique*, vii (1971/2), pp. 55–80: p. 56.

[1] *Language and the Study of Language*, 1868, quoted by O. Jespersen, *Language: Its Nature, Development and Origin*, London, 1934 impr., p. 397, n. 1. Cf Coseriu, loc. cit. pp. 101 and 110. Saussure refers to Whitney in this connexion in op. cit., p. 110.

[3] See E. Benveniste, 'Nature du signe linguistique', *Acta Linguistica*, i (1939), pp. 23–9. On the whole debate, see R. Engler, 'Théorie et critique d'un principe saussurien: L'arbitraire du signe', *Cahiers Ferdinand de Saussure*, xix (1962), pp. 5–66 (supplement: ibid., xxi (1964), pp. 25–32). Among more recent contributions, see—in addition to the articles by Coseriu and Fónagy, mentioned in notes 1 and 2, p. 12 above—G. Gougenheim, 'Sur la motivation en linguistique', *Journal de Psychologie*, lxiv (1967), pp. 257–63; H.-M. Gauger, *Wort und Sprache. Sprachwissenschaftliche Grundfragen*, Tübingen, 1970, ch. 4; Id., *Durchsichtige Wörter. Zur Theorie der Wortbildung*, Heidelberg, 1971; T. De Mauro, *Senso e significato*, Bari, 1971, Part I, ch. 2. Cf. also A. Martinet. *La Linguistique synchronique*, Paris, 1968, ch. 1, section 3.

rustling wings' in *Paradise Lost*[1]), *thwack, zoom*. Elsewhere, the experience thus depicted will be, not an acoustic phenomenon but something belonging to a different sense such as touch or sight; it may even be an abstract action or quality. In this case we shall have 'secondary onomatopoeia', as for example in *snoop* or *sly* and various other words with initial *sn-* and *sl-*, or the famous 'symbolic value' of the vowel [i] where it evokes smallness or small things: *bit, tip, pip, little, wee, teeny-weeny*, French *petit*, Italian *piccolo*, etc.[2] Naturally, there are also examples which do not fit into the pattern: English *big*, as opposed to *small*, German *Riese* 'giant'. There is also some kind of correlation between certain vowels and visual impressions: when ten French schoolboys who did not know any English were told that there are two words, *gleam* and *gloom*, one referring to light and the other to darkness, and were asked which seemed more appropriate to light, they all gave the correct answer.[3]

Four further points may be made about phonetic motivation. Firstly, words motivated by primary onomatopoeia are likely to be broadly similar in different languages. An often quoted example is the name of the *cuckoo* not only in Germanic and Romance idioms but even in more distant ones: Greek κόκκυξ, Russian *kukushka*, Hungarian *kakuk*. On the other hand, the same basic pattern may be conventionalized in different ways, even in the case of obviously onomatopoeic formations: where we say *cock-a-doodle-doo*, the French say *cocorico*, the Spaniards *quiquiriquí*, the Dutch *kukeleku*, the Japanese *kokekokkoo*.[4]

Secondly, motivation, phonetic or otherwise, is a purely synchronic quality: a word may lose or acquire it in the course of its history. As Saussure already pointed out, French *pigeon* is unmotivated whereas the Vulgar Latin *pīpiōnem*, from which it is

---

[1] I, 768 (quoted by the *Shorter Oxford English Dictionary*, s.v. *hiss*).

[2] See in particular M. Chastaing, 'Le Symbolisme des voyelles. Significations des *i*', *Journal de Psychologie*, lv (1958), pp. 403–23 and 461–81. Cf. also Id. 'Nouvelles recherches sur le symbolisme des voyelles', ibid., lxi (1964), pp. 75–88.

[3] M. Chastaing, 'La Brillance des voyelles', *Archivum Linguisticum*, xiv (1962), pp. 1–13: p. 5. Cf. Fónagy, loc. cit., pp. 62f.   [4] Ibid., p. 61.

derived, was an onomatopoeic formation connected with *pīpīre* 'peep, pip, chirp'.[1]

Thirdly, while some onomatopoeic words are widely, or even universally, recognized as such, opinions will vary about others, and in some cases the reactions of certain speakers or writers may be purely subjective. How many people would agree with Keats's impressions about the onomatopoeic quality of the adjective *forlorn*:

> Charm'd magic casements, opening on the foam
> Of perilous seas, in faery lands *forlorn*.
> *Forlorn!* the very word is like a bell
> To toll me back from thee to my sole self.
> > *Ode to a Nightingale.*

There are even purely personal and fanciful idiosyncrasies such as the remark by the German poet Christian Morgenstern that all sea-gulls look as if their name was *Emma*.[2]

A fourth point to be noted concerning onomatopoeia is that it only exists where there is some sort of correspondence or harmony between name and sense. This becomes clear when one compares certain pairs of homonymous words: *peal* 'ringing of a bell' is onomatopoeic whereas *peel* 'strip' is not; similarly *ring* 'give out a resonant sound' and *ring* 'circle'. A slight modification in the sound pattern may so alter the meaning that all onomatopoeic overtones are destroyed; thus it has been pointed out that if Tennyson's line: 'And murmuring of innumerable bees' is changed to 'And murdering of innumerable beeves', the onomatopoeia is completely lost.[3]

(b) *Morphological motivation.*—Compounds like *handful, hotplate, yes-man* are motivated by their morphological structure:

---

[1] Op. cit., p. 102; cf. O. Bloch–W. v. Wartburg, *Dictionnaire étymologique de la langue française*, 5th ed., Paris, 1968, *s.v. pigeon*, and Lewis and Short, *s.v. pīpio*.

[2] Cf. P. Trost, 'Zur Theorie des Eigennamens', in *Omagiu lui Iorgu Iordan*, Bucharest, 1958, pp. 867–9: p. 869, n. 1.

[3] C. F. Hockett, *A Course in Modern Linguistics*, New York, 1958, pp. 298f.

if one knows their components one will understand their meaning even if one hears them for the first time. Derivatives like *re-decorate* and *dreamer* are motivated in the same way. The components themselves (*hand, full, dream,-er* etc.) may be opaque but this does not affect the transparency of their combinations.[1]

Morphological motivation is one of the great creative devices in language. Transformational-generative grammar has emphasized our ability to produce and to understand an infinite number of grammatically well-formed sentences. Although there are obvious differences,[2] derivation, composition and other types of word-formation enable us to accomplish something similar in the lexical sphere. It is thanks to this device that we are able to create and understand neologisms like *dam-buster, brinkmanship, mini-budget, trendy, pro-marketeer* and many others. Even more unorthodox coinages can be transparent and self-explanatory: portmanteau words like *stagflation*, back-formations like *enthuse*. Occasionally, however, the transparency of a compound may be deceptive: its meaning cannot be deduced from that of its constituents. Words like *bluebottle, lady-bird, nightmare* or *black-mail* are examples of such 'pseudo-motivation'. The same problem may arise in the sphere of derivation: a *supper* is not a man who sups, and although a *disclaimer* can mean 'one who disclaims' it can also signify 'disavowal'.

(c) *Semantic motivation.*—Some words are motivated semantically: they are based on a metaphor or some other transparent figure of speech. This is another highly important creative device whose significance in literary style will be considered in the next chapter. It underlies such everyday metaphors as *trigger off, spark off, chain-reaction*, to be on the same *wavelength*, to *over-heat* the economy, *think-tank*, and many more.

---

[1] On 'relative motivation' see Saussure, op. cit., pp. 180ff., and L. Zawadowski, 'The So-called Relative Motivation in Language', *Omagiu lui Iorgu Iordan*, pp. 927–37.

[2] See recently J. Rey-Debove, op. cit., pp. 65, 69, 120ff. On the creative aspects of morphological motivation, see now Gauger, *Durchsichtige Wörter*, ch. 5 and pp. 179f.

An interesting aspect of motivation, on which Saussure had already remarked,[1] is that languages may differ from each other, or even from an earlier stage in their own history, in the preference they show for opaque or transparent words. Morphological motivation provides particularly useful criteria for such contrastive studies. As Fichte had already emphasized in his *Speeches to the German Nation*, German is particularly fond of forming words from elements already in the language.[2] To take two often-quoted examples, it has *Handschuh*, 'hand'+'shoe', where English and French have the opaque, unanalysable terms *glove* and *gant*; similarly *Fingerhut*, 'finger'+'hat', as opposed to *thimble* and *dé*. It is interesting to note that *Handschuh* and *Fingerhut* have a double motivation: they are transparent compounds as well as picturesque metaphors. This makes them not only self-explanatory but also easy to remember.

In many other cases, German compounds or derivatives correspond to Greek, Latin or even Graeco-Latin formations in English and French. Where we say *agriculture*, whose motivation lies in Latin, not in English, German has *Landwirtschaft*, a compound of *Land* and of *Wirtschaft* 'economy'. The latter is itself a derivative made up of the word *Wirt* 'landlord' and of the suffix *-schaft* forming abstract nouns. An example of a Graeco-Latin formation in English and French whose German equivalent is a transparent compound is *television* (from Greek τῆλε 'far'+ Latin *vīsio*), which has been translated into German as *Fernsehen*, 'far'+'see'. The existence of a series of similar classical formations such as *telephone*, *telegraph*, *telescope*, etc. constitutes a kind of secondary motivation in English and French, but once again the ultimate explanation of these combinations will be found, not in the modern idioms but in Latin, Greek or both.[3]

Yet another facet of these tendencies is the existence of mixed

[1] Op. cit., pp. 183f.

[2] See M. Wandruszka, 'Etymologie und Philosophie', in *Etymologica. W. v. Wartburg zum 70 Geburtstag*, Tübingen, 1958, pp. 857–71: pp. 866f.

[3] Cf. A. Martinet, *A Functional View of Language*, Oxford, 1962, pp. 88f.

pairs in English and French. To form an adjective from *mouth*, English has recourse to the Latin terms *oral* and *verbal*; it is true that *mouthy* exists, but it means 'bombastic'. In German, the ordinary adjective associated with *Mund* 'mouth' is the regular derivative *mündlich*.

While there is thus an obvious affinity between French and English in matters of word-formation, examples are not lacking where English has a transparent derivative whereas French prefers a classical formation: *day, daily—jour, quotidien*;[1] *week, weekly—semaine, hebdomadaire*, etc.

These differences between languages may have far-reaching implications in several fields. The ease with which compounds and derivatives are formed in some idioms may be exploited for purposes of purism and linguistic chauvinism, the systematic avoidance of foreign words for political reasons. There are also pedagogical implications: a language where morphological motivation is widely used and where there exist many formal links between words will be taught by different methods than one whose vocabulary is more opaque. Even for the native speaker, the existence of many learned formations drawn from, or based on, Greek and Latin may create certain problems and give rise to what has been called a 'language bar':[2] such words will be far more intelligible to people who have had a classical education than to those who have not had the benefit of such a background.

II. COMPLEX SEMANTIC SITUATIONS: LEXICAL AMBIGUITY

Complex semantic situations, where two or more senses are connected with the same name, have two cardinal types: one word with several senses, and several words identical in form.

The situation where one and the same word has two or more different senses is known in linguistics as '*polysemy*'. There are innumerable examples of this condition: *order* 'sequence, dis-

---

[1] The transparent formation *journalier* also exists.
[2] V. Grove, *The Language Bar*, London, 1949.

position' and 'regulation, direction'; *letter* 'alphabetic character' and 'epistle', and thousands of similar cases.

The other situation, where several different words have the same form, is more complicated since there are three possibilities:

(a) The words in question may be pronounced alike but spelt differently ('*homophones*'): *pale—pail, plane—plain, peak—pique.*

(b) They may be spelt alike but pronounced differently ('*homographs*'): *tear, read.*

(c) They may be identical both in their spoken and their written forms ('*homonyms*'): *peer* 'look narrowly'—*peer* 'member of the nobility'; *rail* 'bar'—*rail* 'utter abusive language'.

In practice, it is customary to refer to both types (a) and (c) as 'homonyms'.

The crucial problem in this area of semantics is the boundary between polysemy and homonymy.[1] This boundary is often fluid, and lexicographers, for example, may hesitate whether to record two forms as one lexical item with two senses or as two separate words. Needless to say, historical considerations will be irrelevant to a purely descriptive dictionary: the fact that *port* 'harbour' and *port* 'a kind of wine' ultimately have the same etymology does not affect their status in present-day English where the

---

[1] On this problem see my *Language and Style*, pp. 32ff. To the references given there, the following may now be added: H. Frei, 'Désaccords', *Cahiers Ferdinand de Saussure*, xviii (1961), pp. 33–51: pp. 42ff.; K. Heger, 'Homographie, Homonymie und Polysemie', *Zeitschrift für Romanische Philologie*, lxxix (1963), pp. 471–91; E. Buyssens, *Linguistique historique*, Brussels, 1965, section 1; J. Klare, 'Zum Problem der Differenzierung von Homonymie und Polysemie', *Omagiu lui A. Rosetti*, Bucharest, 1965, pp. 445–50; O. Ducháček, *Précis de sémantique française*, Brno, 1967, pp. 69ff.; H. Koziol, *Grundzüge der englischen Semantik*, Vienna–Stuttgart, 1967, pp. 44ff.; B. Trnka, 'Words, Semantemes and Sememes', in *To Honor Roman Jakobson*, The Hague–Paris, 1967, pp. 2050–4; K. Baldinger, *Teoría semántica*, pp. 42f.; H. Geckeler, *Zur Wortfelddiskussion. Untersuchungen zur Gliederung des Wortfeldes 'alt–jung–neu' im heutigen Französisch*, Munich, 1971, pp. 124ff.; Rey-Debove, op. cit., pp. 122ff.; L. Zgusta, *Manual of Lexicography*, Prague–The Hague–Paris, 1971, pp. 85ff.

ordinary speaker would undoubtedly regard them as two homonymous words. The difficulty is that the distinction between polysemy
and homonymy is based on a semantic criterion: the existence of
a link between two or more senses in the contemporary language.
But this criterion is obviously imprecise and subjective; in Bloomfield's words, 'the degree of nearness of the meanings is not subject
to precise measurement'.[1] A glance at descriptive dictionaries will
show many inconsistencies and discrepancies in the treatment of
these border-line cases. A number of examples have been collected
in a recent book on the theory and practice of lexicography: it
shows, for instance, that two dictionaries of contemporary French
record *balle* as one lexical item with five different senses whereas
another dictionary treats them as five separate words, and there
are also intermediate solutions between these two extremes.[2]

To bring some order into this chaos, modern semantics and
lexicography have tried to establish some precise and objective
criteria for deciding the issue. Apart from incidental indications
derived from rhymes and repetition,[3] three main criteria have
been suggested:

(a) Where two or more identical names give rise to different
derivatives they should be regarded as belonging to separate
lexical items. To take again the example of the various *balle*-s in
French, *balle* 'ball' has the derivative *ballon* 'balloon', and *balle*
'bale, large parcel' is connected with *ballot* 'bundle, package',
which would seem to indicate that these two *balle*-s are two
separate words.[4]

(b) If two or more identical names enter into collocations with
totally different items, we have to do with homonymy, not
polysemy. Such an example would be the form *suit* in '*suit* in
law'—'to wear a *suit*'—'the highest card of one's longest *suit*.'[5]

(c) It has also been suggested that one may test the reactions of

---

[1] Op. cit., p. 436.   [2] Rey-Debove, op. cit., p. 125.
[3] Cf. my *Language and Style*, pp. 32f. See also P. Rickard, 'Semantic
Implications of Old French Identical Rhyme', *Neuphilologische Mitteilun-
gen*, lxvi (1965), pp. 355–401.   [4] Rey-Debove, op. cit., p. 130.
[5] Cf. ibid., pp. 131ff., and Sinclair, loc. cit., pp. 425f.

native speakers in order to find out whether they would regard an ambiguous form as one or more lexical items. An American linguist has argued that 'social science has workable techniques for studying subjective opinions, which could be applied to homonymy problems (if it is granted that they are a matter of speakers' opinions) as well as to political issues'.[1] This procedure would be somewhat similar to the experiment in 'measuring' meaning which was referred to in the first section of this chapter.

These criteria, though useful, do not by any means solve every problem, and they may even lead to contradictory results. Meanwhile, however, the two cardinal types, polysemy and homonymy, remain distinct in spite of the existence of border-line cases. Polysemy is not a defect of language but an essential feature of it. If we were unable to use the same word with different senses only one of which will normally fit into a particular context, we would need a vastly increased vocabulary. It would even seem that there is a correlation between the frequency of a word and the number of senses it possesses; one scholar has actually put forward a mathematical formula for this correlation, claiming that 'different meanings of a word will tend to be equal to the square root of its relative frequency (with the possible exception of the few dozen most frequent words)',[2] so that

$$m = F^{1/2}$$

Homonymy, on the other hand, is certainly not essential to the functioning of language: though it is harmless in most cases, it has no positive advantages except for purposes of punning and rhyming.

Both polysemy and homonymy can, under certain circumstances, give rise to conflicts due to ambiguity or to undesirable

[1] See Uriel Weinreich's review of my *Précis de sémantique française* in *Language*, xxxi (1955), pp. 537–43: pp. 541f. Cf. also his article, 'On the Semantic Structure of Language', in J. H. Greenberg (ed.), *Universals of Language*, 2nd ed., Cambridge, Mass., 1966, pp. 142–216: pp. 177ff.

[2] G. K. Zipf, 'The Meaning-Frequency Relationship of Words', *The Journal of General Psychology*, xxxiii (1945), pp. 251–6: p. 255. Cf. J. Whatmough, *Language. A Modern Synthesis*, London, 1956, p. 73.

associations. But here again there are significant differences. Contrary to what was believed at one time,[1] polysemy rarely leads to the disappearance of a word. A Swedish semanticist has investigated the history of 120 English adjectives affected by polysemy at some stage in their development and found that only three have been discarded altogether.[2] Usually it is sufficient to eliminate one or more of the conflicting senses. The adjective *vivacious*, for example, could once mean 'continuing to live; long-lived', as in this quotation from the seventeenth century which strikes the modern reader as distinctly odd: 'Hitherto the English Bishops had been *vivacious* almost to wonder.'[3] Undesirable associations due to polysemy can be avoided in the same way. *Undertaker*, for example, had at one time a number of meanings which gradually fell into disuse as the word became specialized in its present sense; it could mean, not only 'contractor' but 'publisher', 'dramatic producer or impresario', or 'one who undertakes the preparation of a literary work'. Hence the odd effect produced by Swift's sentence where the word is used in the last of these meanings: 'The *undertaker* himself will publish his proposals with all convenient speed.'[4]

'Homonymic clashes', which have been extensively investigated by linguistic geographers,[5] often require a more drastic solution:

[1] See J. Gilliéron, *Généalogie des mots qui désignent l'abeille*, Paris, 1918, p. 157.

[2] A. Rudskoger, '*Fair, Foul, Nice, Proper*': *A Contribution to the Study of Polysemy*, Stockholm, 1952, p. 439. Cf. also his book on *Plain*, mentioned on p. 3, n. 3. For a new approach to polysemy, see recently D. Bolinger, 'Semantic Overloading: A Restudy of the Verb *Remind*', *Language*, xlvii (1971), pp. 522–47.

[3] Quoted by the *Shorter Oxford English Dictionary;* cf. Rudskoger, '*Fair, Foul, Nice, Proper*', pp. 463ff.

[4] Quoted by the *Shorter Oxford English Dictionary*.

[5] See for example the discussion in W. v. Wartburg, *Problems and Methods in Linguistics*, English translation, Oxford, 1969, ch. 3, section 1. See also the controversy between the late J. Orr and W. Rothwell: J. Orr, 'On Homonymics' (first published in 1939, reprinted with notes in his *Words and Sounds in English and French*, Oxford, 1953, and again in his booklet, *Three Studies on Homonymics*, Edinburgh, 1962); W. Rothwell,

one of the two terms in conflict has to be sacrificed. Thus, the old word *near* 'kidney' has disappeared because of the possibility of confusion between *a near* and *an ear*. In some areas, the ambiguity was resolved in a different way: by dropping *ear* and using *lug* in its place.[1] A homonymic clash may also be due, as in the case of polysemy, to undesirable associations. It has been reported, for example, that a group of six players in an orchestra was called a *quintet* because *sextet* would have been too suggestive.[2]

Both polysemy and homonymy are the source of countless puns many of which are exploited for literary purposes; these will be discussed in the next chapter.

C. RELATIONS BETWEEN WORDS AND THE STRUCTURE OF THE VOCABULARY

According to a recent estimate, there are thirty-seven consonant and vowel phonemes in one variety of English, and a leading French linguist has stated that the French spoken by him has thirty-four phonemes.[3] Others may put the figures somewhat higher but the difference is not very substantial. The limited

---

'Homonymics and Medieval French', *Archivum Linguisticum*, xiv (1962), pp. 35–48; J. Orr, 'On Homonymics', ibid., xvii (1965), pp. 77–90; W. Rothwell, *'Rectus Vindicatus?'*, *History and Structure of French. Essays in the Honour of Professor T. B. W. Reid*, pp. 203–22. On a famous homonymic clash, that between *aimer* and *esmer<aestimare* in French, which was discussed in an article by Orr reprinted in *Words and Sounds* and *Three Studies on Homonymics*, see recently D. McMillan, 'Remarque sur *esmer-aimer*', *Travaux de Linguistique et de Littérature*, ix, 1 (1971), pp. 209–28. On a related problem see W. A. Coates, 'Near-homonymy as a Factor in Language Change', *Language*, xliv (1968), pp. 467–79.

[1] See E. R. Williams, *The Conflict of Homonyms in English*, Yale Studies in English, 100 (1944), pp 47ff.

[2] A. W. Read, 'The Lexicographer and General Semantics', *Papers from the Second American Congress on General Semantics*, Chicago, 1943, pp. 33–42: pp. 41f.

[3] See G. Price, *The French Language: Present and Past*, London, 1971, p. 26. The French linguist referred to is A. Martinet, *Elements of General Linguistics*, English translation, London, 1964, p. 29.

C

number of phonemes contrasts very sharply with the size of the vocabulary: the *Oxford English Dictionary* is said to include nearly 415,000 words.[1] A comparison between vocabulary and grammar would reveal a similar contrast: in grammar, as in phonology, we have to do with 'closed sets' of relatively small membership, as opposed to the 'open sets' and indeterminately large inventories found on the lexical plane (cf. above, p. 5). The situation has been aptly summed up in the following formula: 'we can think of grammar as few items in complex patterns, lexis as many items in simple patterns'.[2]

This contrast goes a long way to explain why the concept of language as a 'structure'—a highly integrated system of interdependent elements—has been much more readily applicable to phonology and grammar than to the lexical side of language. Nevertheless, 'structural semantics' has already obtained some interesting and promising results at three different levels: that of single words, that of conceptual spheres, and that of the vocabulary in its entirety.

I. SINGLE WORDS AND THEIR ASSOCIATIVE FIELDS

At the level of single words, the basic concept evolved by structural semantics is that of the 'associative field'. This was first developed by Saussure though it is one of his disciples who gave it its name.[3] The associative field of a word is a network of associations—formal, semantic or both—which surround it. To take a

---

[1] S. Potter, *Modern Linguistics*, London, 1957, p. 101.

[2] Halliday, McIntosh, Strevens, op. cit., p. 34. Cf. also Halliday's article, 'Lexis as a Linguistic Level', in *In Memory of J. R. Firth*, pp. 148–62. On the problem of lexical inventories see A. de Vincenz, 'Zur Frage der "begrenzten Inventare" in der Semantik', in *Orbis Scriptus. Festschrift für D. Tschiževskij*, Munich, 1966, pp. 865–93.

[3] See Saussure, op. cit., pp. 173ff., and Ch. Bally, 'L'Arbitraire du signe', *Le Français Moderne*, viii (1940), pp. 193–206: pp. 195f. On Saussure's analysis of the associative field of *enseignement* and subsequent discussions of this problem, see H. G. Schogt, 'Quatre fois *enseignement*', in *Linguistic Studies Presented to A. Martinet, II, Word*, xxiv (1968), pp. 433–45. Asso-

concrete example, the English verb *read* is at the focal point of three types of associations:

(1) Formal: *reed*; *red*.

(2) Semantic: *peruse*; *write*; *book*, *newspaper*, etc.

(3) Formal and semantic: *reader*, *readership*, *reading*, *readable*, *re-read*, etc.

Experiments have shown that type (1) is marginal in normal subjects but becomes more prominent under the influence of fatigue, headaches and influenza, and also in mentally retarded children.[1]

Although associative fields are unstable, variable and idiosyncratic mental structures, they have a common core which may influence the development of words. Many changes which traditional philology had interpreted, quite correctly, as cases of analogy, popular etymology or ordinary shifts in meaning, may find their ultimate explanation in this factor. To return to the associative field of the verb *read*, it enables us to explain the anomalous development of a French verb in the same area, *écrire* 'write'. This comes from the Latin *scrībere* which originally gave *escrivre* in French. Subsequently the verb lost its *v*, not because of any sound law reducing *-vre* to *-re* (cf. the closely similar *vivre*, *livre*, *suivre*, etc.), but under the influence of two verbs in the same associative field, *lire* 'read' and *dire* 'say'.[2]

Other cases are more complicated and may involve more than

ciative fields are discussed in my *Semantics*, pp. 238ff., and *Language and Style*, pp. 10ff. and 35ff.; see now also P. Guiraud, *Structures étymologiques du lexique français*, Paris, 1967; E. de Bustos Tovar, 'Anotaciones sobre el campo asociativo de la palabra', in *Problemas y principios del estructuralismo lingüístico*, Madrid, 1967, pp. 149–70; and my article, 'Où en sont les études de sémantique historique', in *Le Réel dans la littérature et dans la langue. Actes du X⁰ Congrès de la Fédération Internationale des Langues et Littératures Modernes*, Paris, 1967, pp. 105–22: pp. 108ff. On the whole problem of the part played by associations in language, see J. Deese, *The Structure of Associations in Language and Thought*, Baltimore, 1965.

[1] A. R. Luria–O. S. Vinogradova, 'An Objective Investigation of the Dynamics of Semantic Systems', *British Journal of Psychology*, L (1959), pp. 89–105.

[2] Cf. Bloch-Wartburg's dictionary, *s.v. écrire*.

one type of association and even more than one associative field. A classic example is the change from Latin *coxa* 'hip' to French *cuisse* 'thigh'. At first sight this looks like a perfectly straightforward process: the name of one part of the body is used to denote a neighbouring part. On closer inspection, however, it turns out to have been but one phase in a kind of chain-reaction which involved both formal and semantic associations, including a homonymic clash between Latin *fĕmur* 'thigh' and Vulgar Latin *fĕmus* (Classical Latin *fimus*) 'dung, excrement'.[1]

II. CONCEPTUAL SPHERES

In the linguistic study of conceptual spheres, the most fruitful notion elaborated by structural semantics is that of the '*lexical field*'. The field theory had its predecessors[2] but the concept itself was not clearly formulated till 1924, and the first major monograph based on it was Trier's work on intellectual terms in mediaeval German, which appeared in 1931.[3] A lexical field is a closely integrated sector of the vocabulary which corresponds to a

[1] For details, see my *Semantics*, p. 242.

[2] See recently E. Coseriu, 'Zur Vorgeschichte der strukturellen Semantik: Heyses Analyse des Wortfeldes "Schall"', in *To Honor Roman Jakobson*, pp. 489–98, and Geckeler, op. cit., pp. 86ff.

[3] J. Trier, *Der deutsche Wortschatz im Sinnbezirk des Verstandes. Die Geschichte eines sprachlichen Feldes. I: Von den Anfängen bis zum Beginn des 13.Jahrhunderts*, Heidelberg, 1931. On the field theory and in particular on the ideas of Trier and Weisgerber, see my *Principles of Semantics*, ch. 3, section 2; for later developments cf. my *Semantics*, ch. 9, section 2, and *Language and Style*, pp. 12ff., 58ff., 94f., 222ff. Among more recent works, the following may be mentioned: H. Gipper, *Bausteine zur Sprachinhaltsforschung*, Düsseldorf, 1963; N. C. W. Spence, 'The Basic Problems of Ethnolinguistics', *Archivum Linguisticum*, xvi (1964), pp. 145–56; J. D. Apresjan, 'Analyse distributionnelle des significations et champs sémantiques structurés', *Langages*, i (1966), pp. 44–74; R. A. Waldron, *Sense and Sense Development*, London, 1967, Part I, ch. 5; R. L. Miller, *The Linguistic Relativity Principle and Humboldtian Ethnolinguistics*, The Hague–Paris, 1968; L. Seiffert, *Wortfeldtheorie und Strukturalismus. Studien zum Sprachgebrauch Freidanks*, Stuttgart etc., 1968; Id., 'Neo-Humboldtian Semantics in Perspective: "Sprache und Gemeinschaft"', *Journal of Linguistics*, iv (1968), pp. 93–108; Baldinger, op. cit., pp. 101ff.; Geckeler,

particular sphere of experience. The elements of such a field delimit each other and derive their significance from their place within the system; to take a trivial example, the meaning of *captain* is defined by its position in the military hierarchy between *lieutenant* and *major*. Some fields are mere nomenclatures and therefore of limited interest; in others, however, the raw material of experience is analysed and classified in a unique manner. In this sense, some lexical fields may be said to embody a certain *Weltanschauung*, a particular way of looking at the world and organizing its elements. Nor are these fields merely the expression of a *Weltanschauung* and a scale of values, but they crystallize them, perpetuate them and pass them on to future generations, thus influencing their whole way of thinking. At this point there is a remarkable affinity between the field theory and the Sapir-Whorf hypothesis concerning the influence of language upon thought; as Whorf himself has said, 'we dissect nature along lines laid down by our native languages'.[1]

It will be convenient to distinguish between three kinds of lexical fields: concrete and continuous ones, concrete ones made up of discrete elements, and abstract ones. Each type will be briefly illustrated by one example on which a great deal of research has been done.

(a) *Concrete and continuous fields.*—A typical example of such a field is the system of colours. The spectrum is a continuous band

op. cit.; L. M. Vasiliev, 'Teorija semanticheskich polei', *Voprosy Jazykoznanija*, 1971/5, pp. 105–13. On the various types of linguistic 'fields' see O. Ducháček, 'Différents types de champs linguistiques et l'importance de leur exploration', in W. Th. Elwert (ed.), *Probleme der Semantik*, Wiesbaden, 1968, pp. 25–36; Id., *Précis de sémantique française*, pp. 30ff.; W. H. Veith, 'Zum Terminus *Feld* in der Linguistik', *Zeitschrift für Dialektologie und Linguistik*, 1971/3, pp. 347–55. Cf. also Y. Ikegami, 'Structural Semantics', *Linguistics*, xxxiii (1967), pp. 48–67. Since 1962, H. Gipper and H. Schwarz have been publishing, in instalments, a *Bibliographisches Handbuch zur Sprachinhaltsforschung*, Cologne–Opladen.

[1] J. B. Carroll (ed.), *Language, Thought, and Reality. Selected Writings of Benjamin Lee Whorf*, New York–London, 1956, pp. 212f. See recently H. Gipper, *Gibt es ein sprachliches Relativitätsprinzip? Untersuchungen zur Sapir–Whorf–Hypothese*, Frankfurt am Main, 1972.

which can be divided up in many different ways.[1] There are obvious discrepancies between the organization of this sphere in various languages. Thus, Latin had no single word for 'brown' or for 'grey'; French *brun* and *gris* are of Germanic origin. Russian, on the other hand, distinguishes between two kinds of 'blue': *sinij* 'dark blue' and *goluboj* 'azure, sky-blue'. The contrast is even more marked if we compare the names of some colours in English and Welsh:[2]

green	*gwyrdd*
blue	*glas*
grey	
brown	*llwyd*

The rôle of this particular lexical field in the organization of our sense-impressions is confirmed by the observations of neurologists. They found that aphasics suffering from colour amnesia reacted erratically to colour tests: when faced with a heap of skeins in many nuances of various colours, they had great difficulty in picking out similar ones. Having lost the linguistic categories which introduce some kind of order into the continuum of colours, they 'did not sort, but simply matched'.[3]

[1] Cf. John Lyons's comments on what he calls 'the semantic aniso-morphism of different languages' (*Introduction to Theoretical Linguistics*, p. 457) and in particular his remarks on colour terms (ibid., pp. 56ff. and 429ff.). On systems of colours very different from our own, see for example I. Meyerson (ed.), *Problèmes de la couleur*, Paris, 1957, and H. C. Conklin, 'Hanunóo Color Categories', *Southwestern Journal of Anthropology*, xi (1955), pp. 339–44.

[2] This example is taken from L. Hjelmslev, *Prolegomena to a Theory of Language*, English translation, revised ed., Madison, 1963, p. 53. I am grateful to my colleague, Professor I. Ll. Foster, Jesus Professor of Celtic in the University of Oxford, for explaining the Welsh system to me.

[3] K. Goldstein, *Language and Language Disturbances*, New York, 1948, pp. 255f. Cf. my *Language and Style*, pp. 208ff.

Research in this area has tended to concentrate on differences between languages in the structure of the same lexical field. Yet a book published in 1969 on *Basic Color Terms*[1] suggests that there are some constant features underlying this diversity. Experimental data from twenty languages and information about seventy-eight others have revealed, the authors claim, that there are eleven basic colour categories: white, black, red, green, yellow, blue, brown, purple, pink, orange and grey. The distribution of these basic colours shows some totally unexpected features. All languages have terms for white and black. Those with three terms also have one for red; those with four have either green or yellow; those with five have both of these; languages with six terms possess one for blue; those with seven terms one for brown; those with eight or more terms have a word for purple, pink, orange, grey or some combination of these.[2] Diagrammatically, there are thus two possible orders:[3]

$$\left.\begin{array}{l}\text{white}\\\text{black}\end{array}\right\} \rightarrow\text{red}\rightarrow\text{green}\rightarrow\text{yellow}\rightarrow\text{blue}\rightarrow\text{brown}\rightarrow \left\{\begin{array}{l}\text{purple}\\\text{pink}\\\text{grey}\\\text{orange}\end{array}\right.$$

and

$$\left.\begin{array}{l}\text{white}\\\text{black}\end{array}\right\} \rightarrow\text{red}\rightarrow\text{yellow}\rightarrow\text{green}\rightarrow\text{blue}\rightarrow\text{brown}\rightarrow \left\{\begin{array}{l}\text{purple}\\\text{pink}\\\text{orange}\\\text{grey}\end{array}\right.$$

(b) *Concrete fields with discrete elements.*—While the spectrum of colours is a continuum into which we can introduce a greater or lesser number of distinctions, another lexical field, the system

---

[1] B. Berlin–P. Kay, *Basic Color Terms. Their Universality and Evolution*, Berkeley–Los Angeles, 1969. See also some further data in the review of this book by W. R. Merrifield, *Journal of Linguistics*, vii (1971), pp. 259–68. Cf., however, some critical remarks by N. B. McNeill, 'Colour and Colour Terminology', ibid., viii (1972), pp. 21–33.

[2] Berlin–Kay, op. cit., pp. 2f.   [3] Ibid., p. 104.

of family relations, is totally different: it consists of elements
which are already separate in the non-linguistic world. Yet even
here language does not play the role of a simple inventory: kinship terms can be categorized in various ways and based on
different criteria.[1] American linguists and anthropologists have
investigated the great diversity of these terminologies in American
Indian languages. Even in Europe, there are surprising differences. Hungarian, for example, has a traditional distinction
between words for 'younger brother', 'elder brother', 'younger
sister' and 'elder sister'. Not until the nineteenth century was it
felt necessary to form two neologisms denoting 'brother' and
'sister' without specifying their age. Hungarian also has a global
term for 'sibling', *testvér*, literally 'body+blood': this time it is
the opposition between male and female which is neutralized.
Swedish has separate words for paternal and maternal grand-
father and grandmother: *farfar, morfar, farmor, mormor*. In
Latin, the two kinds of uncle and aunt were designated by different terms: *patruus* 'father's brother', *avunculus* 'mother's
brother', *amita* 'father's sister', *matertera* 'mother's sister'; only
the two middle terms have survived, in an extended sense, in
uncle and *aunt* (French *oncle—tante*).[2] In the same language,
nepos could mean 'grandson' and 'nephew', and *neptis* 'grand-
daughter' and 'niece'.

(c) *Abstract fields.*—In view of the vital importance of language
in the formation of abstract concepts, the role of such fields is
even more significant than that of their concrete counterparts.

[1] Cf. my *Semantics*, pp. 247f., and *Language and Style*, pp. 13f. See also
A. F. C. Wallace–J. Atkins, 'The Meaning of Kinship Terms', *American
Anthropologist*, lxii (1960), pp. 58–80; F. G. Lounsbury, 'The Structural
Analysis of Kinship Semantics', *Proceedings of the Ninth International
Congress of Linguists*, The Hague, 1964, pp. 1073–93; E. A. Hammel (ed.),
Formal Semantic Analysis, special number of *American Anthropologist*,
lxvii (1965); L. Irigaray–J. Dubois, 'Les Structures linguistiques de la
parenté et leurs perturbations dans les cas de démence et de schizophrénie',
Cahiers de Lexicologie, viii (1966), pp. 47–69.

[2] R. Harris, 'The Semantic Prehistory of the Romance Progeny of Latin
Avunculus–Amita', *Romance Notes*, vii (1965), pp. 95–100.

One sphere which has received particular attention is the terminology of intellectual qualities. This, it will be remembered, was the area in which Trier obtained his early successes. In the monograph already referred to and in subsequent studies, he and one of his disciples showed the 're-structuring' which this field underwent in German between 1200 and 1300. Around 1200, it was based on two main principles: feudalism and universality. Feudalism was responsible for a sharp distinction between courtly and non-courtly attainments whereas universality was reflected in the existence of a global term, *wîsheit*, denoting all aspects of human wisdom, theological as well as mundane. A hundred years later, German mystical vocabulary shows a totally different structure. The feudal criterion has ceased to be relevant; *wîsheit* has lost its universality and is now reserved for religious and mystical experiences, and the rest of the field has also been re-organized.[1]

More than thirty years after the appearance of Trier's mono-graph, John Lyons published a study on intellectual terminology in Plato;[2] the results of this enquiry were subsequently developed in the last two chapters of his *Introduction to Theoretical Linguistics*. Lyons's approach is based on his definition of the 'sense' of a word as 'its place in a system of relationships which it contracts with other words in the vocabulary'.[3] Consequently, he proposes to describe the semantic structure of 'lexical systems' 'in terms of the sense-relations holding between the lexical items'.[4] The sense-relations he explores are: synonymy; 'hyponymy' ('the "inclusion" of a more specific term in a more general term':[5] *tulip—flower, scarlet—red*); incompatibility (*red*

[1] For further details, see my *Semantics*, pp. 248f.

[2] *Structural Semantics. An Analysis of Part of the Vocabulary of Plato*, Oxford, 1963.

[3] *Introduction to Theoretical Linguistics*, p. 427.   [4] Ibid., p. 429.

[5] Ibid., p. 453. There are some affinities between this scheme and the one put forward by F. R. Adrados in his article, 'Estructura del vocabulario y estructura de la lengua', *Problemas y principios del estructuralismo lingüístico*, pp. 193–229 (see also the same author's *Estudios de lingüística general*, Barcelona, 1969, ch. 2). Cf. also Schippan, op. cit., ch. 7, section 2.

—*green*); finally, antonymy (*big—small*) and other types of 'oppositeness' of meaning.

Yet another approach to lexical fields is more socio-linguistic in orientation: it seeks to analyse and interpret the vocabulary as an expression of the structure of society.[1] Two concepts with which this school operates are 'witness-words' and 'key-words'. The former are of particular importance in the hierarchical organization of socio-linguistic fields; thus, in French commercial life around 1830, *magasin* 'shop' and *négociant* 'merchant, trader' were typical witness-words.[2] 'Key-words' are terms which crystallize the ideals of a particular society: in the same period, *individualisme, organisation, bourgeois, artiste* and *prolétaire* held such a key position in the French vocabulary.[3]

In recent years, a wide variety of lexical fields have been investigated: aesthetic, moral and religious terms; those denoting hostile attitudes; the terminology of dwelling, cooking and domestic animals; verbs of motion; adjectives for 'old' and 'young', and other spheres.[4] This is certainly one of the most active and most promising areas of structural semantics, and of

[1] See esp. two books by G. Matoré: *Le Vocabulaire et la société sous Louis-Philippe*, Geneva–Lille, 1951, and *La Méthode en lexicologie. Domaine français*, Paris, 1953.

[2] On 'witness-words' ('mots-témoins'), see *La Méthode en lexicologie*, pp. 65ff.

[3] On 'key-words' ('mots-clés'), see ibid., pp. 67ff. For a recent application of Matoré's method, see G. S. Burgess, *Contribution à l'étude du vocabulaire pré-courtois*, Geneva, 1970. On key-words see also the series, *Europäische Schlüsselwörter*, Munich, 1963ff.

[4] To the works listed on p. 250 of my *Semantics*, the following may now be added: H. E. Brekle, *Semantische Analyse von Wertadjektiven als Determinanten persönlicher Substantive in William Caxtons Prologen und Epilogen*, Tübingen, 1963; H. Meschonnic, 'Essai sur le champ lexical du mot *idée*', *Cahiers de Lexicologie*, v (1964), pp. 57–68; G. Mounin, 'Essai sur la structuration du lexique de l'habitation', ibid., vi (1965), pp. 9–24; Id., 'Un Champ sémantique: la dénomination des animaux domestiques', *La Linguistique*, i (1965), pp. 31–54 (see now also his *Clefs pour la sémantique*, Paris, 1972); E. H. Bendix, *Componential Analysis of General Vocabulary: The Semantic Structure of a Set of Verbs in English, Hindi,*

semantics in general. The wise remarks made recently by a German semanticist ought to be heeded by those who engage in premature speculations about the structure of the vocabulary: 'Semantic analysis must . . . start with small, clear sub-systems, developing thereby the necessary basic concepts. Such islands might then be extended to larger complexes and more intricate problems.'[1]

III. THE VOCABULARY

The total structure of the vocabulary is an extremely complicated and elusive problem, and the methods which exist at present in this area are still tentative and rudimentary. Two approaches may be briefly noted: the classification of concepts and 'componential analysis'.

(a) *The classification of concepts.*—In his *Aspects of the Theory of Syntax*, Chomsky states that 'it is important to determine the universal, language-independent constraints on semantic features—in traditional terms, the system of possible concepts. . . It is surely our ignorance of the relevant psychological and physiological facts that makes possible the widely held belief that there is little or no a priori structure to the system of "attainable concepts".'[2] Roget's *Thesaurus* was an early experiment in this field, and authors of conceptual dictionaries need a broad framework for the classification of concepts. The problem was on the

and *Japanese*, Bloomington–The Hague, 1966; W. Kühlwein, *Die Verwendung der Feindseligkeitsbezeichnungen in der altenglischen Dichtersprache*, Neumünster, 1967; Id., *Modell einer operationellen lexikologischen Analyse: Altenglisch 'Blut'*, Heidelberg, 1968; R. Ostrá, *Le Champ conceptuel du travail dans les langues romanes. Domaines français, espagnol et roumain*, Brno, 1967; A. Lehrer, 'Semantic Cuisine', *Journal of Linguistics*, v (1969), pp. 39–55; Y. Ikegami, *The Semological Structure of the English Verbs of Motion. A Stratificational Approach*, Tokyo, 1970; Geckeler, op. cit.

[1] M. Bierwisch, 'Semantics', in J. Lyons (ed.), *New Horizons in Linguistics*, Harmondsworth, 1970, pp. 166–84: p. 184.

[2] N. Chomsky, *Aspects of the Theory of Syntax*, Cambridge, Mass., 1965, p. 160. See also recently his Russell Lectures, *Problems of Knowledge and Freedom*, London, 1972, p. 21.

agenda of the seventh international congress of linguistics, held in London in 1952. A general scheme put forward in the same year[1] classifies concepts under three headings, each with numerous subdivisions: 'the Universe', 'Man', and 'Man and the Universe'. This has already been applied to several French texts and non-French dialects, and whatever the merits of this particular scheme, there would be obvious advantages in using the same broad and flexible framework in a series of enquiries whose results could then be compared and any significant differences easily detected.

(b) *Componential analysis.*—This approach was briefly referred to at the end of the first section of this chapter (p. 11). It will be remembered that componential analysis represents a return to a referential-denotational concept of meaning; it differs, however, from earlier analytical theories in that it tries to break down meaning into its minimal components. A critic of one of these methods has actually characterized this approach as an 'atomization of meaning'.[2] There are several varieties, American and European, not all of which would be described by their practitioners as componential analysis.[3]

The best-known experiment in this kind of analysis is the theory of Katz and Fodor, which is designed to provide the semantic component of a transformational-generative grammar. This was first put forward in 1963 but has since undergone

---

[1] R. Hallig–W. v. Wartburg, *Begriffssystem als Grundlage für die Lexikographie. Versuch eines Ordnungsschemas*, Deutsche Akademie der Wissenschaften zu Berlin, 2nd ed., 1963. Cf. my *Semantics*, pp. 255f., and K. Heger, 'Les Bases méthodologiques de l'onomasiologie et du classement par concepts', pp. 15ff.

[2] D. Bolinger, 'The Atomization of Meaning', *Language*, xli (1965), pp. 555–73.

[3] Cf. T. Todorov, 'Recherches sémantiques', *Langages*, i (1966), pp. 5–43. For a general survey of these trends, see esp. G. Wotjak, *Untersuchungen zur Struktur der Bedeutung*, Berlin, 1971. Cf. also H. Yamaguchi, *Essays Towards English Semantics*, 2nd ed., Tokyo, 1969, pp. 466ff.; F. Hundsnurscher, *Neuere Methoden der Semantik*, 2nd ed., Tübingen, 1971, and Geckeler, op. cit., ch. 7. On componential analysis in general, see also Lyons, *Introduction to Theoretical Linguistics*, pp. 470ff.

several modifications.[1] The Katz-Fodor scheme has been so widely discussed that there is no need to give a detailed account of it here. Its essential feature is that it breaks down each sense of a word into a series of elementary components arranged in such a way that they progress, like a Porphyrian tree, from the general to the particular. If these components also occur elsewhere in the dictionary, they are called 'semantic markers'; if they are idiosyncratic, peculiar to a particular sense of one lexical item, they are termed 'distinguishers'. Not every sense has a distinguisher; if there is one, it always stands at the end of the series. No two senses of the same word will have identical components, so that the device may also help in the removal of ambiguities. There is also a third type of component: a 'syntactic marker' specifying the part of speech to which the word belongs. Two simple examples may illustrate the procedure. The meaning of *boy* may be analysed as involving the following components, the first of which is a syntactic marker while the rest are semantic markers: 'noun—animate—human—male—young'. *Girl* will have the same components, except that here we shall have 'female' instead of 'male'. Lexical entries also include 'selection restriction rules' showing the kind of items with which a word in a particular sense may combine: thus the adjective *honest*, in the old sense of 'chaste', would have the selection restriction 'female'.

The Katz-Fodor theory has several weaknesses.[2] To mention only one or two, the number and order of semantic markers is

---

[1] J. J. Katz–J. A. Fodor, 'The Structure of a Semantic Theory', *Language*, xxxix (1963), pp. 170–210 (reprinted in Fodor–Katz (eds.), *The Structure of Language: Readings in the Philosophy of Language*, Englewood Cliffs, N.J., 1964). See also J. J. Katz–P. M. Postal, *An Integrated Theory of Linguistic Descriptions*, Cambridge, Mass., 1964; Katz, *The Philosophy of Language*, New York, 1966; Id., 'Recent Issues in Semantic Theory', *Foundations of Language*, iii (1967), pp. 124–94; Id., *Semantic Theory*, New York, 1972.

[2] See especially the criticisms of D. Bolinger (in the article mentioned in n. 2, p. 34 above) and of U. Weinreich, 'Explorations in Semantic Theory', in T. A. Sebeok (ed.), *Current Trends in Linguistics*, vol. III, The Hague–Paris, 1966, pp. 395–477: pp. 397ff. (published as a separate book in 1972).

somewhat arbitrary; the presence or absence of distinguishers is unpredictable;[1] there is no provision in the theory for derived and metaphorical meanings;[2] no distinction is made between 'fortuitous homonymy and lexicologically interesting polysemy'.[3] Nor is it easy to see how this model of meaning can be reconciled with the theory of lexical fields. Chomsky himself has recognized this difficulty and has mentioned colour as an example of a 'field property that cannot be described naturally in terms of separate lexical entries, though it obviously plays a rôle in semantic interpretation'.[4] In spite of these and other limitations, the Katz-Fodor experiment has played a valuable part in the development of structural semantics. It was the first detailed and explicit semantic theory to be put forward in America for a long time; it focused attention on the semantic component of a transformational-generative grammar,[5] and gave rise to a lively and searching discussion of a number of fundamental problems.

[1] On the distinction between semantic markers and distinguishers, see Bolinger, loc. cit., pp. 558ff., and Weinreich, loc. cit., pp. 405f. The concept of distinguisher has varied in the course of the development of the theory; cf. Katz's formulation in Foundations of Language, iii, p. 159, and Semantic Theory, pp. 87f.

[2] On this problem see D. Bickerton, 'Prolegomena to a Linguistic Theory of Metaphor', Foundations of Language, v (1969), pp. 34–52, and R. J. Matthews, 'Concerning a "Linguistic Theory" of Metaphor', ibid., vii (1971), pp. 413–25.

[3] Weinreich, 'Explorations in Semantic Theory', p. 402. Cf. Bolinger, 'The Atomization of Meaning', p. 562; Hundsnurscher, op. cit., pp. 17ff.; J. D. McCawley, 'The Role of Semantics in a Grammar', in E. Bach–R. T. Harms (eds.), Universals in Linguistic Theory, New York etc., 1968, pp. 124–69: pp. 125ff.; Katz, Semantic Theory, pp. 68ff. This problem is connected with the lack of a clear-cut boundary between polysemy and homonymy, which was discussed above (pp. 19ff.).

[4] Aspects of the Theory of Syntax, p. 160. Cf. K. Baumgärtner, 'Die Struktur des Bedeutungsfeldes', in H. Moser (ed.), Satz und Wort im heutigen Deutsch, Düsseldorf, 1967, pp. 165–97, and Katz, Semantic Theory, pp. 346ff.

[5] There is no need to go here into this problem, and in particular into the controversy between 'interpretative' and 'generative' semantics. On these matters, see for example the discussion between Katz and McCawley

European semanticists, using very different methods, have also been trying to reduce meaning to minimal components or, as they call them, *'semes'*. A 'seme' is an elementary constituent of meaning comparable in function to distinctive features in phonology. Just as the phoneme /b/ in *bale* differs from the /p/ in *pale* in respect of voice, the meaning of *boy* differs from that of *girl* in respect of sex. The opposition between /b/ (voiced) and /p/ (voiceless) corresponds to that between *boy* (male) and *girl* (female): 'male' and 'female' are therefore 'semes'—in Katz-Fodor's terminology, semantic markers.[1] A French semanticist has given an illuminating example of the distinctive function of semes by analysing the meaning of four French words for various kinds of seats[2] (see table overleaf). It will be noted that no two words have exactly the same components. The first two semes, however, are shared by all four terms, and it so happens that

in *Foundations of Language*, 1970 and 1971 (cf. also Katz, *Semantic Theory*, pp. 384ff.); the contributions by Fillmore and McCawley to the volume *Universals in Linguistic Theory*, mentioned in n. 3, p. 36 above; those by Chomsky and G. Lakoff in D. D. Steinberg–L. A. Jakobovits (eds.), *Semantics. An Interdisciplinary Reader in Philosophy, Linguistics and Psychology*, Cambridge, 1971. On the whole issue see now Brekle, *Semantik*, pp. 116ff., and Chomsky, *Studies on Semantics in Generative Grammar*, The Hague–Paris, 1972.

[1] See A. J. Greimas, *Sémantique structurale*, Paris, 1966, p. 22. Cf. now also by the same author, *Du Sens. Essais sémiotiques*, Paris, 1970. On Greimas's semantic theory, see my review article in *Lingua*, xviii (1967), pp. 296–303; E. U. Grosse, 'Zur Neuorientierung der Semantik bei Greimas. Grundgedanken, Probleme und Vorschläge', *Zeitschrift für Romanische Philologie*, lxxxvii (1971), pp. 359–93; Wotjak, op. cit., pp. 144ff. On the analogy between phonological and semantic analysis, see ibid., pp. 67ff.; E. Coseriu, 'Pour une sémantique diachronique structurale', *Travaux de Linguistique et de Littérature*, ii, 1 (1964), pp. 139–86: pp. 150ff.; A. Neubert in *Zeichen und System der Sprache*, vol. III, Berlin, 1966, pp. 106–16.

[2] See B. Pottier, 'La Définition sémantique dans les dictionnaires', *Travaux de Linguistique et de Littérature*, iii, 1 (1965), pp. 33–9: p. 34 (cf. also Geckeler, op. cit., p. 428, on the meaning of *pouf*). On these and other recent European theories, cf. my article on 'Semantics' in vol. IX (Western Europe) of *Current Trends in Linguistics*, The Hague–Paris, 1972,

	to sit upon	with leg(s)	for one person	with a back	with arms
canapé 'sofa'	+	+	—	(+)	(+)
fauteuil 'arm-chair'	+	+	+	+	+
chaise 'chair'	+	+	+	+	—
tabouret 'stool'	+	+	+	—	—

there exists a word in French, *siège* 'seat', whose meaning consists of these two components and no others.

In the light of this highly selective survey of recent developments in semantics, it is possible to make some general remarks on the present state and the prospects of this discipline. Five impressions seem to stand out very clearly:

(1) Semantics was under a cloud in the post-Bloomfieldian era, but in recent years there has been a dramatic change in its status, and it has become one of the most important growing-points in linguistics. This applies not only to semantics in the wider sense but also to the study of word-meanings.

(2) Present-day semantics tends to lean too heavily towards theoretical speculations. A better balance between theory and practice is urgently needed, especially when claims are made about alleged universals of semantic structure.[1]

(3) Traditional semantics had a purely historical orientation. Modern semantics has gone to the other extreme and has become

pp. 375ff. To the references given there, the following may now be added: E. Coseriu, *Einführung in die strukturelle Betrachtung des Wortschatzes*, Tübingen, 1970, and K. Heger, *Monem, Wort und Satz*, Tübingen, 1971. See also above, p. 11, n. 2.

[1] Cf. Lyons's comments in his *Introduction to Theoretical Linguistics*, pp. 472f. On 'semantic universals', see U. Weinreich's article in J. H. Greenberg (ed.), *Universals of Language*, mentioned in n. 1, p. 21 above; my own contribution to the same volume has appeared in a modified form as chapter 5 of my *Language and Style*.

a predominantly descriptive science. Once again we need a healthier balance between two equally legitimate approaches.

(4) One of the most promising developments in recent years has been the establishment of close contacts between semantics and syntax.[1]

(5) Semantics stands at the focal point of many converging interests. Philosophers, psychologists, anthropologists, historians, students of literary style and many other scholars are all concerned with various aspects of meaning. In recent years, the advent of computers, machine translation, information theory and other developments have also made an impact on our field. It is this central position which makes semantics an eminently educative discipline.

[1] Cf. above, p. 36, n. 5, and my article in *Current Trends*, vol. IX, pp. 377f. See also on these problems S. Abraham–F. Kiefer, *A Theory of Structural Semantics*, The Hague–Paris, 1966; G. N. Leech, *Towards a Semantic Description of English*, London, 1969; W. L. Chafe, *Meaning and the Structure of Language*, Chicago, 1970.

CHAPTER II

STYLISTICS AND SEMANTICS

Opinions differ as to what constitutes the essence of style. Some would agree with Proust that style is to the writer what colour is to the painter: it is a matter not of technique but of a highly personal mode of vision.[1] Others would regard style as the product of conscious or unconscious choices, on the lines of a formula found in a well-known textbook: 'two utterances in the same language which convey approximately the same information, but which are different in their linguistic structure, can be said to differ in style'.[2] A third group would consider deviation from a 'contextually related norm' as fundamental to the concept of style;[3] some of these critics would merely note and interpret deviations whereas others would try to state them in statistical terms. A recent article on the subject suggests that a complex

[1] See below, ch. 6, p. 128, n. 3.

[2] C. F. Hockett, *A Course in Modern Linguistics*, p. 556. This idea is fully developed in B. Dupriez, *L'Étude des styles*, Paris, 1969. For a recent critique of this concept, see B. Gray, *Style. The Problem and its Solution*, The Hague, 1969, ch. 7. Cf. also L. T. Milic, 'Rhetorical Choice and Stylistic Option: The Conscious and Unconscious Poles', in S. Chatman (ed.), *Literary Style: A Symposium*, Oxford University Press, 1971, pp. 77–88.

[3] N. E. Enkvist, 'On Defining Style', in J. Spencer (ed.), *Linguistics and Style*, Oxford University Press, 1964, p. 28. Cf. also K. D. Uitti, *Linguistics and Literary Theory*, Englewood Cliffs, N.J., 1969, pp. 211ff.; M. Riffaterre, *Essais de stylistique structurale*, Paris, 1971, ch. 1; A. E. Darbyshire, *A Grammar of Style*, London, 1971, ch. 3.

factor which may be described as 'general purport' lies at the root of style.[1] Perhaps the most neutral of all definitions is the one which equates style with '*expressiveness*' as distinct from cognitive meaning. Valéry had already advocated a study of 'les inventions expressives et suggestives qui ont été faites pour accroître le pouvoir et la pénétration de la parole',[2] and a Latin American critic has tried to define this factor in purely negative terms, by arguing that 'stylistics is the study of what is extra-logical in language'.[3]

However different these various approaches may seem to be—and some are really complementary rather than mutually exclusive—they have one thing in common: they all assume the existence of some feature or features which are peculiar to style and distinguish it from language. It follows that stylistics is not a mere branch of linguistics but a parallel discipline which investigates the same phenomena from its own point of view. This would suggest a certain isomorphism between the two sciences: to each main division of linguistics there is likely to correspond a stylistic sector. If, for the sake of simplicity, one adopts the transformational-generative model which distinguishes between three components of grammar: phonology, semantics and syntax,[4] then stylistics will show the same three-level structure. In other models of linguistics, semantics will appear as a subdivision of the study of lexis; elsewhere, the two will be assigned to different levels.[5] Here we are not concerned with the place of

[1] S. Chatman, 'The Semantics of Style', *Social Science Information*, vi (1967), pp. 77–99.

[2] 'The expressive and suggestive devices which have been invented to enhance the power and penetration of speech' (*Introduction à la poétique*, pp. 12f., quoted in R. A. Sayce, *Style in French Prose*, Oxford, 1953, p. 7).

[3] R. Fernández Retamar, *Idea de la estilística*, Havana, 1958, p. 11.

[4] See, for example, Noam Chomsky, *Language and Mind*, pp. 49f., and *Studies on Semantics in Generative Grammar*, p. 12. This model has been challenged in recent years by the so-called 'generative semanticists'; cf. above, ch. 1, p. 36, n. 5.

[5] As in the stratificational model; cf. S. M. Lamb, *Outline of Stratificational Grammar*, Washington, D.C., 1966.

semantics in the general model, but with its internal structure within linguistics and stylistics. The main purpose of this chapter is to identify the 'expressive' values which certain semantic features may acquire: those elements which colour the cognitive meaning of a word, deepen its effect or strengthen its impact.

In the first chapter of this book, certain dominant tendencies in present-day semantics were discussed; these, as well as other features, will now be probed for their stylistic implications. We shall again have to distinguish between two sets of problems: those pertaining to the semantic structure of individual words and those connected with semantic relations between words.

A. THE SEMANTIC STRUCTURE OF INDIVIDUAL WORDS

The distinction between *signifiant* and *signifié*, 'name' and 'sense', which was mentioned in the last chapter, provides a convenient framework for the classification of semantic phenomena in this area. We shall distinguish once again between two kinds of semantic situations: simple ones, in which one name is connected with one sense, and complex ones, where one name is attached to several senses.

I. SIMPLE SEMANTIC SITUATIONS

In this field, semantic research has concentrated on three crucial factors each of which has significant stylistic corollaries: the 'motivation' of the name, the vagueness of the sense, and the overtones which may arise around either the name or the sense or both.

1. Motivation: Transparent and Opaque Words
As we have already seen (pp. 13ff), words can be 'motivated' in three different ways: phonetically, morphologically and semantically. Each of these processes can have powerful stylistic implications.

(a) *Phonetic motivation.*—Here there are, it will be remembered, two possibilities: the phonetic structure of a word may imitate some sound or noise ('primary onomatopoeia'), or it may evoke some non-acoustic experience ('secondary onomatopoeia'), as in the closing lines of Mallarmé's *Le Vierge, le vivace et le bel aujourd'hui* where the accumulation of [i] sounds, reinforced by the rhyme scheme of the whole sonnet, suggests whiteness, coldness, purity and other associations:

> *Il s'immobilise au songe froid de mépris*
> *Que vêt parmi l'exile inutile le Cygne.*[1]

Onomatopoeia, sound symbolism, phonaesthetic effects and kindred phenomena are part of the very fabric of poetry, and although a recent monograph[2] has uttered a salutary warning against auto-suggestion and fanciful speculations, this remains one of the most active areas of stylistic study.[3] It also forms the connecting link between two major divisions of stylistics: the phonological[4] and the semantic component.

(b) *Morphological motivation.*—The existence of morphologically transparent compounds and derivatives is stylistically relevant mainly because of the emotive (pejorative, facetious, etc.) connotations of some of these formations: these can best be handled in the section on overtones. It also happens that words which had become opaque are 'revitalized' by being placed in a suitable context which will restore their transparency and enhance their expressiveness, as in these lines by T. S. Eliot where the term *revision* is rejuvenated:

---

[1] 'It becomes motionless in the cold scornful dream in which the Swan wraps itself in useless exile.'

[2] P. Delbouille, *Poésie et sonorités*, Paris, 1961.

[3] Cf. my *Semantics*, p. 85, n. 3; see also more recently G. N. Leech, *A Linguistic Guide to English Poetry*, London, 1969, ch. 6, and P. Valesio, *Strutture dell'Allitterazione*, Bologna, 1967.

[4] On 'phonostylistics', see already N. S. Trubetzkoy, *Principes de phonologie*, French transl., Paris, 1949, pp. 16–29. Cf. now P.-R. Léon, *Essais de phonostylistique*, Montreal–Paris–Brussels, 1971.

And time yet for a hundred indecisions,
And for a hundred visions and *revisions*.[1]

(c) *Semantic motivation*.—All words based on a metaphor, metonymy or some allied figure are motivated by the similarity or other connexion which exists between the literal and the transferred meaning. This simple and trivial semantic fact has far-reaching consequences for style: it underlies *imagery* in all its countless manifestations. The supreme importance of imagery, and more particularly of metaphor and its explicit variety, simile, has been proclaimed by many writers and thinkers.[2] Aristotle had already declared: 'The greatest thing by far is to have a command of metaphor. This alone cannot be imparted by another; it is the mark of genius.'[3] Some extravagant claims have been put forward on behalf of imagery: Mallarmé has spoken of the 'absolute power' of metaphor; André Breton has compared certain images to an earthquake;[4] Proust, as will be seen in the last chapter, believed that 'metaphor alone can give a kind of eternity to style',[5] and Ezra Pound once stated that 'it is better to present

[1] *The Love Song of J. Alfred Prufrock*. Cf. M. Schlauch, *The Gift of Tongues* (subsequently renamed *The Gift of Language*), London, 1943, pp. 247f. See also J. do Prado Coelho, 'Sôbre a restituição da motivação lexical no português literário', in *Estudos Filológicos. Homenagem a Serafim da Silva Neto*, Rio de Janeiro, 1967, pp. 89–93.

[2] Cf. my books, *Style in the French Novel*, 2nd impr., Oxford, 1964, ch. 6, and *Language and Style*, ch. 9; see now also W. A. Shibles, *Metaphor: An Annotated Bibliography and History*, Whitewater, Wisconsin, 1971. On imagery, see recently D. Bouverot, 'Comparaison et métaphore', *Le Français Moderne*, xxxvii (1969), pp. 132–47, 224–38, 301–16; J. Dubois et al., *Rhétorique générale*, Paris, 1970, Part I, ch. 4; B. Dupriez, op. cit., pp. 50ff.; W. M. Frohock (ed.), *Image and Theme. Studies in Modern French Fiction*, Harvard University Press, 1969; P. N. Furbank, *Reflections on the Word 'Image'*, London, 1970; G. Genette, *Figures I–III*, Paris, 1966–72; A. Henry, *Métonymie et métaphore*, Paris, 1971.

[3] Cf. C. Day Lewis, *The Poetic Image*, London, 1947, p. 17.

[4] On the quotations from Mallarmé and Breton, see G. Antoine, 'Pour une méthode d'analyse stylistique des images', in *Langue et littérature. Actes du VIIIe Congrès de la Fédération Internationale des Langues et Littératures Modernes*, Paris, 1961, pp. 151–62: pp. 151f.

[5] See below, ch. 6, p. 144, n. 2.

one Image in a lifetime than to produce voluminous works'.[1] Even if one discounts some of the more inflated claims, there are at least three very good reasons for metaphor to be regarded as a factor of fundamental importance in style. Firstly, by combining two elements—a 'tenor' and a 'vehicle', a *comparé* and a *comparant*—metaphor (and simile) produce a kind of double vision in which both terms illuminate each other. In Dr Johnson's words, 'as to metaphorical expression, that is a great excellence in style, when it is used with propriety, for it gives you two ideas for one'.[2] A modern philosopher has expressed the same view in these terms: 'The fact that a sign can intend one thing without ceasing to intend another, that, indeed, the very condition of its being an *expressive* sign for the second is that it is also a sign for the first, is precisely what makes language an instrument of knowing.'[3]

Secondly, a really memorable image does not merely state an obvious similarity, but discovers a hidden analogy between two seemingly disparate phenomena; it works, as Wordsworth said,

> By observation of affinities
> In objects where no brotherhood exists
> To passive minds.[4]

Modern writers attach particular importance to this aspect of metaphor. In André Breton's view, for example, 'to compare two objects, as remote from one another in character as possible, or by any other method put them together in a sudden and striking fashion, this remains the highest task to which poetry can aspire.'[5]

---

[1] Quoted by C. Day Lewis, op. cit., p. 25.

[2] Quoted by I. A. Richards, *The Philosophy of Rhetoric*, Oxford University Press, 1936, p. 93.

[3] W. M. Urban, *Language and Reality*, London, 1939, pp. 112f. Cf. G. Genette, *Figures I*, pp. 216ff.

[4] Quoted by C. Day Lewis, op. cit., p. 36.

[5] 'Comparer deux objets aussi éloignés que possible l'un de l'autre, ou, par toute autre méthode, les mettre en présence d'une manière brusque et saisissante, demeure la tâche la plus haute à laquelle la poésie puisse prétendre' (*Les Vases communicants*, Paris, 1955 ed., p. 148). The English translation is by I. A. Richards, op. cit., p. 123.

A quotation from Baudelaire will illustrate the two points made by Breton, the remoteness of the two 'objects' from each other and the striking way in which they are juxtaposed. When Baudelaire writes in one of his 'Spleen' poems:

> Je suis un cimetière abhorré de la lune,
> Où comme des remords se traînent de longs vers
> Qui s'acharnent toujours sur mes morts les plus chers,[1]

the 'angle'[2] of the image, in the second line, is very wide; a comparison between two phenomena as different as remorse and gnawing and crawling worms is quite unusual but none the less convincing. The formal structure of the simile is equally unusual: rather than comparing an abstract tenor to a concrete vehicle ('remorse is like worms'), which is the normal procedure, Baudelaire inverts the two terms and assimilates a painfully concrete and repellent physical experience to an abstract mental process.

The third factor which explains the extraordinary importance of metaphor in style is the freedom of choice which exists in this area. The grammatical choices which a writer can make are as a rule severely limited: he can choose only between a very small number—sometimes no more than two—alternative expressions which are equally well formed and have roughly the same cognitive meaning. In the lexical field, we sometimes have more synonyms to choose from, but even here the scope for choice is very restricted. The only sphere where we can choose with virtually unlimited freedom is imagery, and in particular simile and metaphor: any tenor may be compared to any vehicle as long as there is the remotest resemblance or analogy between them. In fact, the writer may find this experience of absolute

---

[1] 'I am a graveyard abhorred by the Moon, in which long worms crawl like Remorses, always battening on those dead whom I hold most dear' (Francis Scarfe's translation in *Baudelaire*, The Penguin Poets, 1961, p. 175). For the French text, see Pléiade ed., p. 69.

[2] On this concept see R. A. Sayce, op. cit., pp. 62f. Cf. also H. Weinrich, 'Semantik der kühnen Metapher', *Deutsche Vierteljahrsschrift für Literaturwissenschaft und Geistesgeschichte*, xxxvii (1963), pp. 325–44.

freedom somewhat frightening; to quote again André Breton:
'Seule, l'image, en ce qu'elle a d'imprévu et de soudain, me donne
la mesure de la libération possible et cette libération est si complète
qu'elle m'effraye.'[1]

The semantic motivation of words can be restored in the same
way as their morphological transparency. Even where the original
image has been completely forgotten, an attempt can be made to
recreate it: thus Valéry re-establishes the link between the concrete meaning of Latin *scrupulus*, 'small sharp or pointed stone',
and the modern sense of *scruple* by inventing the collocation 'le
ruisseau scrupuleux'.[2] Elsewhere, a faded image is revitalized by
being placed in a suitable context. Thus Ionesco, like Camus
before him, remotivates the various transferred senses of the verb
exécuter when he makes a doctor say in one of his plays:
'*Exécuter*, Majesté, non pas assassiner. J'obéissais aux ordres.
J'étais un simple instrument, un *exécutant* plutôt qu'un *exécuteur*,
et je le faisais euthanasiquement.'[3] There is an obvious connexion
at this point between semantic motivation and ambiguity.

2. *Vagueness*

Vagueness in meaning is a condition due to a variety of factors:
the generic nature of our words which usually stand for class-
concepts and in which individual differences are inevitably
neglected; inconsistencies, looseness and contextual shifts in the
way we use language; absence of clear boundaries in the things

---

[1] 'The image alone gives me, by its unexpectedness and suddenness, a
full sense of potential liberation, and this liberation is so complete that it
frightens me' (quoted by G. Antoine, loc. cit., p. 151).

[2] 'The "scrupulous" brook' (quoted by M. Wandruszka, 'Etymologie
und Philosophie', loc. cit., p. 865). On revitalized metaphors see now
Henry, op. cit., pp. 143ff.

[3] '*Execute*, Your Majesty, not assassinate. I obeyed orders. I was a simple
instrument, an *executant* rather than an *executioner*, and I did it by
euthanasia' (*Le Roi se meurt*, quoted by Th. Buck, 'Ionesco et notre
réalité', in *Recueil commémoratif du X*^e *anniversaire de la Faculté de
Philosophie et Lettres* (Publications de l'Université Lovanium de Kinshasa,
22), Louvain–Paris, 1968, pp. 81–107: pp. 103f.).

we talk about; lack of familiarity with these things, and fumbling or muddled thinking in general.[1] Such vagueness will be a serious disadvantage in all situations where clarity and precision are essential and where concepts have to be sharply delimited. Even poets have denounced vagueness as one of the major shortcomings of language. T. S. Eliot has spoken of the 'intolerable wrestle with words and meanings', and more specifically of

> a raid on the inarticulate
> With shabby equipment always deteriorating
> In the general mess of imprecision of feeling,[2]

and Dylan Thomas has complained:

> Were vagueness enough and the sweet lies plenty,
> The hollow words could bear all suffering
> And cure me of ills.[3]

There are, however, many situations where vague, tentative or suggestive language is preferable to precise formulation. Wittgenstein has an interesting simile about what he calls 'concepts with blurred edges': 'Is a blurred concept a concept at all?—Is an indistinct photograph a picture of a person at all? Is it even always an advantage to replace an indistinct picture by a sharp one? Isn't the indistinct one often exactly what we need?'[4] Many poets would agree with Wittgenstein. Vagueness was in fact one of the basic principles of the Symbolist aesthetic. Verlaine embodied it in the programme outlined in his *Art poétique*:

> Il faut aussi que tu n'ailles point
> Choisir tes mots sans quelque méprise:
> Rien de plus cher que la chanson grise
> Où l'Indécis au Précis se joint.[5]

---

[1] Cf. my *Semantics*, pp. 116ff.

[2] *Four Quartets: East Coker*. This and the next quotation are taken from R. Quirk, *The Use of English*, London, 1962, pp. 231f.

[3] 'Out of the Sighs.'   [4] *Philosophical Investigations*, p. 34.

[5] 'It is also essential that you should not always choose the right word:

Mallarmé put the same idea in a lighter vein in the short poem, *Toute l'âme résumée*:

> Le sens trop précis rature
> Ta vague littérature.[1]

Gide has given a specific example of this attitude. Speaking of his early literary experiments, he writes:

J'affectionnais en ce temps les mots qui laissent à l'imagination pleine licence, tels qu'*incertain, infini, indicible* . . . Les mots de ce genre, qui abondent dans la langue allemande, lui donnaient à mes yeux un caractère particulièrement poétique. Je ne compris que beaucoup plus tard que le caractère propre de la langue française est de tendre à la précision.[2]

In this way, vagueness of meaning can become an important source of stylistic effects, of those 'inventions suggestives' of which Valéry spoke in a passage already quoted.

3. Overtones

It has often been suggested that there exists a fundamental distinction between two uses of language, one referential and cognitive, the other emotive. This dichotomy—the theory of the Great Divide, as it has been called—is clearly oversimplified and even misleading: as a recent critic has pointed out, '"emotive", or "affective", is being used as a catch-all term to refer to a number of quite distinct factors',[3] some of which have very little

nothing is more precious than the grey song where Vagueness and Precision meet.'

[1] 'Too precise a meaning will erase your vague literature.'

[2] 'At that time I was fond of words which give free scope to the imagination, such as *uncertain, infinite, unutterable*. . . Words of this kind, which abound in the German language, gave it in my view a particularly poetic character. I understood only much later that it is in the nature of French to tend towards precision' (*Si le grain ne meurt*, Paris, 1928 ed., p. 246).

[3] J. Lyons, *Introduction to Theoretical Linguistics*, p. 449.

to do with 'emotions' in the ordinary sense of the term. Some scholars have therefore devised a more delicate set of distinctions to handle these complex and elusive phenomena; one recent contribution would distinguish as many as nine different aspects of meaning.[1] From the semantic and stylistic point of view, it is preferable to discard the term 'emotive' altogether and to speak, more neutrally, of 'connotations' or 'overtones': some of these will be directly related to emotional attitudes whereas others will be merely 'expressive', in the broader sense defined at the beginning of this chapter. As far as meaning is concerned, such overtones would seem to fall into three groups: those generated by the name, those connected with the sense, and a third type which involves the word as a whole and depends on what is nowadays called 'register'.

(a) *Overtones connected with the name.*—Quite apart from the onomatopoeic values discussed in a previous section, the phonetic —acoustic as well as articulatory—structure of a word may give rise to pleasant or unpleasant aesthetic overtones. These are particularly noticeable in elements which are on the fringe of organized language: foreign words, neologisms, proper names. A passage in Boileau's *Art poétique* is significant in this respect:

> La Fable offre à l'esprit mille agrémens divers.
> Là tous les noms heureux semblent nés pour les vers,
> Ulysse, Agamemnon, Oreste, Idomenée,
> Helene, Menelas, Paris, Hector, Enée...
> D'un seul nom quelquefois le son dur ou bizarre
> Rend un Poëme entier, ou burlesque ou barbare.[2]

One is reminded of the famous line in *Phèdre*: 'La fille de Minos et de Pasiphaé', where mythological associations of fateful

[1] W. K. Frankena in chapters 5 and 6 of P. Henle (ed.), *Language, Thought, and Culture*, Ann Arbor, 1958.

[2] 'Mythology offers a thousand different pleasures to the mind. There all the happy names seem born for the verse, Ulysses, Agamemnon, Orestes, Idomeneus, Helen, Menelaus, Paris, Hector, Aeneas... Sometimes the hard or bizarre sound of a single name renders a whole poem ludicrous or barbarous.' (Pléiade ed., p. 174.)

heredity are reinforced by the purely aesthetic effect of the names. In ordinary words, where form and sense are indissolubly interlinked and automatically call up one another, such overtones are less common. An interesting example is the theory of sound values evolved by Dante in *De Vulgari Eloquentia*. Dante borrows images from textiles to explain his reactions to words: *amore* or *donna* are *pexa*, like 'fine velvet with its full but evenly and smoothly combed out pile'; *terra* is *hirsutum*, having 'the more abundant and less smoothly finished nap of a high-grade wool'; *corpo* is *reburrum*, 'suggesting the somewhat excessive shagginess of fustian'.[1]

(b) *Overtones connected with the sense.*—There is a whole gamut of these, ranging from particular to general effects. Some overtones are confined to one special context or situation. Others are fairly constant but limited to the language of a single person. As opposed to these idiosyncratic overtones, there are more general ones which arise around the fashionable slogans and key-words of a particular period: they are extremely widespread while they last but are usually short-lived. Terms like *confrontation, escalation, integration, apartheid, permissive, psychedelic* are enjoying such a vogue at the present time. Even more general are the permanent overtones which certain words acquire in a particular community, such as for example *rex* in ancient Rome: 'pulso Tarquinio nomen regis audire non poterat (populus Romanus)', says Cicero in *De Re Publica*.[2] Finally, there are terms whose actual meaning contains an element of evaluation: *gawky, grumpy, slouch, squawk, mawkish* and many others fall into this category. The fact that some at least of these words are also onomatopoeic adds to their expressive force.

Overtones of meaning can also result from certain processes of word-formation. Here belong such cases of 'emotive derivation'

[1] See A. Ewert, 'Dante's Theory of Diction', *MHRA, Annual Bulletin of the Modern Humanities Research Association*, no. 31 (1959), pp. 15–30: pp. 24f.

[2] 'After the expulsion of Tarquinius, (the Roman people) could not bear to hear the word *rex*' (quoted by Lewis and Short, *s.v. rex*).

as the Italian *poveretto*, *poverino* and *poveraccio*, where the diminutive or pejorative suffix modifies not only the denotation but the connotation of *povero* 'poor'. Portmanteau terms coined by such writers as Laforgue, Lewis Carroll or Joyce are also rich in expressive overtones, whereas some of Gerard Manley Hopkins's compounds ('lovely-dumb', 'feel-of-primrose hands'; 'fresh-firecoal chestnut-falls'[1]) are not only striking in their novelty and their unusual appearance but also achieve an extraordinary effect of density.

(c) *Overtones associated with particular registers.*—Words, like other linguistic elements, have the ability to evoke those registers to which they normally belong. Hence the term 'evocative value' which is sometimes employed to denote these overtones. A register has been defined as 'a variety of a language distinguished according to use',[2] and these registers have been classified according to three important criteria: field, mode and tenor of discourse.[3] 'Field' of discourse refers to 'the area of operation' of linguistic activity, and this criterion yields such registers as personal relations, politics, or the various technical languages. 'Mode' denotes the medium of linguistic activity, with spoken versus written language as the fundamental distinction. The 'tenor' of discourse is determined by relations among the participants. The basic dichotomy here is between 'colloquial' and 'polite' (or 'formal') language. It has been suggested that this criterion, rather than yielding distinct registers, 'is best treated as a cline', with such categories as 'casual', 'intimate' and 'deferential' appearing at various points. In addition to these three dimensions, evocative

---

[1] From the poems 'The Habit of Perfection' and 'Pied Beauty'.

[2] M. A. K. Halliday, A. McIntosh, P. Strevens, *The Linguistic Sciences and Language Teaching*, p. 87. On these problems, see also G. N. Leech, *A Linguistic Guide to English Poetry*, ch. 1, and D. Crystal–D. Davy, *Investigating English Style*, London, 1969.

[3] *The Linguistic Sciences and Language Teaching*, pp. 90ff., from where the definitions which follow are taken, distinguishes between 'field', 'mode' and 'style'. J. Spencer and M. J. Gregory, 'An Approach to the Study of Style' (*Linguistics and Style*, p. 87, n.1), suggest 'tenor' instead of 'style'.

overtones can also arise from differences in space (regional, dialectal, foreign elements), or in time (archaisms, neologisms), those between the speech of the two sexes, and various other factors. Local colour and a multiplicity of other stylistic effects can be derived from the existence of registers and the innumerable overtones associated with them.

Each language also possesses certain special devices for intensifying the overtones of words. While the resulting effect will be semantic, the devices themselves may be phonological, lexical or grammatical. A classic example of such a phonological device is the so-called 'emotive accent' in French, which tends to fall on the first syllable of words beginning with a consonant ('C'est 'formidable!')[1] and on the second syllable of those with an initial vowel ('Tu es in'tolérable!').[2] At the lexical level, we have such hyperbolical expressions as *awfully, terrific, tremendous* etc., whose cognitive meaning has been radically modified by emotive use. In grammar, word-order may help to strengthen semantic overtones: the anteposition of the adjective in French provides a very clear example. When Baudelaire wrote, in the opening lines of the sonnet *Correspondances*:

> La Nature est un temple où de *vivants* piliers
> Laissent parfois sortir de *confuses* paroles,[3]

he could have placed the two adjectives after their nouns: the sense would have been the same, but the overtones, the emphasis and emotive impact, would have been different.[4]

It will have been noticed that the whole division of semantics dealing with overtones of meaning lies astride the boundary between linguistics and stylistics and could be regarded as a kind of condominium of the two disciplines.

[1] 'Well, I never!'

[2] 'You are unbearable!'

[3] 'Nature is a temple, in which living pillars sometimes utter a babel of words' (Francis Scarfe's translation, op. cit., p. 36). For the French text, see the Pléiade ed., p. 11.

[4] On the place of the adjective in French, see below, p. 83.

II. COMPLEX SEMANTIC SITUATIONS

In complex semantic situations, where more than one sense is connected with the same name, the ambiguity which results is often exploited for stylistic purposes. As noted in the preceding chapter, these purely lexical ambiguities—as distinct from those due to grammatical factors—have two cardinal types: 'polysemy' (several senses of a single word) and 'homonymy' (several words identical in form). This distinction is fully applicable to stylistic uses of ambiguity, ranging from the humble—and often excruciating—efforts of the punster to the most sublime examples of Shakespearean word-play. Both types have two further subdivisions according to whether the ambiguity is implicit or explicit. Explicitness can be achieved in two ways: by repeating the same form with a different meaning, or by making some explanatory comment; in certain cases the two methods are combined. These criteria yield a system of six types of lexical ambiguity used as a device of style.

1. Polysemy

(a) *Implicit.*—The extreme form of implicitness is found in those cases where the title of a book is itself ambiguous. Since there is no immediate context or situation to help the reader, he may not even notice the pun until it begins to emerge from the text. Such a title is for instance that of Robbe-Grillet's novel, *La Jalousie*, where the word means both 'jealousy' and 'screen, Venetian blind'. A little less cryptic are those examples of double meaning which are clarified by the context or the situation in which they occur; but even here, the reader may not immediately grasp the full implications. A sinister pun of this type is found in the last act of Racine's *Bajazet* when Roxane says to her rival, speaking of the man they both love:

> Loin de vous séparer, je prétends aujourd'hui
> Par des *nœuds* éternels vous unir avec lui,[1]

[1] 'Far from separating you, I intend today to unite you to him with eternal *bonds*.'

a cruel play on the physical and metaphorical meaning of *nœuds*, 'knots' and 'bonds of marriage'.

(b) *Explicit:*

(i) *Repetition.*—In *Paradise Lost*, Book III, ll. 214–15, Milton uses the adjective *mortal* twice, first in the sense 'subject to death', then in the meaning 'deadly':

> Which of ye will be *mortal* to redeem
> Man's *mortal* crime, and just the unjust to save?

It may be noted that the same adjective had been used, in a slightly different sense, at the very beginning of the poem:

> Of man's first disobedience, and the fruit
> Of that forbidden tree, whose *mortal* taste
> Brought death into the world.

(ii) *Explanatory comment.*— A pun on the double meaning of the verb *to eat*, in the ordinary sense and in the expression *to eat one's words*, occurs in *Much Ado About Nothing*, act IV, scene 1, where Benedick gives a witty twist to a question by Beatrice:

> Beatrice: Will you not *eat* your word?
> Benedick: With no sauce that can be devised to it.

2. *Homonymy*

(a) *Implicit.*—A subtle critic has suggested that there is a homonymic pun in the title of Michel Butor's novel, *Passage de Milan*.[1] This is the name of an imaginary street in Paris, which one would naturally connect with the Italian city; it is, however, possible that *milan* in the sense of 'kite' is also relevant. The fact that the bird of prey is mentioned twice in the story lends colour to this interpretation, especially as one of these passages appears quite early in the book: 'Dans le haut de l'air, ailes déployées, si ce n'est un avion, c'est un *milan*.'[2] This will make the reader wonder,

---

[1] L. Spitzer, 'Quelques Aspects de la technique des romans de Michel Butor', *Archivum Linguisticum*, xiii–xiv (1961–62): xiv, p. 65, n.1.

[2] 'High up in the air, with its wings spread, if it is not a plane, it is a kite.'

E

even at this early stage, about the full meaning and symbolic implications of the title.

(b) *Explicit:*

(i) *Repetition.*—There is a pun on the two meanings of *hail* in *Love's Labour's Lost*, Act V, scene 2:

> King: All *hail*, sweet madam, and fair time of day!
> Princess: 'Fair' in 'all *hail*' is foul, as I conceive.

(ii) *Explanatory comment.*—In Hervé Bazin's novel, *Lève-toi et marche*, the narrator, an invalid girl who suffers from an incurable disease but whose intellectual vitality is unimpaired, plays on the two senses of *caillette*, 'young woman of easy virtue, flirt' and 'petrel', and adds a descriptive touch which does not merely explain the pun but develops it into an image: 'la téléphoniste, cette *caillette* à bec pourpre.'[1]

The homonyms mentioned so far were purely lexical: the two forms involved were identical in their ordinary phonetic structure. A different type of homonymy is also exploited by writers: that brought about by syntactic factors. An interesting example is found in *La Jalousie* where the self-effacing narrator, who tells the story without ever referring explicitly to himself, writes: 'Sa phrase se termine par "savoir *la prendre*" ou "savoir *l'apprendre*", sans qu'il soit possible de déterminer avec certitude de qui il s'agit, ou de quoi.'[2]

It is clear from this small selection of examples that semantic ambiguity is often more than a mere witticism: it can help to underline important ideas or implications, portray a character, or play its part in the general structure of the work.

---

[1] 'The telephone operator, this *caillette* with a purple beak.' It is interesting to note that *caillette*, 'frivolous person', came from the name of a sixteenth-century court jester and was originally a masculine noun; it became feminine under the influence of the ending and because it was regarded as a diminutive of *caille* 'quail' (Bloch–Wartburg).

[2] 'His sentence ends with "to know how to take it or her" or "to know how to learn it", and one cannot be sure whom or what it is about.'

B. SEMANTIC RELATIONS BETWEEN WORDS

As we saw in the first chapter, one of the most promising approaches to structural semantics at the present time is concerned with the relations—synonymy, incompatibility, subordination, antonymy, etc.—in which words may stand to each other. These relations can be further analysed in the light of the distinction between 'paradigmatic' and 'syntagmatic' connexions. According to a recent definition, a unit 'enters into *paradigmatic* relations with all the units which can also occur in the same context', and 'into *syntagmatic* relations with the other units of the same level with which it occurs and which constitute its context'.[1] As Saussure put it, syntagmatic relations work *in praesentia*, paradigmatic ones *in absentia*.[2]

I. PARADIGMATIC RELATIONS

A paradigmatic relation which is of crucial importance to stylistics is *synonymy*. Choice between synonyms—or quasi-synonyms—is often dictated by considerations which have nothing to do with cognitive meaning. Various attempts have been made to classify the criteria which determine these choices. A recent suggestion is that we should distinguish between 'complete' synonymy ('equivalence of both cognitive and emotive sense'), and 'total' synonymy (words 'interchangeable in all contexts'). There would thus be four possible combinations: '(1) complete and total; (2) complete, but not total; (3) incomplete, but total; (4) incomplete, and not total.'[3] A more delicate scheme put forward more than thirty years ago[4] comprises nine categories:

(1) One term is more general than another: *refuse—reject*.

[1] Lyons, *Introduction to Theoretical Linguistics*, p. 73.

[2] Op. cit., p. 171.

[3] Lyons, *Introduction to Theoretical Linguistics*, p. 448.

[4] W. E. Collinson, 'Comparative Synonymics: Some Principles and Illustrations', *Transactions of the Philological Society*, 1939, pp. 54–77: pp. 61f.

(2) One term is more intense than another: *repudiate—refuse*.

(3) One term is more emotive than another: *reject—decline*.

(4) One term may imply moral approbation or censure: *thrifty—economical*.

(5) One term is more professional than another: *decease—death*.

(6) One term is more literary than another: *passing—death*.

(7) One term is more colloquial than another: *turn down—refuse*.

(8) One term is more local or dialectal than another: Scots *flesher—butcher*.

(9) One of the synonyms belongs to child talk: *daddy—father*.

It is worth noting that all but one or two of these criteria are connected with emotive overtones, differences of register and other stylistic factors. An even more complex scheme, outlined at a symposium on semantics held at Mainz in December 1966, distinguishes as many as twenty-five criteria.[1]

The position is further complicated by the fact that we may have to choose, not between two or more synonyms, but between a direct and a periphrastic expression. As Pascal said, there are situations where we have to call Paris Paris, and others where we have to call it 'the capital of France'. Periphrasis was a popular figure in traditional rhetoric, and although the Romantics tried to avoid it, it can be the source of valuable stylistic effects. The famous line from *Phèdre*, 'la fille de Minos et de Pasiphaé', with the wide vistas of mythology and heredity which the names open up, has already been mentioned. The same play (Act I, scene 3) provides a striking example of the contrast between periphrasis and direct statement:

[1] K. Baldinger, 'La Synonymie—problèmes sémantiques et stylistiques', in *Probleme der Semantik*, pp. 41–61. See now also his *Teoría semántica*, Part II, ch. 5. Cf. also O. Ducháček, *Précis de sémantique française*, pp. 55–69. On wider implications of the problem, see recently R. Harris, *Synonymy and Linguistic Analysis*, Oxford, 1973, and H.-M. Gauger, *Zum Problem der Synonyme*, Tübingen, 1972.

Phèdre: J'aime . . . À ce nom fatal, je tremble, je frissonne.
   J'aime . . .
Oenone: Qui?
Phèdre: Tu connais ce fils de l'Amazone,
  Ce prince si longtemps par moi-même opprimé?
Oenone: Hippolyte! Grands Dieux!
Phèdre: C'est toi qui l'as nommé. [1]

As a perceptive critic has said, 'the effect may be compared to that of a sword drawn from its sheath.'[2]

II. SYNTAGMATIC RELATIONS

As this last example shows, terms which are in a paradigmatic relationship to one another may sometimes be combined, and a syntagmatic connexion may thus arise between them. *Collocation of synonyms* is a very common stylistic device. It often has an emotive motivation: we may give vent to our indignation, anger, excitement or other strong feelings by piling synonyms on each other. Thus, when we first meet Hamlet, he speaks to his mother of 'all forms, moods, shapes of grief, That can denote me truly'; a little later, when he is on his own, his repressed feelings reveal themselves by accumulations of synonyms or words with closely similar meanings:

> O, that this too too solid flesh would melt,
> Thaw, and resolve itself into a dew! . . .
> How weary, stale, flat, and unprofitable,
> Seem to me all the uses of this world!

Synonyms can also be collocated for emphasis or contrast, to describe one's groping for the *mot juste*, and for other purposes.

---

[1] Phèdre: I love. . . At the mention of that fatal name I tremble, I shudder. I love. . .—Oenone: Whom?—Phèdre: You know the son of the Amazon, that prince so long oppressed by me?—Oenone: Hippolyte! Great Gods!—Phèdre: It's you who have named him.

[2] R. A. Sayce, 'Racine's Style: Periphrasis and Direct Statement', in *The French Mind. Studies in Honour of Gustave Rudler*, Oxford, 1952, pp. 70–89: p. 80.

Combinations of *antonymous* and incompatible terms are also a frequent device underlying some well-known rhetorical figures such as antithesis:

> *Rentre* dans le néant dont je t'ai fait *sortir*[1]
> > (Racine, *Bajazet*, Act II, scene 1);

> Hier la *grande armée*, et maintenant *troupeau*[2]
> > (Hugo, *L'Expiation*).

The purely semantic antithesis may be reinforced by a contrast of tenses:

> Que je le *hais*; enfin, Seigneur, que je *l'aimai*[3]
> > (Racine, *Andromaque*, Act IV, scene 3).

In another traditional figure, the 'oxymoron', two contradictory terms are conjoined, often in an adjectival phrase. Thus Racine revitalizes the hackneyed comparison between love and a fire when he makes Phèdre say:

> Et dérober au jour une *flamme si noire*[4] (Act I, scene 3).

Even the sun can appear as black to the poetic imagination: Nerval speaks of 'le *Soleil noir* de la Mélancolie'[5] (*El Desdichado*) and Hugo of 'ces *noirs soleils* pestiférés'[6] (*La Légende des siècles*, 'Inferi'), and Baudelaire explicitly notes the incongruity: 'Je la (*viz.*, a woman) comparerais à un *soleil noir*, si l'on pouvait concevoir un astre noir versant la lumière et le bonheur'[7] (*Le Spleen de Paris*, XXXVI: 'Le Désir de peindre').

Yet another time-honoured rhetorical device, *repetition*, is

---

[1] '*Go back* to the obscurity from which I *brought you out*.'

[2] 'Yesterday the *Grand Army*, and now a *herd*.'

[3] 'That I *hate* him; indeed, my Lord, that I *loved* him.'

[4] 'And hide from the daylight a *flame so black*.'

[5] 'The *black Sun* of Melancholy.' On this and the next two quotations, see Antoine, loc. cit., p. 161. Cf. also H. Tuzet, *Revue des Sciences Humaines*, fasc. 88 (1957), pp. 479–502.

[6] 'These plague-stricken *black suns*.'

[7] 'I would compare her to a *black sun*, if one could conceive a black star pouring down light and happiness' (Pléiade ed., p. 289).

based on syntagmatic relations between words. Even one repetition may be sufficient to produce an impression of monotony, as in Hugo's *L'Expiation*:

> Après la *plaine blanche*, une autre *plaine blanche* . . .
> Pour cette *immense* armée un *immense* linceul,[1]

with the recurrent verb *il neigeait*, 'it was snowing', providing the key-note of the whole scene. Elsewhere, simple repetition serves to express strong feelings, as in Racine's *Iphigénie*, Act V, scene 4, where lexical and grammatical devices combine to depict Clytemnestra's despair at the impending sacrifice of her daughter:

> Les *vents*, les mêmes *vents*, si longtemps accusés,
> Ne te couvriront pas de ses vaisseaux brisés?
> *Et toi*, Soleil, *et toi*, qui dans cette contrée,
> Reconnais l'héritier et le vrai fils d'Atrée. . .[2]

There are also more complex patterns, as in this sentence from Voltaire's *Candide*:

'il me VENDIT à un autre marchand, qui me REVENDIT à *Tripoli*; de *Tripoli* je fus REVENDUE à *Alexandrie*, d'*Alexandrie* REVENDUE à *Smyrne*, de *Smyrne* à Constantinople'.[3]

In another passage from the same novel, repetition is combined with chiasmus to evoke the melancholy procession of exiled Turkish dignitaries and their successors who are ultimately doomed to the same fate:

'On *voyait* souvent passer . . . des bateaux chargés d'*effendis*, de *bachas*, de *cadis*, qu'on envoyait en exil . . . ; on *voyait* venir d'AUTRES *cadis*, d'AUTRES *bachas*, d'AUTRES *effendis*,

---

[1] 'After the *white plain*, another *white plain*. . . For this *immense* army an *immense* shroud.'

[2] 'The *winds*, the very *winds*, so long decried, will they not cover you with its broken vessels? *And you*, Sun, *and you*, who in this country recognizes the true son and heir of Atreus. . .'

[3] 'He SOLD me to another merchant who RESOLD me in *Tripoli*; from *Tripoli* I was taken to be RESOLD in *Alexandria*; from *Alexandria* I was taken to be RESOLD in *Smyrna*; from *Smyrna* to Constantinople.' (See J. H. Brumfitt's ed. of *Candide*, Oxford University Press, 1968, p. 83.)

qui prenaient la place des *expulsés*, et qui étaient *expulsés* à leur tour.'[1]

In one sentence of Voltaire's *Dictionnaire philosophique*, the verb *assassiner* appears fifteen times.[2] In Proust, Charlus's litany over his dead friends, in which the word *mort* occurs six times, is followed by the comment: 'Et chaque fois, ce mot "mort" semblait tomber sur ces défunts comme une pelletée de terre plus lourde, lancée par un fossoyeur qui tenait à les river plus profondément à la tombe.'[3]

With these syntagmatic relations between words, we have arrived at the boundary between semantics and syntax. As already pointed out, connexions between these two branches of linguistics have aroused a great deal of interest in recent years, and the problem has obvious implications for the study of style. It should also be noted that the entire analysis given in this chapter has been confined to synchronic aspects of meaning. Naturally, all these semantic phenomena are subject to change, and these changes may have direct or indirect stylistic repercussions, so that each of the divisions and subdivisions discussed above will have a diachronic dimension.

Two general conclusions emerge from this rapid survey of relations between semantics and stylistics. Firstly, the initial assumption of some kind of isomorphism between linguistic and stylistic studies has been fully confirmed by our analysis: each major sector of semantics has its counterpart in stylistics. Secondly,

---

[1] 'One could often *see* passing ... boats loaded with *effendis, pashas, cadis* who were being sent into exile ... ; and one could *see* OTHER *cadis*, OTHER *pashas*, OTHER *effendis* who came to take the place of those *expelled* and who were themselves *expelled* in their turn' (ibid., p. 147).

[2] J. R. Monty, *Étude sur le style polémique de Voltaire: Le 'Dictionnaire Philosophique'* (*Studies on Voltaire and the Eighteenth Century*, vol. XLIV), Geneva, 1966, pp. 64f.

[3] 'And each time, that word *dead* seemed to fall on the deceased like a heavier spadeful of earth, thrown by a grave-digger who was anxious to rivet them more tightly to their tombs' (Pléiade ed., vol. III, p. 862— *Le Temps retrouvé*).

there is a considerable amount of overlapping between the two disciplines: in certain areas (onomatopoeia, imagery, overtones and registers, etc.), meaning and style are inextricably interwoven and can hardly be treated in separate compartments. One wonders whether this degree of interpenetration is peculiar to semantics and whether relations between linguistics and stylistics at other levels are quite as intimate and all-pervasive.

CHAPTER III

STYLE AND PERSONALITY

At a conference on 'Style in Language' held in the United States in 1958, it was suggested that the style of a person is as unique as his fingerprints.[1] The analogy is slightly misleading since one's fingerprints do not change whereas one's style may do so; moreover, one cannot alter one's fingerprints but one can adjust one's style to suit the circumstances; one can even modify it for purposes of pastiche, parody or the need to portray a character through his or her speech. Nevertheless, Buffon's principle, 'Style is the man himself', is still widely held and has been echoed by many writers and thinkers. Schopenhauer described style as the 'physiognomy of the mind'. As has been seen or will be seen in other chapters of this book,[2] Flaubert and Proust regarded it as a unique and highly personal mode of vision. Gide gave expression to the same idea in an interesting image. 'Une personnalité neuve,' he claimed, 'ne s'exprime sincèrement que dans une forme neuve. La phrase qui nous est personnelle doit rester aussi particulièrement difficile à bander que l'arc d'Ulysse.'[3] The same writer wrote

[1] Roger Brown in *Style in Language*, ed. by T. A. Sebeok, Cambridge, Mass., repr. 1968, pp. 378ff. For a recent comment on this analogy, see W. Fucks, 'Possibilities of Exact Style Analysis', in *Patterns of Literary Style*, ed. by J. Strelka (Yearbook of Comparative Criticism, vol. III), The Pennsylvania State University Press, 1971, pp. 51–76: p. 53.

[2] See pp. 40, 92, 128.

[3] 'A new personality needs a new form to expresss itself sincerely. The sentence which is peculiar to us must be as particularly difficult to bend as Ulysses's bow' (*Nouveaux Prétextes*, Paris, 1947 ed., p. 169).

in his diary: 'On ne tracera pas aisément la trajectoire de mon esprit; sa courbe ne se révélera que dans mon style et échappera à plus d'un.'[1]

Most students of style would agree that there is an intimate connexion between a writer's language and his personality, in the widest sense of that term. In order to examine this connexion more closely, modern stylistics has evolved a number of methods, five of which will be briefly discussed in this chapter: statistical analysis; the so-called 'psychological' approach; typologies of style; the evidence of key-words; lastly, the study of the sources from which images are drawn.

A. STATISTICAL ANALYSIS

The volume *Linguistics and Style*, which was mentioned in the last chapter,[2] contains a very precise formula for the statistical analysis of stylistic features. 'The style of a text' is defined as 'a function of the aggregate of the ratios between the frequencies of its phonological, grammatical and lexical items, and the frequencies of the corresponding items in a contextually related norm.' More concisely, 'the style of a text is the aggregate of the contextual probabilities of its linguistic items'.[3] The merit of this approach is that it emphasizes the importance of context in the study of style; as the author rightly points out, 'uncontextualized statistics on single items are of no stylistic significance'.[4] There remains the difficulty of establishing a 'contextually related norm', based on a corpus comparable in genre, register and subject-matter to the work whose style one is examining. On a modest scale, a comparison of this kind was attempted in a recent article where the vocabulary of Racine's *Phèdre* was contrasted

---

[1] 'It will not be easy to trace the trajectory of my mind; its curve will be revealed only in my style and will escape the attention of many people' (*Journal, 1889–1939*, Pléiade ed., Paris, 1939, p. 276—Sept.–Oct. 1909).

[2] Ch. 2, p. 40, n. 3.   [3] N. E. Enkvist, loc. cit., p. 28.

[4] Ibid. On the role of context in stylistics, see esp. Riffaterre, *Essais de stylistique structurale*, ch. 2; cf. my *Language and Style*, pp. 127f.

with that of Pradon's *Phèdre et Hippolyte* and Thomas Corneille's *Ariane*.[1] It was found, for example, that although Racine's play is the shortest of the three, he uses about twenty per cent more words than the other two, and about twice as many proper names. Other numerical data, confined to words beginning with the first three letters of the alphabet, are more directly relevant to connexions between style and personality: thus we learn that, among the seventy-nine words peculiar to Racine, there are twenty concrete terms and twelve belonging to the vocabulary of violence.

'Stylostatistics', as it is somewhat pretentiously called, has become very popular of late; at the same time, the use of quantitative methods in a sphere where quality, aesthetic effects and emotive overtones are of supreme importance has aroused understandable misgivings. Yet even those who feel that detailed statistics are both unnecessary and undesirable in these matters would probably agree that a rough indication of frequencies would often be helpful. A distinguished French scholar has spoken, for instance, of Victor Hugo's 'abuse' of images from electricity in some of his later works, but has quoted a bare three examples of this tendency.[2] One would like to know whether there were dozens, scores or hundreds of such images, whether their number was significantly higher than in Hugo's earlier writings, and how his usage compared with that of his contemporaries. Another field where some numerical pointers could be useful is the distribution of a device of style in an entire work. A penetrating American critic has found, for example, that

[1] Th. Aron, 'Racine, Thomas Corneille, Pradon: Remarques sur le vocabulaire de la tragédie classique', *Cahiers de Lexicologie*, xi (1967), pp. 57–74.

[2] F. Brunot, *Histoire de la langue française*, XIII, Part I (by Ch. Bruneau), Paris, 1953, pp. 103f. and p. 185, n.1, where there is a brief comparison between Hugo's and Michelet's usage. As Ch. Bruneau himself points out on p. 104, 'il serait désirable d'étudier l'emploi des mots *voltaïque*, *électrique*, etc., dans la littérature de l'époque (Balzac, en particulier, use et abuse de ce genre d'images)' ('It would be desirable to study the use of the words *voltaic*, *electric*, etc., in the literature of the period (Balzac, in particular, uses and abuses images of this kind)').

Camus's novel *L'Étranger* is—for reasons which will be discussed in the next chapter—singularly poor in images, but that there is a sudden efflorescence of bold and intense similes and metaphors in the scene where the narrator, Meursault, shoots an Arab on an Algerian beach.[1] This anomalous distribution is symptomatic of Meursault's state of mind as portrayed through his style. Dazed by the heat and glare of the sun, he is assailed by all kinds of hallucinations: the light reflected from the Arab's knife hits him on the forehead like a long flashing blade; he feels the 'cymbals' of the sun against his forehead while the burning sword scorches his eyelashes and thrusts into his aching eyes.[2] It is this imagery which suggests the only possible motivation for his crime: in his state of utter confusion, he seems to have mistaken the light reflected from the blade for the blade itself and pulled the trigger from some obscure instinct of self-defence.

Statistics may also help to establish the authorship, unity or chronology of certain works. This method, which classicists have applied for many years to the study of Plato's dialogues, has been widely discussed during the recent debate on the authenticity of St Paul's epistles. The advent of computers has given a powerful impetus to this approach; yet even here there is a great danger of hasty conclusions disregarding the role of context and the complexities of literary creation. An article published a few years ago by two leading French linguists provides an example of these pitfalls.[3] Having noted that the frequency of adjectives rises steadily in Racine's plays from *Andromaque* to *Esther*, the authors point out that there is one exception: *Iphigénie* has fewer

---

[1] W. M. Frohock, *Style and Temper. Studies in French Fiction, 1925–1960*, Oxford, 1967, pp. 107ff.; n. 32 contains references to some other works on the subject.

[2] For a detailed account, see my book, *The Image in the Modern French Novel*, Oxford, repr. 1963, pp. 248ff.

[3] R.-L. Wagner–P. Guiraud, 'La Méthode statistique en lexicologie', *Revue de l'Enseignement Supérieur*, 1959, no. 1, pp. 154–9. On the role of the adjective in Corneille, cf. now I. D. McFarlane, 'Notes on the Rhetoric of *Horace*', in *The French Language. Studies Presented to Lewis Charles Harmer*, London, 1970, pp. 182–210: p. 184.

adjectives than might have been expected. They wonder, therefore, whether *Iphigénie* was not written earlier than is commonly
believed; there is, it would seem, some external evidence to support this view. However that may be, the number of adjectives in
the play need have no bearing whatever on the date of its composition: it may be connected with the dramatic structure of the
work or may even be due to a temporary change in Racine's
style. Numerical data are no more than a starting-point for the
critic; they must be tested for qualitative differences and carefully examined in the light of the context and the whole situation
before any conclusions can be drawn from them. The position
was neatly summed up in these terms in a review of a recent book
on the subject: 'Fully-automated analysis of "style", the plotting
of the complex co-ordinates of literary genius, is clearly utopian
(as those engaged in Machine Translation sadly concluded of
their field). However, a morganatic marriage of perceptive sub-
jectivity with ancillary quantification certainly is not.'[1]

B. THE 'PSYCHOLOGICAL' APPROACH

The most influential exponent of this doctrine was the late Leo
Spitzer. Combining Croce's and Vossler's philosophy of language
with some Freudian ideas, Spitzer evolved his famous theory of
the 'philological circle' which he expounded in a long series of
books and articles, and especially in the volume *Linguistics and
Literary History* (1948). Although the concept of the philological
circle has a respectable ancestry,[2] the term itself is rather un-

---

[1] In a review of *Statistics and Style* (ed. by L. Doležel and R. W. Bailey,
New York, 1969), by D. R. Tallentire in *The Modern Language Review*,
lxvi (1971), pp. 164f. Cf. on these problems, in addition to this book and
the ones mentioned in my *Language and Style*, p. 120, R. Posner, 'The
Use and Abuse of Stylistic Statistics', *Archivum Linguisticum*, xv (1963),
pp. 111–39; S. Chatman, 'Stylistics: Quantitative and Qualitative', *Style*,
i (1967), pp. 29–43; W. Fucks, loc. cit., and the works listed in R. W.
Bailey–D. M. Burton, *English Stylistics: A Bibliography*, Cambridge, Mass.,
1968, pp. 85–102.

[2] In *Linguistics and Literary History*, Princeton University Press, 1948,

fortunate because it suggests that there is an element of circularity in the method, whereas in fact there is none.[1] It simply means an operation in three phases moving from the periphery to the centre and then back to the periphery. In the first phase the critic, who must be equipped with 'talent, experience, and faith',[2] will read and re-read the text until he is struck by some persistently recurring peculiarity of style. In the next phase, he will try to discover some psychological feature which would account for this peculiarity. In the final phase, he will make the return journey to the periphery and look for further manifestations of the same mental feature. To quote Spitzer himself, 'the scholar will surely be able to state, after three or four of these "fro voyages", whether he has found the life-giving centre, the sun of the solar system (by then he will know whether he is really permanently installed in the centre, or whether he finds himself in an "excentric" or pericperic position).'[3]

To take a concrete example, when reading Diderot, Spitzer noticed a certain rhythmic pattern: 'a self-accentuating rhythm, suggesting that the "speaker" is swept away by a wave of passion which tends to flood all limits.'[4] The psychological explanation was clearly indicated: this rhythm was the linguistic expression of Diderot's nervous temperament which, 'instead of being tempered by style, was allowed to energize style'.[5] Nor was it difficult to discover further manifestations of this temperament in Diderot's philosophy of mobility, his efforts to transcend all rational boundaries. There was thus, in this author, a very neat correspondence between three different planes: his temperament, his philosophy and his style.

The philological circle has been criticized on various grounds. Some observers objected to the intuitive nature of the method and to the slenderness of the linguistic evidence on which such far-

---

p. 19 and p. 33, n.10, Spitzer mentions as his predecessors Dilthey, Schleiermacher, and ultimately Plato.

[1] Cf. Spitzer, ibid., p. 19 and pp. 33f., notes 9 and 10. See more recently R. A. Hall, Jr., *Idealism in Romance Linguistics*, Ithaca, 1963, p. 73.

[2] Spitzer, op. cit., p. 27.   [3] Ibid., p. 19.   [4] Ibid., p. 135.   [5] Ibid.

reaching conclusions were built. Others pointed out that some peculiarities of style need have no psychological background: they may be mere mannerisms or tics. It has also been suggested that the sequence of events may not always be the one foreseen by the theory: 'many relationships professing to be thus established are not based on conclusions really drawn from the linguistic material but rather start with a psychological and ideological analysis and seek for confirmation in the language.'[1] In the final stages of his long career, Spitzer himself tended to move away from his earlier positions. In a lecture given a short time before his death,[2] he emphasized that the psychological approach could be more easily applied to modern literature than to earlier periods which often aimed at a more impersonal style. He also pointed out that 'psychoanalytical stylistics' was merely a special form of the 'biographical fallacy'—a criticism which will be examined more closely at the end of this chapter. To correct these weaknesses, Spitzer recommended a truly 'structural' approach where stylistic analysis is subordinated to an interpretation of the work of art 'as a *poetic organism in its own right*', without any recourse to psychology.[3]

C. TYPOLOGIES OF STYLE

On an even more ambitious scale, some critics have devised more or less elaborate typologies of style on psychological grounds.

[1] R. Wellek–A. Warren, *Theory of Literature*, London, repr. 1954, pp. 187f. On Spitzer's method see recently, in addition to the works listed in my *Language and Style*, p. 124, n.1, Hall, op. cit., pp. 71–8; B. Terracini, *Analisi stilistica. Teoria, storia, problemi*, Milan, 1966, pp. 81–106; H. A. Hatzfeld, *Saggi di stilistica romanza*, Bari, 1967, ch. 1; B. Gray, *Style. The Problem and its Solution*, ch. 4; G. Hough, *Style and Stylistics*, London, 1969, pp. 59–68; K. D. Uitti, *Linguistics and Literary Theory*, pp. 132–41.

[2] 'Les Études de style et les différents pays', in the volume *Langue et littérature* (mentioned in ch. 2, p. 44, n. 4), pp. 23–38: p. 27.

[3] 'Subordonner l'analyse stylistique à l'explication de leurs œuvres particulières en tant qu'*organismes poétiques en soi*, sans recours à la psychologie de l'auteur' (ibid., pp. 27f.).

Some of these are centred on imagery and are inspired by Freudian or Jungian ideas: they posit a fundamental distinction between 'animizing' and 'deanimizing' images,[1] classify metaphors according to the four elements—earth, water, air and fire—from which they are drawn,[2] etc. A French scholar distinguishes between two classes of image-makers: the 'chemists' and the 'inspired' type.[3] The former include intellectual poets like Mallarmé and Valéry, whereas writers who express themselves in irrational or visionary imagery—Rimbaud, Apollinaire, Éluard—belong to the inspired category. Other typologies are more broadly based. A Spanish critic believes that there are three essential ingredients of literary style: reason, feeling and imagination;[4] we thus have six cardinal types, according to the relative importance of the three factors. A far more sophisticated scheme was put forward in 1959 by a Swiss scholar, Henri Morier, in his entertaining book, *La Psychologie des styles*. He distinguishes between no less than eight classes of style, each corresponding to a certain temperament and mental make-up: weak, delicate, balanced, positive, strong, hybrid, subtle, and defective. Each class has several subdivisions, yielding a grand total of seventy different styles. These essays in typology are certainly interesting and stimulating, but they are too abstract and schematic to be of much help in the stylistic study of particular texts or authors.[5]

[1] On this theory, propounded by H. Pongs, see Wellek and Warren, op. cit., pp. 210ff.

[2] On this typology, associated with G. Bachelard, cf. recently C. G. Christofides, 'Gaston Bachelard's Phenomenology of the Imagination', *Romanic Review*, lii (1961), pp. 36–47, and G. Poulet, 'Bachelard et la critique contemporaine', in *Currents of Thought in French Literature. Essays in Memory of G. T. Clapton*, Oxford, 1965, pp. 353–7. For an introduction to Bachelard's thought, see now P. Ginestier, *La Pensée de Bachelard*, Paris, 1968.

[3] Ch. Bruneau, 'L'Image dans notre langue littéraire', in *Mélanges A. Dauzat*, Paris, 1951, pp. 55–67.

[4] Dámaso Alonso, *Poesía española; ensayo de métodos y límites estilísticos*, Madrid, 1950.

[5] For a critique of the typological approach to stylistics, see L. T. Milic,

F

D. THE EVIDENCE OF KEY-WORDS

As we saw in the first chapter, key-words play an important part in a certain type of structural semantics.[1] They can also be used in the study of literary style. As early as 1832, Sainte-Beuve had declared, in his essay on Senancour: 'Chaque écrivain a son mot de prédilection, qui revient fréquemment dans le discours et qui trahit par mégarde, chez celui qui l'emploie, un vœu secret ou un faible.'[2] It is probable that Baudelaire was referring to this passage when he wrote, in an essay of Banville: 'Je lis dans un critique: "Pour deviner l'âme d'un poëte, ou du moins sa principale préoccupation, cherchons dans ses œuvres quel est le mot ou quels sont les mots qui s'y représentent avec le plus de fréquence. Le mot traduira l'obsession." '[3] In our own century, Valéry has spoken of 'des mots dont la fréquence, chez un auteur, nous révèle qu'ils sont en lui tout autrement doués de résonance, et, par conséquent, de puissance positivement créatrice, qu'ils ne le sont en général', adding the interesting comment: 'C'est là un exemple de ces évaluations personnelles, de ces *grandes valeurs-pour-un-seul*, qui jouent certainement un très beau rôle dans une production de l'esprit où la singularité est un élément de première

---

'Against the Typology of Styles', in *Essays on the Language of Literature*, ed. by S. Chatman and S. R. Levin, Boston, 1967, pp. 442–50. On a new typological criterion, see recently E. F. Timpe, 'The Spatial Dimension: a Stylistic Typology', in *Patterns of Literary Style* (referred to in n. 1, p. 64 above), pp. 179–97.

[1] See above, p. 32.

[2] 'Each writer has his favourite word which frequently recurs in his style and inadvertently betrays some secret wish or some weakness of the user' (*Portraits contemporains*, vol. I, Paris, 1855, pp. 115f.).

[3] 'I read in a critic: "To discover the mind of a poet, or at least his main preoccupation, let us find out in his works which is the word or which are the words which occur most frequently. The word will express the obsession"' (Pléiade ed., p. 735; cf. p. 1676 on the source of this passage). I am indebted to Professor P. Bénichou for drawing my attention to Sainte-Beuve's essay on Senancour.

importance.'[1] For Valéry, a key-word is thus a purely relative concept: it is a term whose frequency is significantly higher in a particular author than in his contemporaries. It is perhaps conducive to clarity to distinguish, as does one mathematical linguist, between 'thematic-words' (*mots-thèmes*) and 'key-words' (*mots-clés*). The former are the terms most frequently employed by a given writer, whereas key-words are those lexical items whose frequency rises significantly above the normal.[2] Since key-words in this restricted sense are based on relative, not on absolute, frequencies, they cannot be identified until we have established the norm from which they deviate. Even so, the discovery of key-words will be a delicate operation. One must carefully avoid what have been called 'contextual words' whose frequency is due to the subject-matter rather than to any deep-seated stylistic or psychological tendency.[3] As Spitzer once remarked, the frequent occurrence of terms like *love, heart, soul, God* in poetry is hardly more surprising than that of *car* in a report on motor racing or of *penicillin* in a medical journal.[4]

Some enquiries concerned with key-words are statistically orientated, but the concept can also be defined in qualitative terms. It will be remembered that for the semanticist, key-words are lexical items expressing the ideals of a particular society.[5]

---

[1] 'Words whose frequency in a writer shows that they possess for him a resonance and, therefore, a positively creative power far stronger than in ordinary usage. This is an example of those personal evaluations, those *great private values*, which certainly play a significant part in a product of the mind where singularity is an element of prime importance' (*Variété V*, Paris, 1945 ed., p. 318).

[2] P. Guiraud, *Les Caractères statistiques du vocabulaire*, Paris, 1954, p. 64. See also the extract reprinted in *La Stylistique, Lectures*, ed. by P. Guiraud and P. Kuentz, Paris, 1970, pp. 222ff. For an application of this approach, see M. Parent, *Saint-John Perse et quelques devanciers. Études sur le poème en prose*, Paris, 1960, ch. 1.

[3] Cf. Posner, loc. cit., p. 136. See, however, M. A. K. Halliday, 'Linguistic Function and Literary Style: An Inquiry into the Language of William Golding's *The Inheritors*', in the volume *Literary Style: A Symposium* (cf. above, ch. 2, p. 40, n. 2), pp. 330–65: pp. 345f.

[4] 'Les Études de style et les différents pays', p. 36.   [5] See above, p. 32.

This approach can also be applied to individual authors. In this way, Corneille has been re-examined in the light of a small number of terms epitomizing his ideals and aspirations: *mérite, estime, devoir, vertu, générosité*—and of course the famous *gloire* which is the central preoccupation of the Cornelian hero.[1]

E. THE SOURCES OF IMAGERY

The paramount importance of imagery in stylistic studies was discussed at some length in the last chapter. Here we are concerned with the psychological significance of images and more particularly of similes and metaphors. The range and nature of a writer's imagery will obviously be conditioned by various personal factors: his experiences, his reading, his environment, his circle of friends and acquaintances. An author without Proust's encyclopaedic culture and aesthetic sensibility could never have thought of the famous analogies from painting and other arts which run like *leit-motivs* through his cycle: the parallel between Odette and Botticelli's Zephora, between the kitchen-maid and Giotto's Charity, and many more. Some writers have obtained valuable effects by portraying their characters through their choice of imagery. A well known example occurs at the end of Victor Hugo's poem, *Booz endormi,* which is based on the Book of Ruth. After a day spent working on the land, Ruth is gazing up at the night sky, but her mind is still full of the things she saw during the day: she wonders

> Quel dieu, quel *moissonneur* de l'éternel été,
> Avait, en s'en allant, négligemment jeté
> Cette *faucille* d'or dans le *champ* des étoiles.[2]

[1] O. Nadal, 'De quelques mots de la langue cornélienne ou d'une éthique de la gloire', in the appendix of his book, *Le Sentiment de l'amour dans l'œuvre de Pierre Corneille,* Paris, 1948. Cf. now G. S. Burgess, 'Some Thoughts on Roland and Rodrigue', *Modern Language Review,* lxvi (1971), pp. 40–52. For a recent application of this approach, cf. N. Page, *The Language of Jane Austen,* Oxford, 1972, ch. 2.

[2] 'What god, what *harvester* of the eternal summer had, when leaving, casually thrown this golden *sickle* on the *field* of the stars.'

In the same way, the narrator in Gide's *L'Immoraliste*, a young historian and former student of the École des Chartes, sums up his quest for a deeper self in an image admirably attuned to his interests and his background: 'Je me comparais aux palimpsestes; je goûtais la joie du savant qui, sous les écritures plus récentes, découvre sur un même papier un texte très ancien infiniment plus précieux.'[1]

Some critics have gone considerably further and have tried to interpret recurrent images as symptoms of a writer's deeply rooted likes and dislikes, aspirations, fixations and obsessions. The vogue of psychoanalysis in literary studies has naturally encouraged this tendency. On the other hand, the controversy to which Miss Spurgeon's book on Shakespeare's images gave rise[2] has cast considerable doubt on psychological inferences from imagery. There are cases where an author's most crucial experiences, interests and preoccupations left no trace whatever in his similes and metaphors. Thus one would hardly know from the imagery of the fourteenth-century poet and composer Guillaume de Machaut that he was a musician, nor is there any analogy drawn from fishing in Izaak Walton's *Life of Donne*.[3] In Camus's novels there is only one image connected with tuberculosis, an illness which played such an important part in his life. It is also worth noting that Proust—whose keen interest in metaphor will be discussed in the last two chapters of this book—clearly saw that there was no necessary connexion between the tastes of an author

[1] 'I compared myself to a palimpsest; I experienced the joy of the scholar who, underneath more recent writing, discovers on the same paper a very old and infinitely more valuable text' (Paris, 1926 ed., p. 83).

[2] See esp. L. H. Hornstein, 'Analysis of Imagery: a Critique of Literary Method', *Publications of the Modern Language Association of America*, lvii (1942), pp. 638–53. Cf. also Wellek and Warren, op. cit., pp. 214ff. On a more recent experiment of this kind, see Ch. Mauron, *Des Métaphores obsédantes au mythe personnel. Introduction à la psychocritique*, Paris, 1963, and G. Genette's comments in the chapter 'Psycholectures' of his book *Figures*, vol. I, pp. 133–8.

[3] Hornstein, loc. cit., p. 651.

and the images he uses: he maliciously pointed out that Sainte-Beuve was anything but attracted to sport, army life or the sea, although he did derive metaphors from these spheres.[1]

At the same time it would be wrong to deny the existence of obsessive images rooted in some highly personal traumatic experience. Such cases may be rare, but they do occur. An interesting example which has been widely discussed is the frequent recurrence of insect imagery in Sartre. In *La Nausée*, a hand is likened to a crab, with the fingers moving like the animal's legs, whereas a human tongue is transformed into a centipede.[2] The same motif reappears in some of Sartre's later writings; in the play *Les Mouches (The Flies)*, it provides the central symbol enshrined in the title. The novel *La Mort dans l'âme*, which deals with the French collapse of 1940, contains a number of insect images some of which have a hallucinatory and surrealist quality. In the account of the great exodus from Paris, the people and vehicles on the overcrowded roads are assimilated to painfully crawling insects:

... les longues *fourmis* sombres tenaient toute la route ... Les *insectes* rampaient devant eux, énormes, lents, mystérieux . . . les autos grinçaient comme des *homards*, chantaient comme des *grillons*. Les hommes ont été changés en *insectes* . . . nous ne sommes plus que des pattes de cette interminable *vermine*.[3]

The persistence of this theme is truly remarkable. In *Le Diable et le bon Dieu*, Goetz, the proud idealist, implores God to deliver him from his thoughts and turn him into an insect (VI, 2). In *Les Séquestrés d'Altona*, we find a Nazi war criminal pleading his case before an imaginary tribunal of crabs in the thirtieth century.[4] Sartre himself has admitted that he was influenced by

---

[1] See Proust's preface to Paul Morand's *Tendres Stocks*.

[2] 81st ed., Paris, pp. 128 and 199.

[3] 'The long dark *ants* covered the whole road ... *Insects* were crawling in front of them, huge, slow, mysterious . . . the cars creaked like *lobsters*, chirped like *crickets*. Men have been turned into *insects* . . . now we are merely the legs of this endless *vermin*' (Paris, 1949, pp. 20f. and 24).

[4] Act II, scene 1 (pp. 88ff. in P. Thody's edition, London, 1965).

Kafka in some of this imagery, and there are various reasons, aesthetic and philosophical, which explain the frequency of these disturbing parallels between men and insects.[1] At the same time it is impossible to separate these images, and the specific forms in which they appear, from certain experiences recorded by Simone de Beauvoir in her autobiographical volume, *La Force de l'âge*. Here we are told that, a few years before the publication of *La Nausée*, Sartre asked a doctor to give him an injection of mescaline so that he could watch the effects of the drug on himself. As a result he experienced all kinds of semi-hallucinatory states: 'il avait vu des parapluies-vautours, des souliers-squelettes, de monstrueux visages; et sur ses côtés, par derrière, grouillaient des *crabes*, des *poulpes*, des choses grimaçantes'; on several occasions he actually thought that he was being followed about by a lobster.[2]

One could probe even further into the past although, needless to say, 'pathology as such is outside the domain of the literary critic',[3] and all this motivation has nothing to do with the philosophical validity or the artistic merits of the imagery. It has been pointed out that 'the doctors whom Sartre consulted argued that the particular form which these hallucinations took could in no way be attributed to mescaline, and Sartre himself told Kenneth Tynan that his detestation of sea-food went right back to his childhood.'[4] Certain passages in Sartre's autobiography, *Les Mots*, may be relevant here, in particular the following:

[1] See esp. S. John, 'Sacrilege and Metamorphosis: Two Aspects of Sartre's Imagery', *Modern Language Quarterly*, xx (1959), pp. 57–66, and M.-D. Boros, 'La Métaphore du *crabe* dans l'œuvre littéraire de Jean-Paul Sartre', *Publications of the Modern Language Association of America*, lxxxi (1966), pp. 446–50.

[2] 'He had seen umbrellas turned into vultures, shoes which looked like skeletons, monstrous faces; and by his side, from behind, *crabs*, *octopuses*, grimacing creatures were crawling' (Paris, 1960, p. 216; cf. also pp. 217, 228, 282).

[3] G. T. Clapton, *Baudelaire, the Tragic Sophist*, Edinburgh, 1934, p. 8.

[4] P. Thody, op. cit., p. 196, n. 7. See now also his *Sartre. A Biographical Introduction*, London, 1971, p. 28.

Je pensai m'évanouir un jour, dans le train de Limoges, en feuilletant l'almanach Hachette: j'étais tombé sur une gravure à faire dresser les cheveux: un quai sous la lune, une longue *pince* rugueuse sortait de l'eau, accrochait un ivrogne, l'entraînait au fond du bassin... J'eus peur de l'eau, peur des *crabes* et des arbres.[1]

Even this very selective and perfunctory survey will have shown that modern stylistics possesses a number of procedures for studying an author's personality through his style.[2] Neither of these procedures is entirely satisfactory in itself: while each has at least a grain of truth, they are all tentative and have their inherent limitations, even though, on occasion, they can lead to interesting results. There are, however, two essential difficulties about the whole approach. Carried to unreasonable lengths, it may easily

[1] 'One day I thought I would faint, in the Limoges train, while glancing through the Hachette almanac: I had come across a picture which made one's hair stand on end: a quay in the moonlight, a long rough *claw* stood out of the water, caught a drunkard, pulled him down to the bottom of the basin . . . I was frightened of the water, frightened of the *crabs* and the trees' (Paris, 1964, p. 125. The trees refer to a horrifying story he had read in *Le Matin*).

[2] Two other methods may be briefly mentioned here. In his recent book, *L'Étude des styles* (cf. above, ch. 2, p. 40, n. 2), B. Dupriez has evolved a procedure for studying the personal style of an author through the choices he has made among the various ways of expressing the same idea. Cf. my review of this book in *French Studies*, xxvi (1972), pp. 489f. There have also been some experiments in applying transformational-generative criteria to style. See in particular S. R. Levin, 'Poetry and Grammaticalness', reprinted in S. Chatman–S. R. Levin, op. cit., pp. 224–230; R. Ohmann, 'Literature as Sentences', reprinted ibid., pp. 231–8; Id., 'Generative Grammars and the Concept of Literary Style', reprinted from *Word*, xx (1964) in G. A. Love–M. Payne, *Contemporary Essays on Style*, Glenview, Ill., 1969, pp. 133–48; J. P. Thorne, 'Stylistics and Generative Grammars', *Journal of Linguistics*, i (1965), pp. 49–59; Id., 'Generative Grammar and Stylistic Analysis', in *New Horizons in Linguistics* (see above, ch. 1, p. 33, n. 1), pp. 185–97. For a detailed application of transformational-generative concepts in this field, see now S. Chatman, *The Later Style of Henry James*, Oxford, 1972. Cf. also A. E. Darbyshire, *A Grammar of Style*. ch. 2.

become a new form of the 'biographical fallacy', the naïve assumption that there must exist a close connexion between the life of an author and his writings. One is reminded of what Dr Johnson wrote about an admirer of the poet Thomson:

She could gather from his works three parts of his character: that he was a great lover, a great swimmer, and rigorously abstinent; but, said [his intimate] Savage, he knows not any love but that of the sex; he was perhaps never in cold water in his life; and he indulges himself in all the luxury that comes within his reach.[1]

There is also some danger that the critic, mesmerized by the connexions, alleged or real, between the mind of an author and his style, may lose sight of what remains his chief task: the aesthetic evaluation of the text. Spitzer himself was keenly aware of this temptation and warned against it in the lecture, already referred to, which he gave shortly before his death:

Même dans les cas où le critique a réussi à rattacher un aspect de l'œuvre d'un auteur à une expérience vécue, à une *Erlebnis*, il n'est pas dit, il est même fallacieux d'admettre que cette correspondance entre vie et œuvre contribue toujours à la beauté artistique de cette dernière. L'*Erlebnis* n'est en somme que la matière brute de l'œuvre d'art, sur le même plan que, par exemple, ses sources littéraires.[2]

The critic should therefore constantly remind himself that attempts to reach a writer's personality through his language will interest stylistics only if they can throw light on the aesthetic qualities of the text. The ultimate aim of style studies must be the one foreshadowed by Valéry, in a passage part of which has

[1] Wellek and Warren, op. cit., p. 214.

[2] 'Even where the critic has succeeded in connecting one aspect of an author's work with some personal experience, some *Erlebnis*, it does not follow, it would even be wrong to assume, that such correspondence between life and work will always contribute to the artistic beauty of the latter. After all, the *Erlebnis* is no more than the raw material of the work of art, in the same way as are, for example, its literary sources' ('Les Études de style et les différents pays', p. 27).

already been quoted: to investigate the 'strictly literary effects of language' and to examine the 'expressive and suggestive devices which have been invented to enhance the power and penetration of speech'.[1]

---

[1] 'La recherche des effets proprement littéraires du langage, l'examen des inventions expressives et suggestives qui ont été faites pour accroître le pouvoir et la pénétration de la parole' (cf. above, p. 41).

CHAPTER IV

TWO APPROACHES TO STYLE

Nearly thirty years ago, Leonard Bloomfield declared: 'In all study of language we must start from forms and not from meanings.'[1] This statement is far too categorical. Whenever we have to do with meaningful elements—bound morphemes, words, phrases, clauses, sentences or even higher units of discourse—we may take either the form or the meaning, either the *signifiant* or the *signifié* as our starting-point. As one linguist has put it, 'in the first case we take the sound (of a word or of some other part of a linguistic expression) and then inquire into the meaning attached to it; in the second case we start from the signification and ask ourselves what formal expression it has found in the particular language we are dealing with. If we denote the outward form by the letter O, and the inner meaning by the letter I, we may represent the two ways as O→I and I→O respectively.'[2] In lexical studies the I→O approach, usually known as 'onomasiology', has been widely and successfully applied in dialectology and linguistic geography; it also underlies Roget's *Thesaurus* and conceptual dictionaries in general; more recently it has given rise to the theory of lexical fields which was discussed in the first chapter of this book. In syntax, the I→O method is, for obvious reasons, rather more difficult to apply, even though Ferdinand Brunot

---

[1] L. Bloomfield, 'Meaning', *Monatshefte für deutschen Unterricht*, xxxv (1943), pp. 101–6: p. 103.

[2] O. Jespersen, *The Philosophy of Grammar*, London, repr. 1929, p. 33.

demonstrated many years ago, in his monumental *La Pensée et la langue*, that it can yield interesting results. In the preface to that work, he gave a striking example of how such a change of perspective could provide a rational basis for linguistic description:

Entre les formes les plus diverses de l'expression, entre les signes les plus disparates, il y a un lien, c'est l'idée commune que ces signes contribuent à exprimer. Si on la prend pour centre, ... tout s'ordonne autour d'elle; elle groupe des éléments linguistiques venus de toutes parts. . . . Tout se complète, s'organise, se classe. De la sorte, QUELQUES *hommes* cesse d'être aux indéfinis, pendant que DES *hommes* est à l'article, UNE POIGNÉE *d'hommes* au nom, VINGT *hommes* aux noms de nombre; les expressions de quantité précises ou imprécises se cataloguent dans le langage, comme le font ailleurs les nombres et les mesures.[1]

In stylistics—one of whose founders, Charles Bally, was an advocate of the I→O method—there exists a similar choice between two alternative approaches; the terms of the problem are, however, rather different. Here we have to do, not with form and meaning, *signifiant* and *signifié*, expression and content, but rather with stylistic devices and with the effects which they produce. Moreover, stylistic phenomena are usually polyvalent: the same device may give rise to several effects and conversely, the same effect may be obtained from several different devices.[2] To

---

[1] 'Between the most diverse forms of expression, between the most disparate signs, there is a link: the common idea to whose expression these signs contribute. If one takes this idea as one's centre, ... everything falls into place; it groups together linguistic elements from all directions... Everything becomes complete, organized, classified. In this way, QUELQUES *hommes* 'a few' men' will no longer appear among the indefinites while DES *hommes* 'men' is recorded as an article, UNE POIGNÉE *d'hommes* 'a handful of men' as a noun, VINGT *hommes* 'twenty men' as a numeral; expressions of quantity, precise or imprecise, are catalogued in language just as numbers and measures are catalogued elsewhere' (2nd ed., Paris, 1926, p. xviii). There is some similarity between this category and what the late Uriel Weinreich ('Explorations in Semantic Theory', loc. cit., pp. 426ff.) called 'delimitation', although the latter is even wider.

[2] On polyvalency, see recently Riffaterre, *Essais de stylistique structurale*, p. 59.

take a specific example, the mobility of the adjective in modern French constitutes a valuable device of style which can be used for a wide variety of effects.[1] In some contexts, the anteposition of the adjective will generate powerful emotive overtones:

Les plus *lumineuses* et *éclatantes* et *réchauffantes* nouvelles (Proust).[2]

Elsewhere, the same device will help to emphasize an inherent quality, as when Proust speaks of 'la *grise* vieillesse du portail',[3] or Cocteau of 'cette *française*, lourde et légère torpeur.'[4] The adjective in anteposition may also form part of a chiasmus designed to produce a subtle contrast:

Passant difficilement du rang de *jeune* femme au rang de femme *jeune* (Françoise Sagan);[5]
Un autre homme *jeune*, presque un *jeune* homme (Montherlant),[6]

or it may become a vehicle for irony:

Les *rituelles* consultations de M. Vincent Auriol (*Le Monde*);[7]
Ce *superbe* et *grotesque* et *doux* prince (Cocteau).[8]

This is the way stylistic analysis usually proceeds: it takes a particular device in a language or in a limited corpus and

[1] On the whole problem of the place of the adjective in French (cf. above, p. 53), see now E. Reiner, *La Place de l'adjectif épithète en français*, Vienna, 1968. Cf. also J. A. Hutchinson, 'Le Désordre des mots: la place de l'adjectif', *Le Français dans le Monde*, lxii (Jan.–Febr. 1969), pp. 15–23, and E. Faucher, 'La Place de l'adjectif, critique de la notion d'épithète', *Le Français Moderne*, xxxix (1971), pp. 119–27.

[2] 'The most *brilliant* and *splendid* and *heart-warming* news.'

[3] 'The *grey* oldness of the portal.'

[4] 'This *very French*, heavy and light torpor.'

[5] 'Passing with difficulty from the status of a *young* woman to that of a woman *young* in spirit.'

[6] 'Another man *young* in age, almost a *young* man.'

[7] 'The *ritual* consultations of M. Vincent Auriol.'

[8] 'This *superb* and *grotesque* and *gentle* prince.' The two examples from Cocteau are quoted by F. Jones, *La Langue et le style dans la poésie de Jean Cocteau*, unpublished Ph.D. thesis, University of Leeds, 1961; the sentence from Montherlant is taken from A. Lorian, *L'Ordre des propositions dans la phrase française contemporaine: La cause*, Paris, 1966.

examines the various effects which result from it. But one could also reverse the process and study, for example, the different devices through which an ironical effect is produced in the language or corpus in question. Leaving aside such obvious forms of irony as special intonations or clichés of the type: 'a nice kettle of fish!', 'a fat lot of good that will do you!',[1] irony can be conveyed in modern French by a variety of devices, some lexical, others syntactical. One of the latter is word-order: anteposition of the adjective, as already mentioned, or inversion of the subject:

Ainsi arriva à midi, un paon blanc grattant du bec sa queue,... *l'académicien Henri de Régnier . . . Ainsi vint,* le soir même du jour,... *l'académicien René Boylesve* (Giraudoux).[2]

Another syntactical device is the use of highly literary Past Historics and Imperfect Subjunctives in ordinary conversation:

Malheureux ami, pourquoi *commençâtes*-vous Paludes? (Gide);[3]
Oh! par exemple!... on te pince avec mon concurrent... et il faudrait que je te *remerciasse* (V. de Cottens–P. Veber).[4]

To these and other syntactical devices must be added the whole gamut of lexical ones conducive to irony. Some of these— antiphrasis, oxymoron—are among the best known figures of traditional rhetoric. Some neologisms owe their very existence to irony, such as three of Voltaire's coinages: the science of *métaphysico-théologo-cosmolo-nigologie*,[5] professed by Pangloss in *Candide*; *folliculaire* 'hack writer', which is one of Voltaire's permanent contributions to the French vocabulary;[6] and his

---

[1] On the stylistic role of clichés, see Riffaterre, op. cit., ch. 6.

[2] '*Thus arrived* at noon, a white peacock scratching with its beak the train of his robe,... *Academician Henri de Régnier....Thus came,* the same evening,... *Academician René Boylesve.*'

[3] 'My poor friend, why *did* you *start* on Paludes?'

[4] 'Upon my word!...you get pinched with my rival...and you want me to *thank* you.'

[5] Cf. Professor J. H. Brumfitt's comments in his edition of *Candide*, (mentioned in ch. 2, p. 61, n. 3), p. 162.

[6] On this word see Bloch–Wartburg's etymological dictionary, 5th ed., 1968.

description of Geneva as a '*parvulissime* république'.[1] Foreign words can also be used ironically, as in this early specimen of 'franglais' by Musset:

> Dans le *bol* où le *punch* rit sur son trépied d'or,
> Le *grog* est *fashionable*.[2]

Elsewhere, irony is expressed obliquely, but all the more effectively, through the medium of imagery, as in Proust's devastating caricature of M. de Palancy 'qui, avec sa grosse tête de carpe aux yeux ronds, se déplaçait lentement au milieu des fêtes en desserrant d'instant en instant ses mandibules comme pour chercher son orientation.'[3]

It is clear, then, that there are two alternative approaches to style. Bearing in mind the polyvalency of stylistic phenomena, the two methods may be represented in the following simple diagram:

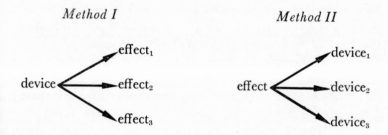

Method I   *Method II*

The question now arises as to how the two methods work in practice and what their respective advantages are. The answer will depend on the nature and scope of any particular enquiry.

[1] Quoted by Ch. Bruneau in F. Brunot, *Histoire de la langue française*, vol. XII, Paris, 1948, p. 214.

[2] 'In the *bowl* where *punch* is smiling on its golden tripod, *grog* is *fashionable*.'

[3] 'Who, with his large carp's head and round eyes, moved about slowly in the midst of the party, continually opening his mandibles as if to find his bearings' (*Du Côté de chez Swann*, Pléiade edition, vol. I, p. 327).

If it is concerned with the stylistic resources of an entire language, then Method II will be clearly inappropriate. Effects of style *in vacuo*, divorced from the devices on which they are normally based, are too vague and general, and also too numerous and diverse, to provide an orderly framework for description and analysis. On the other hand, certain effects are sufficiently precise to be approached by Method II; in this way, monographs have been published on the various ways in which symmetry can be achieved in modern French,[1] and on the devices available for emphasizing an idea in seventeenth-century French and in the contemporary idiom.[2] Other problems, such as possibly irony, could be attacked from the same angle. On the whole, however, this kind of stylistic enquiry.[3] Within the compass of a single anchored in linguistic devices—phonological, lexical or grammatical—around which the effects which they subserve can be grouped.

The position is radically different where the critic deals with a finite corpus, in particular with a single work or with the writings of an author as a whole, which are the two most popular forms of this kind of stylistic enquiry.[3] Within the compass of a single work, which provides in many ways the ideal context for stylistic analysis,[4] major effects of style are easily identifiable and highly significant because they are closely bound up with the thematic

---

[1] G. Schlocker, *Équilibre et symétrie dans la phrase française moderne*, Paris, 1957.

[2] M. L. Müller-Hauser, *La Mise en relief d'une idée en français moderne*, Geneva, 1943; M. Mangold, *Études sur la mise en relief dans le français de l'époque classique*, Mulhouse, 1950.

[3] There are of course also intermediate forms such as stylistic studies of the works of an author in a certain *genre* or within a particular period of his life; cf., for example, Seymour Chatman's monograph on the style of Henry James's later novels, mentioned in ch. 3, p. 78, n. 2.

[4] See on this problem Riffaterre, op. cit., ch. 2, and my *Language and Style*, pp. 127f. On the related phenomenon of 'convergence', defined by Riffaterre as 'the accumulation at a given point of several independent stylistic devices', see op. cit., pp. 6off., and Y. Louria, *La Convergence stylistique chez Proust*, Geneva–Paris, 1957.

structure of the book.[1] To take but one example, several critics have shown how, in Camus's *L'Étranger*, a number of seemingly disparate devices concur to endow the narrator, Meursault, with a language of his own.[2] Meursault is the embodiment of a peculiar human type, that of the 'absurd' man, and all the features of his language have to be in keeping with his psychology and outlook. Short, *staccato* sentences, with a bare minimum of causal links; simple, concrete vocabulary; avoidance of images except in one crucial scene, the murder on the beach, where, as we saw in the last chapter, they reflect the narrator's confused and semi-hallucinatory state of mind; a peculiar choice of tense, replacing the traditional Past Historic by the more direct, inconclusive and conversational Past Indefinite:[3] these and other idiosyncrasies form a kind of linguistic syndrome of the absurd man; without them, the novel would not exist. Such an approach is certainly more interesting and more rewarding than would be the study of the various effects produced by tenses, sentence-structure, imagery and other devices in *L'Étranger*.

Where the enquiry transcends the limits of single works and covers the writings of an author as a whole, it can still be profitably focused on major effects of style rather than on the devices which help to achieve them. These effects will be identified and interpreted as expressions of some fundamental quality, general attitude or abiding preoccupation of the writer. In a monograph

---

[1] On the latter concept, see recently E. H. Falk, *Types of Thematic Structure: The Nature and Function of Motifs in Gide, Camus, and Sartre*, Chicago–London, 1967. Cf. also the volume *Image and Theme. Studies in Modern French Fiction*, mentioned in ch. 2, p. 44, n. 2.

[2] See for example J. Cruickshank, *Albert Camus and the Literature of Revolt*, London, 1959, ch. 7, and W. M. Frohock, *Style and Temper. Studies in French Fiction, 1925–1960*, pp. 103ff. Cf. I. Feuerlicht, *Publications of the Modern Language Association of America*, lxxviii (1963), pp. 606–21.

[3] On this feature, noticed already by Sartre in his review of *L'Étranger*, see now H. Weinrich, *Tempus. Besprochene und erzählte Welt*, Stuttgart, 1964, pp. 262ff. Cf. also M.-G. Barrier, *L'Art du récit dans 'L'Étranger' de Camus*, Paris, 1962.

G

published over forty years ago on 'classical restraint' in Racine's style,[1] Leo Spitzer gave a spectacular demonstration of this procedure. He brought together a multiplicity of linguistic elements which all have one feature in common: they all play their part in the vast process of 'klassische Dämpfung', classical discipline, toning down and understatement, which Spitzer subsequently defined as a 'continuous repression of the emotional by the intellectual', adding that, in his view, 'the alternation between these two conflicting tendencies is the most distinctive characteristic of Racine's style.'[2] It is illuminating to discover that so many widely different devices have a common denominator, that time-honoured rhetorical figures like periphrasis, chiasmus, antithesis as well as conventional metaphors and metonymies have basically the same stylistic function as some delicate grammatical nuances such as the replacement of the first or second person pronoun or possessive adjective by a less direct and intimate form:[3] the indefinite article:

> Voilà ce qu'*un* époux m'a commandé lui-même[4]
> > (*Andromaque*, IV, 1);

the indefinite third-person pronoun *on*:

> Qu'entends-je? Quels conseils ose-t-*on* me donner?[5]
> > (*Phèdre*, IV, 6);

or even a proper name which a character uses when speaking of himself:

> *Néron* impunément ne sera pas jaloux[6]
> > (*Britannicus*, II, 2).

[1] 'Die klassische Dämpfung in Racines Stil', reprinted in *Romanische Stil- und Literaturstudien*, vol. I, Marburg, 1931, pp. 135–268. See now also P. France, *Racine's Rhetoric*, Oxford, 1965.

[2] *Linguistics and Literary History*, p. 110.

[3] Cf. R. Barthes, *Sur Racine*, Paris, 1963 ed., pp. 45f.

[4] 'This is what *a* husband himself bade me do.'

[5] 'What do I hear? What advice am I being given?' (Literally: 'What advice dare *people* give me?')

[6] '*Nero* shall not be made jealous with impunity.'

Works of this kind have amply demonstrated the advantages of an approach based on major stylistic effects when dealing with the language of a book or an author. Needless to say, there will be many cases where the converse method is equally legitimate or even more appropriate. Most students of literary style tend, in fact to take the linguistic data as their starting-point, whether they concentrate on a single device, a group of devices, or on the entire system of stylistic resources in a particular work or writer. Some may aim even higher and investigate the style of a group of authors, a school, movement, period, tradition or literary *genre*. E. R. Curtius's study of the history of various key images in European literature is a classic example of this method.

There is one highly important element of style which raises special problems with respect to the two approaches discussed so far. Imagery—metaphor, simile, metonymy and allied figures—may be regarded as a stylistic device which fits into the alternative models described on p. 85. Under Method I, it can, and often does, serve as a focal point around which various effects produced by images can be grouped: the latter may provide a symbolic expression for some major theme or motif; they may transcribe highly complex abstract experiences in concrete terms; they may, as already noted, serve as a vehicle for irony, imply other value-judgments, play their part in the linguistic portrayal of a character, and have all kinds of other functions.[1] Conversely, imagery may take its place, in accordance with Method II, among the various devices designed to produce the same stylistic effect; in *L'Étranger*, for instance, its peculiar distribution forms, as we have already seen, an integral part of the linguistic portrait of Meursault. Apart from this fundamental duality in which all devices of style are involved, images also have a dual structure which is peculiar to them. What we have here is not a *signifiant* and a *signifié*, but—as noted in the second chapter—a *comparant* and a *comparé*, a 'tenor' and a 'vehicle'. The tenor is the subject

---

[1] On these effects, see ch. 9 of my book, *Language and Style*.

we are talking about, and the vehicle is the element to which the tenor is compared.[1] In the famous image in *Julius Caesar:*

> There is a *tide* in the affairs of men
> Which, taken at the *flood*, leads on to fortune,

tide and *flood* are the vehicles whereas the tenor could be expressed, more prosaically, as 'great opportunities'.

Since imagery has such a dual structure, it can be approached either through the tenor or through the vehicle. The approach through the vehicles, which analyses the images of a work or writer according to the sources from which they are drawn, is very popular; in some cases it has led to the discovery of 'obsessive' metaphors and other significant clusters of imagery which certain critics have interpreted in psychological or psychoanalytical terms; these were discussed in the last chapter. The alternative method, which approaches imagery through the tenors, the great themes which attract similes and metaphors from other spheres, can also yield illuminating results: some recent studies have shown, for example, what kinds of analogies Proust employs in his untiring efforts to describe the complex and elusive phenomena of time and memory with the maximum of precision and evocative force.[2] Both approaches are equally legitimate, and the critic will have to weigh up their relative advantages in each particular case. He may even decide to combine them: in a recent monograph on Proust's imagery, the two central sections, of about equal length, are devoted to the themes and the sources of the images.[3]

[1] See above, p. 45. This analysis is also applicable to metonymies; the word *crown*, for example, is often used metonymically as the 'vehicle' for the 'tenor': 'the rule, position, or empire of a monarch' (*Shorter OED*). The discussion which follows will, however, be confined to images based on analogy, i.e. to metaphors and similes. In recent years, there has been a renewal of interest in metonymy and synecdoche; cf. for example J. Dubois et al., *Rhétorique générale*, Part I, ch. 4; B. Dupriez, op. cit., pp. 51f. and 6off.; G. Genette, op. cit., esp. vol. III, pp. 21–63; A. Henry, op. cit., pp. 17–50; T. Todorov, 'Synecdoques', *Communications*, no. 16 (1970), pp. 26–35; M. Le Guern, *Sémantique de la métaphore et de la métonymie*, Paris, 1973.   [2] For further details, see below, ch. 5.

[3] V. E. Graham, *The Imagery of Proust*, Oxford, 1966.

One leading authority on metaphor has expressed strong doubts about splitting images into their components. 'Metaphor', he argues, 'is by definition the combination of a vehicle with a tenor; what will remain of it if we methodically isolate the vehicles on the one hand and the tenors on the other?'[1] The answer is that such separation is methodologically justified as a discovery procedure capable of revealing significant patterns and tendencies which could not have been noticed in any other way. At the same time, the critic will have to bear in mind the fundamental unity of the two elements: he will have to pay attention to the 'ground' of the image, the feature or features which tenor and vehicle have in common, and also to any other characteristic relationships which may arise between sources and themes of imagery in a given literary work. To mention but one or two of these relations, there exist cases of 'correlative' imagery where one sphere of experience is consistently described in terms of another (for example love compared to illness in Proust);[2] 'serial' images where, once a firm connexion has been established between a tenor and a vehicle, changes in the former are paralleled by the development of the latter (for instance the analogy between human life and the flight of a bird in *The Divine Comedy*);[3] 'reciprocal' images where two different spheres are interrelated and provide metaphorical equivalents for each other: in the poetry of Donne, for example, 'the interchange between the spheres of sex and religion recognizes that sex is a religion and religion is a love'.[4]

What is true of the duality of tenor and vehicle is equally true of the wider dichotomies discussed in this chapter: the distinction between form and meaning in language, and that between device and effect in style. The linguist and the literary critic may have

---

[1] H. Weinrich, *Romanische Forschungen*, lxxiii (1961), p. 201.

[2] Cf. my book, *The Image in the Modern French Novel*, pp. 133ff.

[3] See M. Hardt, *Das Bild in der Dichtung*, Munich, 1966, ch. 2. The book also discusses other examples of such 'serial images' in Dante himself as well as in Aeschylus, Shakespeare and Flaubert.

[4] Wellek and Warren, op. cit., p. 214.

to separate the two components but they must never lose sight of their essential unity and interpenetration. At one time it was customary to regard style as something external and ornamental: Lord Chesterfield defined it as 'the dress of thoughts.' Flaubert protested vigorously against this view: 'Ces gaillards-là s'en tiennent à la vieille comparaison: La forme est un manteau. Mais non! la forme est la chair même de la pensée, comme la pensée est l'âme de la vie.'[1] Nor could this be otherwise if style is regarded as a unique and idiosyncratic mode of vision or, as Flaubert himself put it, 'une manière absolue de voir les choses.'[2]

[1] 'These fellows stick to the old comparison: form is a cloak. No indeed! form is the very flesh of thought, just as thought is the soul of life.'

[2] 'An absolute way of looking at things.' The quotation from Chesterfield is taken from the *Shorter OED*; those from Flaubert are cited in W. v. Wartburg, *Évolution et structure de la langue française*, 5th ed., Berne, 1958, p. 226. For a slightly different wording of the first passage from Flaubert, see the German translation of my *Principles of Semantics*, by Mrs. S. Koopmann (2nd ed., Berlin, 1972), p. 88 and n. 203. Cf. also Ionesco's statement: 'L'expression est pour moi fond et forme à la fois' ('Expression for me is form and substance at the same time') (quoted by A. Henry, 'La Stylistique littéraire', *Le Français Moderne*, xl (1972), pp. 1–15: p. 4).

CHAPTER V

THE BEGINNINGS OF A STYLE: IMAGES OF TIME AND MEMORY IN PROUST'S *JEAN SANTEUIL*[1]

'Tous les à peu près d'images ne comptent pas. L'eau (dans des conditions données) bout à 100 degrés. À 98, à 99, le phénomène ne se produit pas. Alors mieux vaut pas d'images.'[2] On reading *Jean Santeuil*, the student of Proust's imagery is often reminded of these words which he wrote many years later, in his preface to Paul Morand's *Tendres Stocks*. The pages of *Jean Santeuil* are densely packed with similes and metaphors; indeed, the richness of the figurative element is, if anything, greater than in *À la recherche du temps perdu*;[3] its quality, however, is very uneven. There are many images of great poetic beauty, intellectual brilliance and an unmistakably Proustian ring, but there are also

[1] The material for this chapter, and for the article on which it is based, was collected from the 1952 edition of *Jean Santeuil*, long before the Pléiade edition (1971) became available. All the quotations have, however, been checked against the Pléiade text, and it is to this edition that the page numbers refer.

[2] 'Approximate images do not count. Water, under given conditions, boils at 100 degrees. At 98, at 99, the phenomenon does not occur. In that case it is better to have no images at all.'

[3] This at least is the conclusion reached in Elfi Zeblewski's unpublished thesis, *Prousts Bildersprache in 'Jean Santeuil'*, Marburg, 1957, summarized in an article by the same author, 'Zur Bildersprache in Marcel Prousts *Jean Santeuil*', *Die Neueren Sprachen*, N.F., vii (1958), pp. 324–37: p. 324.

many others which do not quite come off, which fail to convince and to illuminate, or which do not play any useful part. Gide once complained in his diary: 'Quoi de plus de fatigant que cette manie de certains littérateurs, qui ne peuvent voir un objet sans penser aussitôt à un autre';[1] in *Jean Santeuil* we see the inexperienced young writer yielding all too frequently to this temptation.

Even if one bears in mind the immaturity, the lack of polish and revision, which are so obvious in the style of *Jean Santeuil*, the proportion of idle and abortive analogies is somewhat surprising in a novel which shows the author fully alive to the dangers inherent in the use of images. There are in the text a number of references to imagery, several of which are either ironic or openly critical. A sweeping condemnation comes from Beulier, the 'professeur de philosophie', who is modelled on Proust's own teacher Darlu: 'Il faudra soigneusement bannir toutes ces métaphores, toutes ces images qui, mieux choisies que les vôtres, peuvent plaire au poète, mais que même alors la philosophie ne tolère pas. Mais même pour le professeur de lettres, ne grossissez pas la voix pour dire des banalités'[2] (p. 263). Beulier himself carefully avoids the vice against which he warns his pupil: 'Jean . . . ne trouva dans toute la leçon aucune de ces images splendides et parfumées auxquelles il aurait pu pendant cette rude course intellectuelle faire halte comme auprès de reposoirs de fleurs'[3] (p. 261). Jean, on the other hand, has a juvenile infatuation for this kind of imagery. He adorns his French essays with images borrowed from various poets (p. 230); he looks for two things

[1] 'What could be more tiresome than this mania of certain men of letters who cannot see an object without immediately thinking of another' (20th August 1926—p. 822 of the Pléiade edition).

[2] 'One should carefully avoid all these metaphors, all these images which, if better chosen than yours, may please the poet but which even in that case philosophy will not tolerate. But even for the teacher of literature, do not raise your voice in order to say commonplaces.'

[3] 'In the whole lesson, Jean . . . did not find any of those splendid and fragrant images at which he might have halted in this stiff intellectual race as at temporary altars made of flowers.'

only in poetry: 'la richesse de leur sens' and 'l'éclat de leurs images'[1] (p. 240). When reading *Le Capitaine Fracasse*, he is intoxicated with 'certaines phrases retentissantes à la fois et imagées'[2] (p. 314), much as the young narrator in the *Temps perdu* will be fascinated by the striking metaphors of Bergotte.[3] In Leconte de Lisle, 'les images brillantes, le style enflammé . . . excitaient en lui une ardeur matinale'[4] (p. 236), but he is a little disturbed by the style of *Colomba* 'où à tous moments une facétie venait empêcher la vague poésie des images de le ravir'[5] (pp. 307f.).

Proust is equally critical of another type of idle imagery: the similes and metaphors with which the conversation of certain intellectuals is sprinkled. A Professor of the École des Sciences Politiques hazards the image: 'une orchestration fouillée de main d'ouvrier', which strikes a more conservative colleague as a little unusual: 'L'image est un peu hardie, . . . cela ne s'écrirait pas, ni vous ni moi ne nous risquerions même à le dire'[6] (p. 275; cf. also p. 274). In the *Temps perdu*, the same idea will be developed in the caricature of Professor Brichot. Even more interesting is the case of Bergotte, who is an artist, not a writer, in *Jean Santeuil*. When listening to music, Bergotte will note certain passages on which he can comment with an unexpected epithet or a prettily turned comparison, whereupon he will lose interest in the music and think of other things (p. 798).

All these remarks on the more superficial aspects of imagery show that the young writer had given some thought to these matters. There are also some passages which foreshadow the role

---

[1] 'The richness of their sense . . . the brilliance of their images.'

[2] 'Certain resounding as well as figurative sentences.'

[3] Vol. I, p. 95 of the Pléiade edition (*Du Côté de chez Swann*).

[4] 'The brilliant images, the fiery style . . . aroused in him a youthful ardour.'

[5] 'Where some facetious remark would constantly prevent the vague poetry of the images from enchanting him.'

[6] 'An elaborate orchestration showing the hand of a craftsman. . . The image is a little bold, . . . one would not write this way, neither you nor I would even risk using it in speech.'

of analogy in the process of involuntary memory. In a description of hawthorns, which was later on transmuted into one of the great metaphorical themes of the *Temps perdu*, the author speculates on the reasons for Jean's interest in the pink variety: 'Était-ce qu'ayant vu auparavant de l'épine blanche, la vue d'une épine rose et dont les fleurs ne sont plus simples mais composées, le frappa à la fois de ces deux prestiges de l'analogie et de la différence qui ont tant de pouvoir sur notre esprit?'[1] (p. 331). In the later work, Proust's technique will be far more subtle and effective; as Professor Cocking has put it, we shall be given 'not the wherefores of the experience, but the experience itself'.[2] More closely related to the literary image is another passage which, though banal in itself, is of some interest in the light of Proust's later ideas on the role of metaphor in the recapture of the past: 'les objets qui furent aimés pour eux-mêmes autrefois, sont aimés plus tard comme symboles du passé et détournés alors de leur sens primitif, comme dans la langue poétique les mots pris comme images ne sont plus entendus dans leur sens primitif'[3] (pp. 723f.).

Another passage shows that Proust was aware of the ambiguity of the term 'image', and of the danger of confusion between the sense 'mental picture or impression' and other meanings of the word. It is in the former sense that 'image' must be taken in this simile which Proust was to use again, with slight modifications, in *Combray*:

C'est roulées pour ainsi dire dans cette image qu'il emportait ses pensées, comme un jeune pêcheur rapporte au soleil, sans qu'il en

[1] 'Was it because, having previously seen white hawthorns, the sight of a pink thorn, whose flowers are no longer simple but composite, struck him at once by the twofold magic of analogy and difference which have so much influence on our minds?'

[2] J. M. Cocking, *Proust*, London, 1956, p. 48. See also by the same author: '*Jean Santeuil* et *À la recherche du temps perdu*', *Bulletin de la Société des Amis de Marcel Proust*, no. 6 (1956), pp. 181–97: pp. 190ff.

[3] 'The objects which we loved once for their own sake, we love them later as symbols of the past, and they are thus diverted from their original sense, as in the language of poetry words taken as images are no longer understood in their original meaning.'

souffre, sous un lit frais d'herbe, de l'herbe arrachée au fond de l'étang où il l'a pris, le poisson qu'il vient de pêcher. Ainsi ne connaissant pas encore ses idées, les gardant cachées sous l'image qu'il voyait devant ses yeux ... [1] (pp. 701f.).

He goes on to develop the same idea, and at one point finds it necessary to emphasize that 'image' does not mean anything symbolic in this context: 'Une fois devant son papier, il écrivait ce qu'il ne connaissait pas encore, ce qui l'invitait sous l'image où c'était caché (et qui n'était en quoi que ce soit un symbole) et non ce qui par raisonnement lui aurait paru intelligent et beau'[2] (p. 703).

I

The imagery of *Jean Santeuil* has a twofold interest for the critic. It can be studied—to borrow two terms from modern linguistics —'synchronically' and 'diachronically': in its own right, without any reference to the major work that followed, and as an important stage in the development of Proust's metaphorical vision. The main purpose of the present chapter is to examine it synchronically, by concentrating on a significant group of intellectual images: those which discuss the workings of memory and time. First, however, it might be useful to consider briefly some of the diachronic problems raised by the imagery. In the words of one critic, to move from Proust's early exercises 'to the shapeless mass of *Jean Santeuil* is to enter the workshop where the real labour is going ahead.'[3] In the field of figurative language this

---

[1] 'It is wrapped, so to speak, in this image that he took away his thoughts, as a young fisherman brings to the sunlight the fish he has just caught, without the latter suffering in any way, underneath a fresh layer of weeds, weeds pulled up from the bottom of the pond where he had caught it. Thus, unaware as yet of his ideas, keeping them hidden underneath the image which he saw before his eyes...' Cf. *À la recherche du temps perdu*, vol. I, p. 179 (*Du Côté de chez Swann*).

[2] 'Once in front of his paper, he wrote what he did not yet know, what appealed to him underneath the image where it was hidden (and which was not in any way a symbol), and not what might have seemed intelligent and beautiful to him by a process of reasoning.'   [3] Cocking, *Proust*, p. 12.

approach is particularly fruitful since it can grant us unique insights into the emergence of individual images and of some of the tendencies which govern the movement of Proust's imagery as a whole.

One is struck, first of all, by the fact that some experiences already have the same, or very nearly the same, metaphorical expression as in the *Temps perdu*. The mother's good-night kiss is already described as 'le viatique, attendu si fiévreusement que Jean s'efforçait de ne penser à rien en se déshabillant, pour franchir plus vite le moment qui l'en séparait'[1] (p. 205). Another great Proustian theme, the 'petite phrase'—identified here as coming from a Saint-Saëns sonata—is also presented in metaphorical terms which all readers of the cycle will immediately recognize: 'il écoutait cette phrase dont le divin sourire déjà au temps de leur bonheur lui paraissait désenchanté ... ils la sentaient passer comme une caresse ... à la phrase désolée qui disait que tout passe, la tristesse paraissait rester aussi légère'[2] (p. 817). A similar persistence of metaphorical motifs is found in the passage on hawthorns, which has already been mentioned. These crucial experiences obviously found their figurative equivalents at an early stage, and the images in which they were clothed remained firmly associated with them in the author's mind.

More incidental analogies may also persist, either because of their graphic quality and expressive force or because of their emotive overtones. Take these descriptions of two women listening to music—first Madame Cresmeyer in *Jean Santeuil*:

... qui depuis le commencement du morceau balançait sa tête avec son corps très vite et sans presque le déplacer, comme un balancier

---

[1] 'The viaticum, awaited so feverishly that Jean tried not to think of anything while undressing, so as to pass faster the moment which separated him from it.'

[2] 'He listened to this phrase whose divine smile had seemed wistful to him even at the time of their happiness ... they felt it pass like a caress ... for the disconsolate phrase which said that everything passes, the sadness seemed to remain as light as in earlier days.' Cf. also pp. 843f.

très rapide mais [qui] s'écarte si peu de son centre de gravité qu'il semble plutôt trembler par lui-même[1] (p. 800);

then Madame de Cambremer in *Du Côté de chez Swann*:

battant la mesure avec sa tête transformée en balancier de métronome dont l'amplitude et la rapidité d'oscillations d'une épaule à l'autre étaient devenues telles . . . qu'à tout moment elle accrochait avec ses solitaires les pattes de son corsage[2] (I, p. 328).

There are obvious differences, but the basic image is the same. Similarly we see in *Jean Santeuil* 'les arbres stériles s'adresser au ciel avec des gestes immenses'[3] (p. 512), and in *Combray* 'le peuplier de la rue des Perchamps adresser à l'orage des supplications et des salutations désespérées'[4] (I, p. 152). At Éteuilles,[5] as at Combray, the flies perform a kind of 'chamber music' on a hot summer's day, and the whole setting is almost exactly the same: Jean lying on his bed, the shutters drawn against the sun, and the sleepy stillness of the afternoon punctuated only by the noise of hammering in the street (pp. 292f.; cf. *Du Côté de chez Swann*, I, p. 83). Even a rather far-fetched mythological analogy is preserved in the passage from *Jean Santeuil* to the *Temps perdu*. Jean looks in on his mother 'comme Thétis visitée par son fils Aristée au fond des eaux'[6] (p. 271), whereas at the beginning of *Combray* the same analogy is used to describe the two vastly different worlds in which Swann moves (I, p. 18).

---

[1] '. . . who, ever since the beginning of the piece, had been swinging her head with her body, very fast and almost without shifting it, like a very swift pendulum moving away so slightly from its centre of gravity that it seems rather to quiver by itself.'

[2] 'Beating time with her head transformed into the pendulum of a metronome the amplitude and speed of whose oscillations from one shoulder to another had become such . . . that her solitaires got caught all the time in the straps of her corsage.'

[3] 'The barren trees appealing to the sky with immense gestures.'

[4] 'The poplar of the rue der Perchamps addressing desperate entreaties and salutations to the storm.'

[5] On variant forms of this name, see Pléiade ed., p. 1001, n. to p. 277.

[6] 'Like Thetis visited by her son Aristaeus at the bottom of the sea.'

It also happens that Proust has not yet found, in *Jean Santeuil*, the metaphorical equivalent which will eventually satisfy him although the ingredients are all there. Thus the lilacs in the park at Éteuilles remind him of a fairy in an eastern tale (p. 278), and there is a variation on the same theme in a later passage: 'ces beaux lilas, de sang persan, . . . sveltes Shéhérazades immobiles entre les branches'[1] (p. 325). The final stage in the development of this image will be reached in *Combray*: 'ces jeunes houris qui gardaient dans ce jardin français les tons vifs et purs des miniatures de la Perse'[2] (I, p. 135). Even more remarkable are the metamorphoses of another flower. At Éteuilles, 'un coquelicot . . . dressait sur le cordon tendu de sa mince tige verte sa fleur éclatante et simple . . . le vent courbait, faisait trembler à l'ombre sa flamme rouge . . . donnant au rare passant qui aperçoit tout d'un coup son pavillon rouge et élancé le plaisir d'une découverte'[3] (p. 301). In *Combray*, these metaphors are gathered up and developed until they form a striking and unified image:

. . . la vue d'un seul coquelicot hissant au bout de son cordage et faisant cingler au vent sa flamme rouge, au-dessus de sa bouée graisseuse et noire, me faisait battre le cœur, comme au voyageur qui aperçoit sur une terre basse une première barque échouée que répare un calfat, et s'écrie, avant de l'avoir encore vue: 'La Mer!'[4] (I, pp. 138f.).

[1] 'These beautiful lilacs, of Persian blood . . . slim Shahrazads immobile amid the branches.'

[2] 'These young houris who, in this French garden, kept the vivid and pure colours of Persian miniatures.'

[3] 'A poppy . . . raised its bright and simple blossom on the tight cord of its thin green stem . . . the wind bent its red flame and made it flicker in the shade . . . thus giving the pleasure of a discovery to the rare passer-by who suddenly notices its slender red flag.'

[4] '. . . the sight of a single poppy hoisting its red flame at the top of its rope and making it sail in the wind, above its greasy black buoy, made my heart beat faster, like a traveller who notices on low ground the first stranded boat which a caulker is repairing, and exclaims: "The Sea!", even before having seen it.' For a detailed comparison of the two versions, see J. Paque, 'De *Jean Santeuil* à la *Recherche du Temps perdu*: Le coquelicot', *Cahiers d'Analyse Textuelle*, vi (1964), pp. 59–69.

Even more significant than the first appearance or gradual crystallization of particular analogies is the presence in *Jean Santeuil* of some of the fundamental forms and tendencies of Proust's imagery, only a few of which can be mentioned here.[1] He is already fond of borrowing similes and metaphors from physics, chemistry and other sciences. Some of these are brief and incisive:

La pensée est une espèce de télescope qui nous permet de voir des spectacles éloignés et immenses[2] (p. 874);

. . . le désir de l'un avait découvert le désir de l'autre, et, comme ce soufre s'unissant à ce phosphore, s'en était enflammé[3] (p. 509).

Elsewhere the analogy is more fully developed. In the 'preface' we are told that the author of *Jean Santeuil* never wrote letters to friends:

Il les considérait comme des sortes de paratonnerres qui tirent à l'esprit son électricité et ne lui permettent [pas] de s'accumuler jusqu'à ces véritables orages intérieurs où peut seulement jaillir le véritable éclair du génie, où la parole humaine prend une puissance qui la fait retentir au loin comme le tonnerre[4] (p. 187).

As in the *Temps perdu*, some of the scientific analogies in *Jean Santeuil* have an ironical twist resulting from the contrast between the grandeur of the image and the mediocrity of the subject described. Thus Jean's father is thrilled to hear of a society

---

[1] On the part played by these types of imagery in the *Temps perdu*, see V. E. Graham, *The Imagery of Proust*; J. Mouton, *Le Style de Marcel Proust*, 2nd ed., Paris, 1968, ch. 3; and my book, *The Image in the Modern French Novel*, ch. 3.

[2] 'Thought is a kind of telescope which enables us to see distant and immense scenes.'

[3] '. . . the desire of the one had discovered the desire of the other and had burst into flame like sulphur combining with phosphorus.'

[4] 'He regarded them as a kind of lightning-conductor which draws the electricity from the mind and does not allow it to accumulate to the point of producing those veritable internal storms from which alone the true flash of genius can shoot forth, where human speech acquires a power which makes it resound far away like thunder.'

scandal which had been common knowledge for many years, 'comme nous trouvons du plaisir en recevant la lumière d'une étoile en voyage peut-être depuis des milliers d'années'[1] (p. 735).

Medicine is already an important source of imagery in *Jean Santeuil*, as it was to remain in the *Temps perdu*. Some of the medical analogies are almost technical in their precision:

> . . . ces paroles qu'elle redisait si souvent étaient comme la petite dose de morphine qui, ayant peu à peu anesthésié sa conscience, la faisait vivre en paix avec elle-même[2] (p. 737).

The association between illness and love, which was to become the main metaphorical theme of *Un Amour de Swann*, is already in evidence in *Jean Santeuil*:

> . . . cet amour n'était plus. On pouvait le toucher aux points jadis sensibles sans que Jean éprouvât rien, comme une peau morte que nous portons encore avec nous, mais qui désormais ne ressentira plus ni caresses ni piqûres, qui n'est plus nous, qui est morte[3] (p. 674);
>
> . . . pareilles à ces maladies d'où un jeune homme se relève plus fort mais auxquelles succombe le tempérament épuisé de celui qui a derrière lui une longue vie, ces querelles, qui rafraîchissent et exaltent un amour naissant, conduisaient de plus en plus vite à sa fin leur amour qui avait tant duré[4] (p. 816).

Images from the various arts are already very prominent in

---

[1] 'As we find pleasure in receiving light from a star, which has perhaps been travelling for thousands of years.'

[2] '. . . these words which she repeated so often were like a small dose of morphia which had gradually anaesthetized her conscience and made her live at peace with herself.'

[3] '. . . this love no longer existed. One could touch it at its once sensitive points without Jean experiencing anything, like dead skin which we still carry with us but which will no longer feel either caresses or pricks, which is no longer part of us, which is dead.'

[4] '. . . like those illnesses from which a young man recovers stronger than before but which prove fatal to the exhausted constitution of one who has a long life behind him, these quarrels, which refresh and excite a nascent love, led faster and faster to the end of their love which had lasted so long.'

Jean Santeuil. Flowers, for example, are repeatedly likened to works of art:

Chacune était large et brillante comme une rose et sa couleur safranée transportait, comme dans un tableau, l'infaillible hardiesse d'un coloriste délicieux[1] (p. 786);

... le petit duvet finement organisé des pistils qui étaient au cœur de la fleur, comme une sorte d'obscur et mystérieux chœur au sein d'une éclatante basilique[2] (pp. 278f.).

In this last example, one wonders whether the homonymy of *cœur* and *chœur* was not the starting-point of the image.

There are already parallels between paintings and human beings, as in this description of M. Beulier: 'Cette essence d'âme, toute la personne de M. Beulier en était comme enduite, comme certains personnages du Titien sont comme enveloppés d'une beauté qui est la beauté de la peinture, et aussi de la vie'[3] (p. 269). This metaphorical motif will give rise to a number of precise and highly differentiated pictorial analogies in the *Temps perdu*, to the parallels which Swann draws between human beings and works of art, and to the close association between certain people and pictures: Odette and Botticelli's Zephora, the kitchen-maid and Giotto's Charity, and others.[4]

Proust's later habit of comparing culinary masterpieces to the major arts is foreshadowed in an image, developed in great detail, where a dinner is compared to an art-gallery: 'Un dîner est une sorte de musée de la gourmandise où les différentes œuvres

---

[1] 'Each was broad and bright like a rose, and its saffron colour was enchanting, as in a picture the unerring boldness of a delightful colourist.'

[2] '... the finely organized slight down of the pistils which were at the very heart (*cœur*) of the flower, like a kind of dark and mysterious choir (*chœur*) in the middle of a brilliant basilica.'

[3] 'It was as though the whole personality of M. Beulier were imbued with this spiritual essence, like some figures of Titian who seem enveloped in a beauty which is the beauty of painting and also of life.'

[4] For details see my book, *The Image in the Modern French Novel*, pp. 154ff. Cf. above, p. 74.

H

auxquelles notre imagination a souvent rêvé . . . se trouvent à notre portée'[1] (p. 570).

Similes and metaphors from mythology are one of the most persistent motifs of Proust's imagery.[2] There are various examples in *Jean Santeuil*, some quite short:

Comme Jupiter, son crâne semblait contenir les mondes[3] (p. 389);
. . . portant plus légèrement qu'Atlas le monde entier sur ses épaules[4] (p. 390);

others developed into an epic simile:

Au plus fort de la mêlée et quand la position devenait vraiment dangereuse, un dieu prenait Ajax par les cheveux et le dérobait aux coups de ses ennemis dans un nuage. C'est ce nuage divin qui flotta pendant quelques jours autour de l'esprit de Marie[5] (p. 613).

Another essential motif of Proust's imagery, personification, is already noticeable in *Jean Santeuil*, though not always with very happy results:

ce devant quoi rôde et aboie notre pensée[6] (p. 756);
L'habitude l'attendait dès la porte et l'ouvrait gaiement pour lui[7] (p. 356).

[1] 'A dinner is a kind of museum of gourmandism where the various works, on which our imagination has often mused . . . are within our reach.' Cf. P. Aschkenasy-Lelu, 'Les Sens mineurs chez Proust', *Bulletin de la Société des Amis de Marcel Proust*, no. 9 (1959), pp. 44–68: pp. 56ff. See also G. Matoré, 'Les Images gustatives dans *Du Côté de chez Swann*', *Mélanges de linguistique et de littérature romanes à la mémoire d'István Frank*, Universität des Saarlandes, 1957, pp. 685–92.

[2] See J. Seznec, *Marcel Proust et les dieux* (Zaharoff Lecture), Oxford, 1962, pp. 9ff.   [3] 'His skull, like Jupiter's, seemed to contain worlds.'

[4] '. . . carrying the whole world on his shoulders more lightly than Atlas.'

[5] 'In the thick of the fight and when the position became really dangerous, a god used to take Ajax by the hair and hide him in a cloud from the blows of his enemies. It is this divine cloud which floated for a few days around Marie's mind.'

[6] 'That which makes our thought prowl and bark.'

[7] 'Habit was waiting for him at the door and cheerfully opened it for him.' Cf. *À la recherche du temps perdu*, vol. I, p. 115 (*Du Côté de chez Swann*). See also Zeblewski, loc. cit., pp. 331ff.

Synaesthetic analogies between the various senses, which Baudelaire's *Correspondances* had erected into an aesthetic principle and which were to play a crucial part in the description of music and other experiences in the *Temps perdu*, occur repeatedly in *Jean Santeuil*:

. . . ce que lui chantait le soleil qui l'accompagnait à son tour de toutes les choses illuminées comme d'instruments retentissants, frémissants d'une musique divine[1] (pp. 777f.).

Yet another great metaphorical theme, the *mystique* of proper names, which will be discussed in the next chapter, is adumbrated in a dithyrambic passage on the name Fontainebleau:

Fontainebleau, nom doux et doré comme une grappe de raisin soulevée . . . ses lettres portent sur le timbre de la poste, comme une obscurité de sous-bois ou une figure de grappe, ce nom glorieux et doux Fontainebleau[2] (pp. 570f.).

It is clear, then, that many characteristic tendencies of the imagery of the *Temps perdu* are already present in *Jean Santeuil*, either in a fully developed or in an embryonic form. Needless to say, there are also very great differences between the two works, both in the quality of the images themselves—in their appropriateness, precision and novelty, in the density and complexity of their texture—and in the way in which they are used. In the *Temps perdu*, many of the major metaphorical themes—hawthorns, the 'petite phrase', parallels between love and illness and between people and paintings, certain forms of personification, the magic of proper names, and others—are closely integrated into the structure of the work; some recurrent images are very much like Wagnerian *leitmotivs*. In *Jean Santeuil*, the integration of imagery into the structure of the novel does not arise since the novel has

[1] '. . . what the sun sang to him, to the accompaniment of all the illuminated objects which were like instruments resounding and vibrating with a divine music.'

[2] 'Fontainebleau, a name soft and golden like a raised bunch of grapes . . . her letters bear on the postmark, like the darkness of underwood or the shape of a bunch of grapes, this glorious and soft name, Fontainebleau.'

no structure in the proper sense of the term. As Proust himself says in the unfinished introduction,[1] 'ce livre n'a jamais été fait, il a été récolté' (p. 181).[2] Looked at in this light, the images in *Jean Santeuil*, like other elements of the book, are no more than raw material waiting to be fitted into the grand design of the cycle.

II

According to one critic, 'le principal plaisir qu'on prend à lire *Jean Santeuil* naît de ces promesses, souvent répétées, du chef-d'œuvre futur'.[3] It would, however, be wrong to consider the book solely as a prefiguration of what was to follow; in this way one might miss certain valuable features which were not subsequently embodied in the *Temps perdu*. We shall therefore examine an important group of images in the novel from a strictly 'synchronic' point of view, irrespective of whether or not they passed into the later work. Time and memory play a prominent part in *Jean Santeuil*;[4] they are complex, elusive and highly abstract experiences about which one can hardly talk, and whose essence one can hardly grasp, in other than figurative language. It is therefore of considerable interest to see how, by means of

[1] 'Projet d'introduction inachevé' (Pléiade ed., p. 986, n.1 to p. 181).

[2] 'This book has never been written: it has been gathered in.'

[3] 'One's main pleasure in reading *Jean Santeuil* comes from these frequently repeated promises of the future masterpiece' (R. Pomeau, '*Jean Santeuil* et le temps retrouvé', *Annales Publiées par la Faculté des Lettres de Toulouse*, vi, 1–2 (1957), *Littératures V*, pp. 59–66: p. 64).

[4] See esp. E. R. Jackson, 'The Genesis of the Involuntary Memory in Proust's Early Works', *Publications of the Modern Language Association of America*, lxxvi (1961), pp. 586–94: pp. 588ff., and her book, *L'Évolution de la mémoire involontaire dans l'œuvre de Marcel Proust*, Paris, 1966, ch. 2. On the further development of this imagery, see E. Gülich, 'Die Metaphorik der Erinnerung in Prousts *À la Recherche*', *Zeitschrift für französische Sprache und Literatur*, lxxv (1965), pp. 51–74. Cf. also L. Fasciati, 'Gegenwart, Zukunft und Vergangenheit im Jugendwerk Marcel Prousts', ibid., lxxx (1970), pp. 193–209, and H. Weinrich, 'Typen der Gedächtnismetaphorik', *Archiv für Begriffsgeschichte*, ix (1964), pp. 23–6.

what analogies, Proust tried to formulate these difficult problems at this stage of his development.

Many of Proust's images are connected with water, the sea and allied phenomena,[1] and it was inevitable that these analogies should suggest themselves to him when he was talking of the passage of time. The basic theme of this imagery, the traditional metaphor of the 'flow of time'—the Heraclitean πάντα ρεῖ[2]— appears already in the unfinished introduction: 'Puis-je appeler ce livre un roman? C'est moins peut-être et bien plus, l'essence même de ma vie, recueillie sans y rien mêler, dans ces heures de déchirure où elle découle' (p. 181).[3] Waves in particular provide Proust with three interesting images in which the continuity of time is evoked on three different planes. One of them depicts the apparent stagnation of one period in a man's life:

... comme un homme assis dans une barque qui reste immobile, les yeux fixés sur les petits flots qui passent autour, peu à peu victime d'une sorte de vertige, croit que les flots conspirent à pousser la barque et qu'elle avance, ainsi le temps en passant lui semblait préparer le jour qu'il attendait[4] (p. 616).

Another wave-image describes the biological processes which are constantly at work in our lives and which can be most directly observed in a sleeping man:

[1] See V. E. Graham, 'Water Imagery and Symbolism in Proust', *The Romantic Review*, 1 (1959), pp. 118–28, and also his book, *The Imagery of Proust*, pp. 15ff. and 119ff.

[2] Cf. G. Poulet, *Études sur le temps humain*, Edinburgh, 1949, p. 10. The formula may, however, be apocryphal; cf. B. Russell, *History of Western Philosophy*, 3rd impr., London, 1948, p. 64. See also H. Meyerhoff, *Time in Literature*, Berkeley–Los Angeles, 1960, pp. 14ff.

[3] 'Can I call this book a novel? It is less perhaps and also much more, the very essence of my life collected without mixing it with anything, in those hours when there is a tear through which it flows.'

[4] '... as a man sitting in a boat which remains motionless, his eyes fixed on the small waves which pass around him, is gradually overcome by a kind of dizziness and believes that the waves combine to push the boat and that it is advancing, thus the passage of time seemed to him to prepare the day for which he was waiting.'

... sa poitrine se soulevait régulièrement, ballottée comme une chose inerte sur ces flots de la vie qui le portaient et venaient se briser si près de Jean et de sa mère avec un bruit égal[1] (p. 879).

A little earlier, the change of generations had been pictured in similar terms:

... vous avez vu l'histoire se faire devant vous, c'est-à-dire en deux générations l'espèce humaine se transformer, comme vous ne pouvez pas rester au bord de la mer quelques minutes, à regarder le flot se soulever, se jeter en avant, reculer et recommencer, sans voir, marquée par les flots eux-mêmes qui semblaient n'être que des flots sans rapport qu'avec celui qui [les] précédait et [les] suivait, l'indication plus vague en apparence, mais au fond plus certaine, plus vaste, de la marée[2] (p. 874).

A few lines further on, the same image is developed into a personification: '. . . si c'est la loi de ces générations . . . de se laisser tendrement dominer par celle qui vient après elles, comme la vague s'infléchit caressante sous la vague qui bondit joyeusement [sur] elle'[3] (p. 875).

Memory and oblivion are also compared to certain experiences at sea:

... les époques de notre cœur sont comme des îles qui s'engloutiraient dans l'océan au moment où le voyageur les quitte et dont ... il ne pourra plus retrouver la trace[4] (p. 820).

---

[1] '. . . his chest rose regularly, tossed about like an inert object on the waves of life which carried him and came to break so near to Jean and his mother, with an even noise.'

[2] '. . . you have seen history being made before your very eyes, that is to say the human species transformed within two generations, as you cannot stand for a few minutes on the sea-shore, watching the waves rising, plunging ahead, withdrawing and starting again, without seeing an apparently vaguer, but basically more certain and vaster indication of the tide, marked by the waves themselves which seemed to be mere waves, each connected only with the one preceding and following it.'

[3] '. . . if it is the law of generations . . . meekly to allow themselves to be dominated by the one following them, as a wave bends affectionately under the wave which jumps joyfully upon it.'

[4] '. . . the epochs of our heart are like islands which are submerged in

... le nom prêt à [être] accueilli par la mémoire ouverte, était comme ces épaves glissantes qu'aucun clou ne peut accrocher, renvoyées par le reflux du doute sur la mer de l'inconnu, en proie [à] des remous sans nombre[1] (p. 738).

Some of these water images have a slightly precious air. A mind which has remained youthful in an ageing body is likened to fresh water underground (p. 270), and the night is visualized as pouring oblivion into our open mouth from its 'outres d'oubli'[2] (p. 296).

Among other forces of nature, the wind plays a vital part in the romantic reveries of Jean Santeuil. In an important passage on involuntary memory, the wind acts as a kind of 'magic carpet'[3] which takes him back into the past, reawakening long-forgotten pictures of seaside holidays:

... le vent, dont le premier bruit ... avait gonflé ses ailes, comme s'il était de la race des mouettes et se [sentait] appelé vers les tempêtes ... l'enfant bien-aimé qu'il avait assis sur ses ailes immenses, caoutchoutées et froides comme des nageoires et bercé de son bruit ... [il l']avait ainsi conduit partout où il avait des souvenirs, où il y avait une idée, quelque chose à trouver, un sentiment qui valait la peine qu'il le déterrât dans le sable[4] (p. 396).

In more simple language we are told: 'Le vent en lui soufflant

the ocean as soon as the traveller leaves them, and of which . . . he will never again find any trace.'

[1] '. . . the name, ready to be received by his open memory, was like those slippery wrecks which no nail can catch, swept back by the ebb of doubt into the sea of the unknown, at the mercy of innumerable eddies.'

[2] 'Water-skins of oblivion.'

[3] Cf. Jackson, art. cit., p. 589.

[4] '...the wind, whose first noise ... had inflated his wings, as if he belonged to the race of gulls and felt drawn towards the storms . . . the beloved child whom it (the wind) had placed on its wings, immense, elastic and cold like floats, and lulled with its noise . . . it had thus taken him everywhere where he had memories, where there was an idea, something to find, a feeling worthy of being unearthed by him in the sand.'

à [la] figure n'entrait pas seulement dans sa poitrine. L'âme de Jean respirait en même temps le souvenir'[1] (p. 390).

Other natural phenomena also suggest analogies for the obscure processes of involuntary memory. When we rediscover a past experience in a present one, we do so by virtue of an 'essence' which the two have in common. These 'eternal' essences, thanks to which we transcend the limitations of time (cf. pp. 400f.), occupy a key position in Proust's idealistic philosophy, and he sums up their nature in a simple but expressive simile: '. . . essence qui nous trouble en ce qu'elle est nous-même, ce nous-même que nous ne sentons pas au moment, mais que nous retrouvons comme un miel délicieux resté après les choses quand elles sont loin de nous'[2] (p. 537). Flowers which take us back into the past seem to have 'une expression morale': they are like an image of an earlier period of our life, which we recognize in them (p. 279). In the same way, a piece of music will carry the memories associated with it, just as a wood keeps the secrets it has overheard (p. 295).

Animal images are also brought into play to portray these experiences. The moments fly past, one after another, 'l'aile basse, emportant au néant le message dont chacun était chargé pour Jean et qu'il n'avait pas eu l'énergie de prendre au vol et d'essayer de comprendre'[3] (p. 418). Other animal images are somewhat bizarre:

. . . les souvenirs lui dressaient une échelle par où, s'il avait la force de la saisir, il pouvait, de réflexion en réflexion ou de créature en créature, s'évader dans ce champ de l'espérance et des siècles où l'esprit peut courir comme un poulain lâché[4] (pp. 210f.);

[1] 'The wind blowing in his face did not merely penetrate into his chest. Jean's soul was breathing memories at the same time.'

[2] '. . . an essence which disturbs us because it is part of our own selves, the selves which we do not feel at the moment, but which we find again like delicious honey left behind by things when they are far from us.'

[3] 'Their wings lowered, taking away into nothingness the message with which each of them was charged for Jean and which he did not have the energy to grasp and try to understand.'

[4] '. . . memories put up a ladder for him by which, if he had the strength to take hold of it, he could, from one reflection or one creature to

... comme une poule que sa nature, sans lui faire connaître si elle réchauffe des œufs de poussin ou des œufs de serpent, force pourtant à leur donner sa vie, il couvait cet avenir inconnu et sa douteuse espérance avec toute la chaleur infatigable de son âme attentive[1] (p. 825).

The scientific bias of Proust's mind comes to the fore in several images connected with memory and time. One of these is drawn from geology, a science which was to become a prolific source of analogies in the *Temps perdu*:

Il fallait... que dans le fond de son passé et de son oubli, qui sait peut-être dans de récentes alluvions de sa mémoire, saignât encore quelque plaie qu'elle lui avait faite[2] (p. 689).

The timelessness of certain human characteristics is compared to a chemical formula:

On dit 'noble de 1830', on dit 'journaliste de 1880', mais, comme le chimiste qui sait que le soufre et le phosphore se combineront éternellement dans les mêmes proportions, vous ne verrez au fond de tout cela que les sentiments[3] (p. 875).

In a passage on the miraculous speed of memory, electric currents and telephones are incongruously associated with medieval pictures of angels:

L'électricité ne met pas moins de temps à conduire à notre oreille penchée sur un cornet téléphonique une voix pourtant bien éloignée,

another, escape to that field of hope and of the centuries, where the mind can run about like a colt which has been let loose.'

[1] '. . . like a hen who, without knowing whether she is warming chicken eggs or eggs of snakes, is forced by her nature to pass on her life to them, he was hatching this unknown future, and his dubious hope, with all the tireless warmth of his attentive mind.'

[2] 'In the depth of his past and his oblivion, or perhaps even in recent alluvia of his memory . . . some wound which she had inflicted on him must still have been bleeding.'

[3] 'We say "a nobleman of 1830" or "a journalist of 1880", but, in the same way as a chemist who knows that sulphur and phosphorus will eternally combine in the same proportions, we realize that fundamentally it is all a question of feelings'. Cf. above, p. 101, n. 3.

que la mémoire, cet autre élément puissant de la nature qui, comme
la lumière ou l'électricité, dans un mouvement si vertigineux qu'il
nous semble un repos immense, une sorte d'omniprésence, est à la
fois partout autour de la terre, aux quatre coins du monde où palpi-
tent sans cesse ses ailes gigantesques, comme un de ces anges que le
Moyen Âge imaginait[1] (p. 243).

Proust is fully aware of the fact, which has been emphasized
by some modern philosophers and linguists, that we tend to
picture time in terms of space.[2] His spatial metaphors have an
abstract, almost geometrical precision:

Il ne cherchait pas à se demander ce qu'elle avait été avant lui, ce
qu'elle serait après, le temps ressemblant pour lui à l'espace et toute
la partie qui ne tombait pas immédiatement sous son rayon visuel
étant cachée derrière cet horizon vague que l'œil, en arrière ni en
avant, ne cherche pas à pénétrer[3] (p. 749);
    Sentiment qui peut-être ne sera pas conservé, mais se rit de
l'être, comme si la conservation si longue qu'elle soit était, dans cette
sphère du temps, si au-dessous de la zone indéterminée dans laquelle
il plane[4] (p. 401).

[1] 'Electricity does not require less time to bring a very distant voice to
our ear bent over a telephone receiver, than memory, that other powerful
element of nature, which, like light or electricity, in a movement so
vertiginous that it seems to us an immense repose, a kind of omnipresence,
is simultaneously everywhere around the earth, in the four corners of the
world where its gigantic wings are constantly fluttering, like one of those
angels pictured by the Middle Ages.'
[2] Cf. esp. B. L. Whorf, op. cit. (cf. above, p. 27, n. 1). On spatial
metaphors see G. Matoré, L'Espace humain, Paris, 1962. Cf. also G.
Poulet, L'Espace proustien, Paris, 1963, esp. pp. 135ff. and 182ff.
[3] 'He did not try to ask himself what she had been like before him and
what she would be like afterwards: time for him was like space, and the
whole part which did not immediately fall within his area of vision was
hidden behind the vague horizon which the eye does not try to penetrate,
either forward or backward.'
[4] 'A feeling which will not perhaps survive but does not care, as if
survival, for however long, were to take place, in the sphere of time, far
below the indeterminate zone where it is hovering.'

Elsewhere, the image becomes impressionistic and heavily charged with emotion:

J'use du bout des doigt de tous ces moments qu'Aujourd'hui m'apporte encore sans pitié, l'un après l'autre. Que la nuit vienne au plus vite enceindre à jamais de ses murailles gigantesques, mettre une forme éternelle et fuyante à Aujourd'hui, passer lentement sur lui son noir déluge[1] (p. 250).

As was only to be expected, Proust's absorbing interest in art colours also his ideas about memory and time. He draws a number of images from the visual arts, including two interesting analogies suggested by photography:

Les lieux ... garderont après notre mort pour quelque temps encore . . . [leur] rideau de saules, ou [leur] chemin montant, ou [le] remous de [leur] eau sous le pont entre les nénuphars, comme les photographies, qui restent dans une maison, de ceux que ne reconnaissent pas ceux qui ne les ont pas connus[2] (p. 535);
... la photographie de tout cela avait pris sa place dans les archives de sa mémoire, des archives si vastes que dans la plus grande partie il n'irait jamais regarder, à moins d'un hasard qui les fît rouvrir[3] (p. 898).

In one of the main passages on the rediscovery of the past, the contrast between involuntary and ordinary memory—'la triste mémoire',[4] as Proust once calls it (p. 401)—is brought out by a series of analogies from painting and drawing. Ordinary memory

[1] 'I use up with my finger-tips all the moments which Today still brings mercilessly along, one after another. May the night come as fast as possible, to enclose Today for ever within its gigantic walls, to give it an eternal and fleeting form, slowly to cover it with its black flood.'

[2] 'Places ... will preserve for some time after our death ... the curtain of willows, or the uphill road, or the eddy in the water underneath the bridge, among the water-lilies, like photographs, left in a house, of people whom those who did not know them will not recognize.'

[3] '... a photograph of all this had taken its place in the archives of his memory, vast archives at most of which he would never look, unless some chance led him to reopen them.'

[4] 'Sorry memory.'

keeps merely 'les croquis rangés du présent',[1] but in some privileged moments of our life the past comes back to us in a flash and we relive our experiences in the fullness and richness of reality: 'au lieu de la tristesse de quelqu'un qui n'a que des collections, . . . je sens la trame de ma vie d'autrefois, . . . non point plate comme une image, mais pleine comme une réalité et vague comme un sentiment'[2] (pp. 400f.).

In a different context, the similarity between people belonging to the same generation is compared to that between portraits from the same period in an art-gallery (p. 875). Elsewhere, sculpture furnishes a somewhat unexpected analogy: 'les mauvais jours . . . persistant seulement dans son souvenir comme ces morts dont nous ne pouvons plus contempler que l'impuissante statue'[3] (p. 615).

In two images, memory is likened to a jewel-case and, in rather questionable taste, to a relic:

. . . trésor qui ne peut se conserver que dans un seul écrin, la mémoire, et ne peut se faire pressentir aux autres que par une sorte d'allusion: la poésie[4] (p. 535).

Un nom qui contient de la voix de ma mère, du temps même en train alors de s'écouler, . . . je le vénère plus, il contient pour moi plus de divin, d'irrefaisable à n'importe quel artiste ou philosophe, que la relique qui contiendrait du sang du Christ[5] (p. 319).

Proust even finds a comparison from his own craft to describe

[1] 'The sketches of the present which have been tidied away.'

[2] 'Instead of the sadness of someone who only has collections . . . I can feel the texture of my past life, . . . not flat like a picture but full like reality and vague like feeling.'

[3] 'The bad days . . . persisting only in his memory, like the dead of whom we can merely contemplate the powerless statue.'

[4] '. . . a treasure which can be preserved only in one jewel-case, that of memory, and can only be indicated to others by one kind of allusion, that of poetry.'

[5] 'A name which contains some of my mother's voice, some of the time itself which was passing just then, . . . I revere it more, it contains for me more of a divine essence, which no artist or philosopher could reproduce, than a relic containing the blood of Christ.'

the effects of time on our memories: 'Les années de notre vie que nous avons vécues avec le plus de passion, une fois révolues, sont pour nous comme un roman que nous avons lu jusqu'à la fin: une fois lu, nous n'avons plus de plaisir à le relire'[1] (p. 387).

Music is one of the principal agencies of involuntary memory, and it also provides some analogies for the description of these processes in *Jean Santeuil*. In a curious passage, which is difficult to reconcile with what we are told elsewhere about the 'petite phrase' (cf. above, p. 98), Proust argues that 'natural music', which has no timeless and universally valid message to convey, will preserve more vividly than human music the atmosphere of the place and time when we heard it. And he goes on:

... ces humbles musiques naturelles ont un rapport profond, une harmonie cachée avec la saison où elles ont été entendues... Nées d'elle, cris d'adieu de l'hirondelle, de ses premiers froids, ou bourdonnement des mouches, de sa chaleur, c'est bien naturellement que ces musiciennes nous parlent d'elle puisque c'est elle-même qui nous parle dans leurs chansons[2] (p. 295).

Another musical image embroiders on the connexion between age and memory:

On dit qu'en vieillissant nos sensations s'affaiblissent. Peut-être, mais elles s'accompagnent de l'écho de sensations plus anciennes, comme ces grandes chanteuses un peu vieilles dont un chœur invisible renforce la voix affaiblie[3] (p. 476).

[1] 'The years of our life which we have lived most passionately, once they are over, are for us like a novel we have read to the end: once we have read it, it gives us no more pleasure to re-read it.'

[2] '... these humble forms of natural music have a deep relationship, a hidden harmony with the season in which we heard them... Born of the season, the farewell cries of the swallow from its first cold days, or the buzzing of flies from its heat, these musicians speak of it very naturally because it is the season itself which speaks to us in their songs.' On the interpretation of the last sentence, see Pléiade ed., p. 1006, n.4 to p. 295.

[3] 'People say that, as we grow older, our sensations become weaker. Perhaps, but they are accompanied by the echo of older sensations, like famous elderly singers whose weakened voice is reinforced by an invisible choir.'

In a very different key, time and memory are sometimes compared to humble everyday objects. An old cloak which his mother used to wear does not simply remind Jean of his own youth but looks like an image of it: 'Troublé, il regarda le manteau qui, dans ses couleurs encore fraîches, son velouté encore doux, ressemblait à ces années qui ne servaient plus à rien, sans rapport avec la vie, mais pas fanées, intactes dans son souvenir'[1] (p. 419). Even an ordinary handkerchief can become an effigy of time:

Chaque heure lui devenant troublante et sacrée, comme ayant reçu l'essence de sa personne et les secrets de son intimité, il la respirait en tremblant ainsi qu'un mouchoir où elle aurait en le tenant dans sa main laissé un peu de son odeur[2] (p. 824).

The contrast between an old body and a young mind is also presented in deliberately prosaic similes: the body will be worn out as an old dressing-gown which is not part of one's personality; it will, however, be kept healthy by the mind just as the freshness of meat is preserved by a grain of salt (p. 270).

The alphabet suggests an unusual image in a discussion of the way in which a writer utilizes the raw material of his experience: 'notre vie, quelle qu'elle soit, est toujours l'alphabet dans lequel nous apprenons à lire et où les phrases peuvent bien être n'importe lesquelles, puisqu'elles sont toujours composées des mêmes lettres'[3] (p. 477).

Other images drawn from ordinary experiences are more poetical. A new day is likened to a mysterious New Year's present:

[1] 'He looked uneasily at the cloak which, with its colours still fresh and its still soft velvety feel, was like those years which were no longer of any use and bore no relation to life, but were not withered and remained intact in his memory.'

[2] 'Each hour became disturbing and sacred for him, as if it had received the essence of her personality and the secrets of her intimacy; he breathed it in, trembling, like a handkerchief which she had held in her hand and in which she had left a little of her scent.'

[3] 'Our life, whatever it is like, is always the alphabet in which we had learnt to read and where the sentences may be of any form because they are always made up of the same letters.'

Demain n'est-il pas là, qui déjà, tandis qu'il dort, repose encore tout enveloppé, comme le grand cadeau mystérieux où une carte se dissimule sous la ficelle, sous la lampe, le matin du jour de l'an[1] (p. 249).

Elsewhere, a parallel is drawn between sleep and a journey— a motif which will be more fully exploited in the *Temps perdu*:

... comme en voyage on se réveille dans un tout autre pays que celui où on s'était endormi, ainsi notre pensée est dans un tout autre site quand nous nous réveillons que quand nous nous sommes endormis ... Il a tant voyagé depuis, pendant cette nuit, que tout a bien changé en lui[2] (p. 864).

A little earlier, dreams about the remote past had been evoked in more romantic terms:

Comme une nuit obscure mais momentanément éclairée, ils (ses rêves) étaient pleins de signes et de présages. La chaîne des circonstances, suite des temps, ne pesant pas sur eux comme sur la vie de la veille, ils convenaient sans doute à cette dernière entrevue, à ce dernier rendez-vous avec un passé déjà trop lointain pour être ressaisi dans la vie. Ce fut donc sou le porche plein d'ombre d'un rêve que Françoise revint une dernière fois à lui[3] (p. 820).

Personification plays a conspicuous part in the description of

---

[1] 'Isn't tomorrow already there, while he is asleep, still resting in its wrapping, like the great and mysterious present where a card is hidden underneath the string, below the lamp, on the morning of New-Year's Day.'

[2] '... as one wakes up on a journey in quite a different country from the one where one had gone to sleep, in the same way our thoughts are in quite a different place when we wake up from the one where we had fallen asleep. .. One has travelled so much since then, during the night, that everything in one has changed.'

[3] 'Like a dark night which is lit up for a moment, they (his dreams) were full of signs and portents. Since the chain of circumstances, the sequence of time were not weighing upon them as they had weighed on his life during the preceding day, they were no doubt well suited to this last meeting, this last appointment with a past already too remote to be recaptured in life. It was thus under the shadowy porch of a dream that Françoise came back to him for the last time.'

time and memory in *Jean Santeuil*. At one point, time itself is endowed with a soul:

... comme si les années passées vivaient encore..., [comme] si l'âme de ce temps flottait encore dans des jardins pareils[1] (p. 473).

The quiet hours of the past are personified and presented as purposeful human beings: '... comme un ouvrage inappréciable qu'auraient ouvré des doigts aimés, ces douces étoffes vertes où sont engainés ces tuyaux au fond du bassin, qu'ont tissées ces mêmes heures silencieuses'[2] (p. 318).

To meet a flower which can talk to us of the past is like seeing an old friend: 'nous avons senti . . . dans ces bonnes fleurs blanches quelque chose qui nous parlait, comme quand nous rencontrons dans un défilé une personne aimée qui nous sourit, nous fait bonjour'[3] (p. 279).

Places we have seen are similarly personified and given a physiognomy of their own: 'Les lieux sont des personnes, mais des personnes qui ne changent pas et que nous retrouvons souvent après bien longtemps . . . des personnes à qui l'humanité qui est en nous a donné une physionomie'[4] (pp. 534f.; cf. p. 395).

Elsewhere the personification is more discreet, hardly more than a vague attempt to present an abstract phenomenon in a concrete form. In this passage on the role of imagination in involuntary memory, the verb *flotter*, not very metaphorical in itself but strengthened by repetition, provides the key-note of the whole experience:

[1] '. . . as if the years which are past were still alive . . ., as if the soul of that time were still floating over similar gardens.'

[2] '. . . like an invaluable piece of work produced by beloved fingers, these soft green fabrics in which the pipes at the bottom of the pond are ensheathed, woven by the same peaceful hours.'

[3] 'We felt . . . in these nice white flowers something that spoke to us, as when we meet in a mountain pass a person we love who smiles at us and greets us.'

[4] 'Places are persons, but persons who do not change and whom we often meet again after a very long time . . . persons to whom our own human nature has given a physiognomy.'

Serait-ce que la beauté, le bonheur pour le poète, c'est dans cette substance invisible qu'on peut appeler l'imagination . . . qui *flotte* seulement autour de la réalité passée qui se trouve prise dans une réalité présente? De sorte qu'entre l'œil qui la voit, qui la voit aujourd'hui et autrefois, *flotte* cette imagination divine[1] (p. 399).

And the same motif recurs once more at the end of the passage:

Nous ne savons pas quel jour où nous chercherons la beauté dans une montagne ou dans un ciel, nous la trouverons dans le bruit d'une roue de caoutchouc ou dans l'odeur d'une étoffe, dans ces choses qui ont *flotté* sur notre vie où le hasard [les] ramène *flotter* encore[2] (p. 402).

From the examples which have been quoted it is clear that the imagery of time and memory in *Jean Santeuil*, though uneven and at times vague and uncertain, contains many valuable elements some of which will recur in the *Temps perdu*, in a more or less modified form. On reading *Jean Santeuil*, one is alternately amazed to see how much had already been achieved and how much still remained to be done. The problem of involuntary memory, and the images clustering around it, are an example in point. Proust was well aware that he had had his predecessors in this field; in *Le Temps retrouvé* he mentions Chateaubriand, Nerval and Baudelaire,[3] and modern scholarship has added several other names to the list.[4] Proust himself was already exer-

---

[1] 'Is it perhaps the case that for the poet, beauty and happiness are located in that invisible substance which may be called imagination . . . which *floats* only around past reality caught in a present one? So that between the eye that sees it, that sees it today and in the past, this divine imagination is *floating*.' (My italics.)

[2] 'We do not know which day, when looking for beauty in a mountain or in a sky, we shall find it in the noise of a rubber wheel or in the smell of a fabric, in those things which have *floated* over our life where chance brings them back to *float*.' (My italics.)

[3] *À la recherche du temps perdu*, vol. III, pp. 919f.

[4] See esp. J. O'Brien, 'La Mémoire involontaire avant Marcel Proust', *Revue de Littérature Comparée*, xix (1939), pp. 19–36; E. Czoniczer, *Quelques antécédents de 'À la recherche du temps perdu'*, Geneva–New York–Paris, 1957; M. Mein, *Proust's Challenge to Time*, Manchester, 1962.

cised by these problems in *Les Plaisirs et les jours*,[1] and in *Jean Santeuil* there are, as we have seen, a number of detailed and penetrating analyses of these experiences, and the author has also evolved a rich and varied metaphorical language in which to talk about them. But the decisive step still had to be taken: Proust's ideas, and the images in which they were couched, had not only to be further developed but had to be transmuted into a work of art. In this as in other respects, he still had to accomplish all the labours which his narrator foresaw in *Le Temps retrouvé*: 'cet écrivain . . . devrait préparer son livre minutieusement, avec de perpétuels regroupements de forces, comme une offensive, le supporter comme une fatigue, l'accepter comme une règle, le construire comme une église, le suivre comme un régime, le vaincre comme un obstacle, le conquérir comme une amitié, le suralimenter comme un enfant le créer comme un monde.'[2]

The imagery of *Jean Santeuil* thus serves to remind us of a truth which, though obvious enough, is apt to be overlooked. Images, like other elements of style, do not exist in isolation. In a novel without structure, individual figures of great artistic beauty or expressive force may arise, but the imagery as a whole is bound to be shapeless and without any structural value. In the passage almost immediately following the lines which have just been quoted from *Le Temps retrouvé*, the narrator tentatively compares his future book to a cathedral, and although he dismisses the analogy as too ambitious, there can be no doubt that Proust liked to picture his cycle in that way. The images of *Jean Santeuil*, talented but inchoate and amorphous like other elements of that novel,[3] had to be transferred from the workshop to the

---

[1] Cf. E. R. Jackson, *L'Évolution de la mémoire involontaire dans l'œuvre de Marcel Proust*, ch. 1.

[2] 'This writer . . . would have to prepare his book scrupulously, with perpetual regroupings of forces, like an offensive, endure it like fatigue, accept it like a rule, build it like a church, follow it like a diet, overcome it like an obstacle, conquer it like a friendship, feed it up like a child, create it like a world' (*À la recherche du temps perdu*, vol. III, p. 1032).

[3] 'In conception, *Jean Santeuil* was an ambitious, intricate novel; it abounds in skilfully narrated passages, direct and vigorous, ranging from

cathedral, they had to be fitted and integrated into the architecture of a highly complex composition, before they could shine forth in their full lustre and significance.[1]

the delicate to the quasi-Balzacian, and in long and often compelling meditative disquisitions, lyrical, analytical, philosophical. But Proust did not succeed in creating an integrated fictional world, with a coherent set of characters' (G. Brée, *The World of Marcel Proust*, London ed., 1967, p. 63).

[1] I am greatly obliged to Professor J. M. Cocking for bibliographical information, and to Professor H. Flasche for enabling me to consult Miss Zeblewski's thesis, referred to in note 3 on p. 93.

CHAPTER VI

THE WRITER AND HIS TOOLS: PROUST'S IDEAS ON LANGUAGE AND ON STYLE IN HIS LETTERS TO SOME FRIENDS AND CRITICS

Un homme qui par l'usage entièrement nouveau qu'il a fait du passé défini, du passé indéfini, du participe présent, de certains pronoms et de certaines prépositions, a renouvelé presque autant notre vision des choses que Kant avec ses Catégories, les théories de la Connaissance et de la Réalité du monde extérieur...[1]

These words, written by Proust towards the end of his life, in his article on the style of Flaubert,[2] throw a glaring light on his whole attitude to language, on his belief in the fundamental importance of linguistic categories in our mental processes and our vision of the world. Interest in language is very widespread among educated Frenchmen, and in particular among French writers, but a recent critic was no doubt right when he concluded an article on 'Proust linguiste' with the claim: 'Aucun autre écrivain, semble-t-il, n'a accordé tant d'importance aux phéno-

[1] 'A man who, by his entirely new use of the Past Definite, the Past Indefinite, the Present Participle, certain pronouns and certain prepositions, has renewed our vision of things almost as much as Kant had renewed, by means of his categories, the theories of knowledge and of the reality of the external world...'

[2] 'À propos du "style" de Flaubert', *Nouvelle Revue Française*, xiv, 1 (1920), pp. 72–90.

mènes linguistiques.'[1] Remarks on language and style in general,
or on particular aspects of them—the *mystique* of proper names,
the social functions of words, the role of metaphor in the recapture of the past, and many other themes, including minute
details of pronunciation, grammar, vocabulary and etymology—
recur throughout his works; many of them are incidental whereas
others are worked out in great detail. They are already in evidence
in *Jean Santeuil*[2] and reach their supreme expression in *Le Temps
retrouvé* where the narrator, having discovered his vocation as a
writer, makes some of his most significant statements on the nature
of metaphor and on the concept of style as an idiosyncratic and
highly personal mode of vision.

How far is this absorbing interest in things linguistic reflected
in Proust's correspondence? Proust himself was intrigued by the
relationship which exists between a writer's conversation, his
correspondence and his creative activity—a special facet of the
wider problem which he examined in *Contre Sainte-Beuve* and
elsewhere: the connexion between an author's private personality
and his literary work. In *Jean Santeuil* he distinguished between
two possibilities. In some cases, the artistic style of the writer will
overflow into his correspondence and his conversation: 'L'habitude du travail peut faire que la causerie, que la correspondance

[1] 'No other writer, it would seem, has attached so much importance to
linguistic phenomena' (G. Matoré (in collaboration with I. Mecz), 'Proust
linguiste', in *Festschrift Walther von Wartburg zum 80.Geburtstag*,
Tübingen, 1968, vol. I, pp. 279–92: p. 292). On Proust's linguistic ideas,
see also K. D. Uitti, '*Le Temps retrouvé*: sens, composition et langue',
Romanische Forschungen, lxxv (1963), pp. 332–61; R. de Chantal, *Marcel
Proust critique littéraire*, Montreal, 1967, vol. I, Part II, ch. 5: 'Qu'est-ce
que le style?'; J. Milly, 'Les Pastiches de Proust: Structure et correspondances', *Le Français Moderne*, xxxv (1967), pp. 33–52 and 125–41;
Id., *Proust et le style*, Paris, 1970; J. Mouton, *Le Style de Marcel Proust*,
ch. 1: 'Les Idées de Marcel Proust sur le style'; M. Wilmet, 'Marcel
Proust: du côté de la grammaire', *Le Français Moderne*, xl (1972), pp.
126–46.

[2] See my article, 'Les Idées linguistiques de Proust dans *Jean Santeuil*',
in *Hommage à la mémoire de John Orr, Revue de Linguistique Romane*,
xxxi (1967), pp. 134–46.

soient comme des mécanismes inférieurs entraînés dans le vaste mouvement des organismes plus grands et plus hauts, et que la précision, l'élégance, l'esprit mènent d'un doigt, sans même y penser, la conversation et la correspondance.' Elsewhere there will be no connexion, no communication between these various activities: 'Il peut se faire que le travail cérébral s'amorçant uniquement dans la solitude pour cette fin spéciale, le langage intérieur suivi par la plume ne s'amorce pas pour la conversation.' This may happen in particular with writers like Balzac, whose gaze is fixed on external reality, and also with artists like Flaubert 'dont la réalité littéraire (une forme qui les fascine . . .) est si intérieure qu'elle ne peut s'appliquer dans la conversation ou dans la correspondance, de sorte que leur correspondance donne cette matière brute dont ils extraient de la beauté; et par moments en effet on a une phrase d'eux qui se trouve coupée dans cette matière.'[1]

Proust himself was an extremely voluminous correspondent, and although many of his letters deal with private matters, others contain more or less detailed discussions of literary and aesthetic problems, including numerous points of linguistic or stylistic interest which link up significantly with his general theories. Limitations of space make it impossible to cover his entire correspondence in this chapter; the analysis which follows will therefore be confined to four volumes of the *Correspondance générale*, which contain his letters to three people who played a major part

---

[1] 'The habit of work may result in casual conversation and correspondence being drawn, like lower mechanisms, into the vast movement of greater and higher organisms, with precision, elegance and wit leading the conversation and the correspondence lightly and quite spontaneously. . . It may happen that brain-work will start only in solitude for this particular purpose and that internal language, followed by the pen, will not therefore come into play for conversation . . . [great writers like Flaubert] whose literary reality (a form which fascinates them . . .) is so internal that it cannot be applied in conversation or in correspondence, so that their correspondence contains the raw material from which they extract beauty; and at times you have indeed a sentence by them which has been cut out of this material' (Pléiade ed., pp. 485f.).

in his life: the Comte Robert de Montesquiou (vol. I), the Comtesse Anna de Noailles (vol. II), and Mme Émile Straus (vol. VI), as well to several literary critics and some other friends (vol. III).[1]

A. GENERAL REMARKS

One of the most important discussions of linguistic problems in this correspondence is found in a letter to Mme Straus, probably written in January 1908 (VI, pp. 92–4).[2] Practically the whole letter deals with questions of language and of style and raises a number of fundamental issues. Proust opens the argument by defining his own position in the form of a paradox rejuvenating an old cliché: 'Les seules personnes qui défendent la langue française ... ce sont celles qui "l'attaquent".'[3] He boldly denies the existence of a French language in the abstract, independently of the writers who use it. Proust takes what might be described as an existentialist view of the relation between language and individual style: 'Chaque écrivain est obligé de se faire sa langue, comme chaque violoniste est obligé de se faire son "son".'[4] He hastens to add that he does not approve of authors who are

[1] *Correspondance générale de Marcel Proust*, 6 vols., Paris, 1930–36. Vol. I also contains several letters to Montesquiou's secretary, Gabriel d'Yturri, and vol. VI includes some addressed to Mme Straus's husband, M. Émile Straus. On Proust's relations with some of the recipients, see, in addition to R. de Chantal's work, G. D. Painter, *Marcel Proust. A Biography*, 2 vols., London, 1961–65; cf. also L. LeSage, *Marcel Proust and his Literary Friends*, Urbana, Illinois, 1958, and W. A. Strauss, *Proust and Literature*, Cambridge, Mass., 1957. For a precise dating of the letters, see P. Kolb, *La Correspondance de Marcel Proust. Chronologie et commentaire critique*, Urbana, Illinois, 1949. All the dates given in the present chapter are based on this volume. Professor Kolb has now begun the publication of a critical edition of Proust's correspondence.

[2] The beginning of this letter was published by André Maurois in his *À la recherche de Marcel Proust*, Paris, 1949, p. 262; cf. R. de Chantal, op. cit., vol. I, pp. 351f.

[3] The only people who defend the French language ... are those who "attack" it.'

[4] 'Every writer has to create his own language, just as every violinist has to create his own "*tone*".'

original but write badly; he prefers those who write well, but they cannot do so unless they are original and forge their own language: 'La correction, la perfection du style existe, mais au delà de l'originalité, . . . non en deçà';[1] without originality, there can be only clichés, not style in the proper sense of the term. This is because the development of a language is a creative and dialectical process: 'son unité n'est faite que de contraires neutralisés, d'une immobilité apparente qui cache une vie vertigineuse et perpétuelle.'[2] One cannot stand comparison with the great writers of the past unless one tries to write differently from them: Rousseau, Hugo, Flaubert, Maeterlinck hold their own beside Bossuet precisely because they were rebels, and some pedantic critics would no doubt find fault with Racine himself if he were writing today.

The truth is, Proust concludes, that nothing is certain, even in the sphere of grammar. Actually, this situation is to be welcomed since it gives the writer a certain amount of freedom: 'ainsi une forme grammaticale elle-même peut être belle, puisque ne peut être beau que ce qui peut porter la marque de notre choix, de notre goût, de notre incertitude, de notre désir, et de notre faiblesse.'[3]

Students of linguistics and stylistics will recognize some of their most fruitful concepts in this remarkable letter: the contrast between language in the abstract and individual language or 'idiolect'; the principle of creativeness, which has received considerable attention during the last decade or so, in the work of Chomsky and his associates; the neutralization of opposites; the part played by choice and personality in style.

Eleven years later, Proust returned to the same problem in a

---

[1] 'Correctness and perfection in style do exist, but beyond originality, . . . not this side of it.'

[2] 'Its unity consists merely in the neutralization of opposites, in an apparent immobility which conceals a vertiginous and perpetual life.'

[3] 'Thus a grammatical form can in itself be beautiful, for only that can be beautiful which can bear the stamp of our choice, our taste, our uncertainty, our desire and our weakness.'

letter to Jacques-Émile Blanche. Having noticed some mistakes and obscurities of syntax in an article by Blanche in *Le Figaro*, Proust reassures his friend while at the same time giving him some sound advice:

Je vous dirais que, certes, des lapsus grammaticaux n'ont jamais terni un beau style, mais que tout de même il vaut mieux les éviter . . . Pour ma part je ne tiens aucun compte de ces choses-là dans l'appréciation d'un style, c'est à mon avis par une incompréhension absolue de ce qu'est le style qu'on croit que pureté de style a un rapport quelconque avec absence de fautes. L'absence de fautes est une qualité purement subalterne, nullement esthétique. Néanmoins il me semble plus élégant d'effacer ces taches insignifiantes (III, p. 168).[1]

A few months after this letter, Proust published his article on the style of Flaubert where he reiterated the same ideas: 'Laissons de côté, je ne dis même pas les simples inadvertances, mais la correction grammaticale; c'est une qualité utile mais négative.'[2] A subsequent letter to Jacques Boulenger provides an interesting footnote to this essay. In an article in *L'Opinion*, Boulenger had completely misunderstood Proust's attitude, and the latter now finds it necessary to explain his position: 'Chose archi-signifiante, vous me faites dire pour Flaubert exactement le contraire de ce que j'ai dit. J'ai dit que la beauté grammaticale n'avait aucun rapport avec la correction. Jacques Boulenger me fait dire le contraire' (III, p. 211).[3]

[1] 'I would say that grammatical mistakes have certainly never tarnished a beautiful style, but that all the same it is better to avoid them. . . As far as I am concerned, I take no account of these things in the appreciation of a style; in my opinion, to believe that purity of style has anything whatever to do with lack of mistakes shows a complete failure to understand the nature of style. Lack of mistakes is a purely subordinate quality and not in any way an aesthetic one. Nevertheless it seems to me more elegant to remove these unimportant blemishes.'

[2] 'Let us disregard, I would not even say mistakes due to mere careless-ness, but grammatical correctness itself; it is a useful but negative quality.' Cf. R. de Chantal, op. cit., vol. I, p. 355.

[3] 'What is of the utmost significance, you make me say about Flaubert

The idea that the style of a writer is deeply rooted in his personality recurs in several letters. 'Style plus éternel d'être plus personnel',[1] Proust writes in 1905 to Mme de Noailles, when congratulating her on her latest book (II, p. 116). The same notion is expressed in almost mystical terms in a letter to Montesquiou: 'Je pense . . . qu'il existe pour toutes les belles phrases un droit imprescriptible qui les rend inaliénables à tout acquéreur, autre que celui qu'elles attendaient par une destination qui est de leur destinée' (I, pp. 73–4).[2] This conception of style will be further developed in *À la recherche du temps perdu* and will lead to the famous definition of style in *Le Temps retrouvé*: 'Le style pour l'écrivain, aussi bien que la couleur pour le peintre, est une question non de technique mais de vision.'[3]

In another letter to Montesquiou, Proust discusses, again in semi-mystical terms, a problem which looms large in modern linguistics as well as in the philosophy and psychology of language: the influence of words upon thought:[4] 'on sent que mille ombres vagues de pensées qui, au fond de nous, appelaient l'existence comme les ombres des êtres à venir dans *l'Énéide*, se sont enfin incarnées, de par vous qui les avez amenées à la lumière.'[5] Montesquiou's formulas give clarity and consistency to the shapeless thoughts of others: 'un de ces clous d'or par lesquels toute pensée indécise, toute conversation vacillante de nous

the exact opposite of what I said. I said that grammatical beauty had nothing to do with correctness. Jacques Boulenger makes me say the opposite.'

[1] 'A style all the more eternal for being more personal.'

[2] 'I believe . . . there exists for all beautiful sentences an imprescriptible right which makes them inalienable to any acquirer other than the one they had been waiting for, by a destination which is part of their destiny.'

[3] 'Style for the writer, like colour for the painter, is a question not of technique, but of vision' (vol. III, p. 895). Cf. above, p. 40.

[4] For a survey of recent approaches to this problem, see my book, *Language and Style*, ch. 10.

[5] 'One feels that a thousand vague shadows of thoughts which, deep down in our minds, were calling for existence like the shadows of future beings in the *Aeneid*, have at last become incarnate, thanks to you who have brought them to light.'

autres . . . est éblouie et fixée.'[1] And Proust concludes by a striking formula of his own: 'Aussi (votre sagesse) n'écrit-elle pas: elle grave'[2] (I, p. 26).

B. COMMENTS ON HIS OWN STYLE

In several passages, Proust criticizes his own style and in particular his inordinately long sentences. In a letter to Paul Souday, written in June 1921, he recognizes that a sentence criticized by Souday in *Le Côté de Guermantes* is completely unintelligible, and mentions as an extenuating circumstance the deplorable conditions in which his novel is being published: 'si je corrige déjà très mal mes épreuves, quand un livre comme celui-ci paraît imprimé directement d'après mes indéchiffrables brouillons, mes éditeurs ont beau avoir la gentillesse de surveiller de leur mieux cette impression, elle est terriblement fautive.' This does not, however, completely exonerate him: 'Je ne cherche pas à m'absoudre ainsi du reproche fort justifié de faire souvent des phrases trop longues, trop sinueusement attachées aux méandres de ma pensée. J'ai ri de bon cœur à votre: "C'est limpide." Mais je vous ai trouvé trop bienveillant de prétendre qu'à la troisième lecture cela devient clair, car, pour ma part, je n'y comprends rien'[3] (III, pp. 93f.). In an earlier letter to the same critic, Proust had expressed the fear that the reader might be discouraged when told by a reviewer that the book is 'rebutant à lire par l'aspect matériel, par la

---

[1] 'One of those golden nails by which all our vague thoughts, all our uncertain conversations . . . are fixed and illuminated.'

[2] 'Therefore (your wisdom) does not write: it carves.'

[3] 'If I am in any case very bad at correcting my proofs, when a book like this one is printed straight from my illegible drafts, my kind publishers try in vain to supervise the printing, it is terribly defective . . . I am not trying to exonerate myself in this way from the very justified reproach that I often write sentences which are too long, too sinuously attached to the meanderings of my thought. I laughed heartily at your remark: "It is limpid." But I thought you were too kind when you said that at the third reading it becomes clear, for, as far as I am concerned, I cannot make head or tail of it.'

longueur des phrases'[1] (III, p. 74), and as far back as 1905, he had written to Mme Straus about an article which he had just published: 'il est raté et horriblement fatigant à lire, avec des phrases d'une page de longueur que vous défendrait tout spéciale-ment le docteur Widmer'[2] (VI, p. 36).

Proust is also critical of superfluous sentences in his own writ-ings and those of others; he tells Jacques Boulenger: 'Moi qui aurais été un bon professeur de seconde, je vois dans certains (viz. de vos articles) la phrase qu'il faudrait couper, comme un câble, pour que le merveilleux ballon captif s'envolât vraiment. J'ai lu de vos articles tordants, qui eussent "fait date" si une phrase de trop n'eût scellé sur eux une pierre étouffante. D'ailleurs je fais exactement de même. Mais ce n'est pas une raison'[3] (III, p. 211). It is perhaps significant in this context that in a letter to Montesquiou he says that he intends to write some newspaper or magazine articles 'pour simplifier une forme souvent inutile-ment compliquée'[4] (I, p. 44).

Self-criticism becomes a form of courtesy and wit when Proust thanks Souday in these terms for a gift of chocolates: 'Ma prose n'a pas, hélas! la saveur de vos chocolats; elle n'en a pas le "coulant" non plus, le merveilleux fondu'[5] (III, p. 90). This image is reminiscent of a passage in an early letter to Mme de Noailles where he says about something he had written: 'toutes

[1] 'Tiresome to read because of its material aspect, the length of the sentences.'

[2] 'It is a failure and terribly tiring to read, with sentences the length of a page, which Dr Widmer would specially forbid you.'

[3] 'I, who would have made a good fifth form teacher, can see in some (of your articles) the odd sentence which one ought to cut like a cable so that the wonderful captive balloon should really fly off. I have read some extremely funny articles of yours which would have "marked an epoch" if one unnecessary sentence had not sealed them up with a stifling stone. For that matter, I do exactly the same. But that is no reason why you should.'

[4] 'So as to simplify a form which is often unnecessarily complicated.'

[5] 'Alas, my prose does not have the flavour of your chocolates; nor does it have their flowing quality, the marvellous way they melt in the mouth.'

ces pages sont détestables, une espèce de nougat indigeste, où il y
a de tout, et qui reste entre les dents"[1] (II, p. 128). All this banter
need not of course be taken too seriously. The same is true of two
references to the style of his early work, *Les Plaisirs et les jours*:
he wants to send Boulenger a copy of the book 'pour vous montrer
que je peux écrire purement'[2] (III, p. 229), and in a later letter
to the same friend he says that *Les Plaisirs et les jours* are much
better written than *Swann* (III, p. 253).

In spite of his theories about grammar and style, Proust was
very anxious to observe the rules of correct usage and was therefore most sensitive to criticism on these matters. He was particularly hurt by a review of *Du Côté de chez Swann* which Paul
Souday had published in *Le Temps* on 10th December 1913, and
in which the critic had blamed him for a number of misprints as
if they were genuine grammatical mistakes. In a letter written the
day after the publication of the review, he protests: 'Mon livre
peut ne révéler aucun talent; il présuppose du moins, il implique
assez de culture pour qu'il n'y ait pas invraisemblance morale à
ce que je commette des fautes aussi grossières que celles que vous
signalez.' He then deftly turns the tables on his critic: 'Quand,
dans votre article, j'ai lu: "M. Marcel Proust fait preuve d'*une*
sens très aiguisé," etc., je n'ai pas pensé: "M. Souday ignore que
le mot *sens* est du masculin." ' In the same way he assumes that
Souday will not attribute to the author's ignorance the more
obvious misprints in the book. But, he goes on, 'il serait . . . aussi
extraordinaire que j'ignorasse les règles de l'accord des temps. Je
vous assure que si le "vieil universitaire" que vous proposez
d'adjoindre aux maisons d'édition n'avait à corriger que mes
fautes de français, il aurait beaucoup de loisirs.'[3] The indignant

---

[1] 'All these pages are execrable, a kind of indigestible nougat which
contains a bit of everything and sticks between one's teeth.'

[2] 'To show you that I can write purely.'

[3] 'My book may reveal no talent; at least it presupposes, it implies
sufficient culture to make it intrinsically improbable that I should commit
mistakes as glaring as the ones you point out. . . When I read in your
article: "M. Marcel Proust shows a very keen sense (*une* sens)", etc., I did

letter ends with another reference to the difficult conditions under which the proofs of the book had to be corrected (III, pp. 62f.).

The same subject is mentioned from time to time in other letters to the same correspondent: 'sachez bien que les fautes ne sont pas de moi. Je n'aurais jamais écrit quelque chose d'aussi idiot que "rafraîchie de souffles tièdes" '[1] (III, p. 78); 'l'article sur Flaubert . . . vous prouvera que je ne suis pas aussi indifférent que vous le croyez aux questions de grammaire'[2] (III, p. 75). He also notes that 'les fautes de Flaubert (qui ne diminuent en rien mon admiration pour lui) sont bien fréquentes'[3] (III, p. 80).

On a number of occasions, Proust apologizes for the careless language and inadequate style of his letters and attributes these defects to illness, fatigue or nervous exhaustion: 'excusez ce style, je n'ai pas eu la force de signer même une dédicace depuis long-temps'[4] (III, p. 69); 'excusez le style fautif d'un homme qui a 40 degrés de fièvre'[5] (III, p. 172); 'excusez je ne dirai pas seulement les défauts de style, mais les fautes de grammaire de cette lettre de plus de dix pages'[6] (III, pp. 304f.). 'Dans mon état de fatigue je fais tant de fautes de français que je m'arrête',[7] he writes to Mme Straus a few years before his death (VI, p. 179). As early as

not think: "M. Souday does not know that the word *sens* is masculine." . . . It would be . . . just as strange if I did not know the rules of the sequence of tenses. I can assure you that if the "old academic" whom you would like to attach to publishing houses had nothing else to correct but my mistakes in French he would have much leisure.'

[1] 'You may rest assured that the mistakes are not mine. I would never have written anything as idiotic as "refreshed by tepid breezes".'

[2] 'The article on Flaubert . . . will prove to you that I am not as in-different to grammatical questions as you think.'

[3] 'Mistakes in Flaubert (which do not in any way lessen my admiration for him) are very frequent.'

[4] 'Do forgive the style, for a long time I have not had the strength to sign even an autograph.'

[5] 'Do forgive the poor style of a man who has forty degrees of tempera-ture.'

[6] 'Do forgive, I shall not say merely the defects of style, but the gram-matical mistakes in this letter of over ten pages.'

[7] 'In my state of fatigue I make so many mistakes in French that I have to stop.'

1905, he had ended a letter to Mme de Noailles with the plea: 'Je vous écris, Madame, très mal, dans une crise d'asthme terrible, mais j'espère que vous rectifiez mes phrases inexactes et vivifiez mes phrases inertes'[1] (II, pp. 162f.). Even when writing about his own grave state of health he remains sensitive to stylistic nuances; in the middle of the sentence: 'Je suis depuis sept mois alité avec des crises d'urémie alternant avec des troubles différents et aussi graves', he inserts the parenthesis: 'pardon des deux "avec"'[2] (III, p. 301; cf.; also p. 205). Elsewhere he expresses the fear that fatigue may blunt the edge of his mind and lead to over-simplification. 'Tout cela est bien mal dit, en supprimant les nuances, la mise au point nécessaire',[3] he complains to Mme Straus at the end of a long letter (VI, p. 137), and to Montesquiou he writes in a similar vein: 'je sens que je fausse un peu ma pensée, en la figeant dans une lettre où je suis trop fatigué pour apporter les nuances et les complexités nécessaires'[4] (I, p. 197).

The correspondence also contains a number of references to the disorders of speech from which Proust suffered for some time and which must have been particularly painful for such a consummate master and sophisticated student of language. In a late letter to Montesquiou he complains that in a restaurant he had to repeat a name more than ten times before they understood him (I, p. 283). He also apologizes to the Count for what he calls the 'cacography' of a letter which he wrote in the middle of a severe attack (I, p. 288). It is interesting to find that as early as 1913, he had written to Mme de Noailles: 'je suis dans un tel état de fatigue que j'ai—comme on dit aphasie—une espèce

---

[1] 'I am writing to you very badly, Madame, in a terrible attack of asthma, but I hope that you will rectify my inaccurate sentences and enliven by inert sentences.'

[2] 'For seven months I have been in bed with attacks of uraemia alternating with different and equally serious troubles (apologies for the two *with*-s).'

[3] 'All this is very badly put, without nuances, without the necessary details.'

[4] 'I feel that I am somewhat distorting my thought by fixing it in a letter where I am too tired to introduce the necessary nuances and complexities.'

d'agraphie'[1] (II, p. 196). Judging by the frequency of his references to his symptoms of aphasia (cf. III, pp. 45, 82, 87, 268, 312), it is obvious that Proust was very worried about his condition. At one point he actually consulted a well-known neurologist about the possibility of a trepanotomy.[2] Characteristically, he used even these painful experiences as raw material for his novel, by making Bergotte suffer from similar symptoms.[3]

In the correspondence under discussion, Proust comments not only on his own style but also on the language of some of the characters in his novel. Particularly significant in this respect is a letter to Souday in which he contrasts Saint-Simon's references to the 'esprit de Mortemart' with his own, far more detailed portrayal of the 'esprit de Guermantes'. He speaks of his disappointment 'en voyant Saint-Simon nous parler toujours de "l'esprit de Mortemart", du "tour si particulier" à M. de Montespan, à M. de Thianges, à l'abbesse de Fontevrault, de ne pas trouver un seul mot, la plus légère indication qui permît de savoir en quoi consistait cette singularité de langage propre aux Mortemart'. It was this dissatisfaction which made him 'écrire comme un pensum tant de répliques de la duchesse de Guermantes et . . . rendre cohérent, toujours identique, l'esprit des *Guermantes* . . . Hélas! je n'ai pas le génie de Saint-Simon. Mais, du moins, ceux qui me liront sauront ce qu'est "l'esprit des Guermantes", ce qui était tout de même plus difficile à faire que de dire: "cet esprit si particulier" sans en donner la plus légère idée'[4] (III, p. 95). An

---

[1] 'I am in such a state of fatigue that I am suffering from a kind of agraphia—as one says aphasia.'

[2] Cf. Painter, op. cit., vol. II, p. 279.

[3] Vol. II, p. 326 (*Le Côté de Guermantes*). Cf. Painter, op. cit., vol. II, p. 321.

[4] 'When we find Saint-Simon speaking to us all the time of the "Mortemart wit", of the "turn of phrase so peculiar" to M. de Montespan, to M. de Thianges, to the abbess of Fontevrault, never to discover a single word, the slightest indication which might enable us to know what this peculiarity of language proper to the Mortemarts consisted of. . . Write like an imposition so many retorts of the duchesse de Guermantes and . . . make the Guermantes wit coherent and always identical. . . Alas, I do

earlier letter to the same critic identifies Proust's model for the language of the Duchess: 'agacé de voir Saint-Simon parler toujours du langage si particulier aux Mortemart sans jamais nous dire en quoi il consistait, j'ai voulu tenir le coup et essayer de faire un "esprit de Guermantes". Or, je n'ai pu trouver mon modèle que chez une femme non "née", Mme Straus, la veuve de Bizet. Non seulement les mots cités sont d'elle (elle n'a pas voulu que je dise son nom dans le livre), mais j'ai pastiché sa conversation'[1] (III, p. 85). Another letter gives a concrete example of the 'esprit de Guermantes' in the form of a pun originally applied by the Duchess to her brother-in-law, Charlus: 'je vous ai constitué dans ma tête comme l'assemblage 1° d'un homme du cœur le plus délicat . . . et 2° d'un taquin (Taquin le Superbe, dirait, justement cette fois, Mme de Guermantes)'[2] (III, p. 279).

Several other passages in the correspondence show how full Proust's mind was of the characters of his novel and of their linguistic idiosyncrasies. In a letter to Blanche he quotes a favourite expression of Dr Cottard and then apologizes for doing so: 'Je comprends donc qu'on vous ait accusé de "police" quand j'avais écrit de "malice" et *tutti quanti* comme dirait un personnage de Swann qui s'appelle (je n'oserais jamais me citer ainsi

not have Saint-Simon's genius. But at least those who read me will know what is the "Guermantes wit", which was all the same more difficult to do than to say: "this so peculiar wit" without giving the slightest idea of what it was.' Cf. *À la recherche du temps perdu*, vol. II, p. 438 (*Le Côté de Guermantes*).

[1] 'Irritated at always finding Saint-Simon referring to the language so peculiar to the Mortemarts without ever telling us what it consisted of, I wanted to see it through and try to create a "Guermantes wit". Well, the only model I could find was a woman who was not "well-born", Mme Straus, Bizet's widow. Not only are the words quoted hers (she did not want me to mention her name in the book) but I have made a pastiche of her conversation.'

[2] 'I have imagined you in my mind as the combination of (1) a man with the most delicate heart . . . and (2) a tease (*taquin*)—Tarquinius Superbus, as Mme de Guermantes would say, quite properly in this case.' Cf. *À la recherche du temps perdu*, vol. II, p. 465 (*Le Côté de Guermantes*).

K

mais depuis que Bakst et le comte de Marigny . . . mais c'est trop long de vous dire les louanges exagérées de ces deux lecteurs) le docteur Cottard'[1] (III, pp. 144f.). The doctor also appears in a letter to Boulenger: 'Et une fois les funestes sorties passées, je vous "ferai appel", comme disait M. Cottard'[2] (p. 206), and a characteristic feature of the style of his wife is mentioned in an interesting remark on the *mot juste*: 'En principe je suis pour appeler les choses par leur nom et pour ne pas faire consister l'originalité et l'innovation dans l'altération de ce nom. Par exemple Reboux a fait des pastiches. Il a appelé cela: "*À la manière de*" (titre qui je le reconnais a fait fortune). J'ai fait aussi et souvent des *Pastiches*, et je les ai appelés tout simplement: *Pastiches*. Vous verrez que si c'est ma "manière", ce n'est pas celle de Mme Cottard, ou du moins vous le verrez si vous avez la bonté de lire, à supposer qu'ils paraissent jamais, les volumes suivants de Swann'[3] (III, p. 148).

The art of the pastiche is referred to in several other letters. Proust is delighted that his collection of pastiches should have pleased Mme de Noailles but hastens to add: 'C'est un exercice facile et vulgaire. Mais enfin je crois tout de même que j'y ai mis une certaine largeur, que ce sont de bonnes "copies" comme on

---

[1] 'I can see why you were blamed for *police* when I had written *malice*, and *tutti quanti* as a character in *Swann* called Dr Cottard would say (I would never dare quote myself like this, but since Bakst and the Comte de Marigny . . . but it would take too long to tell you about the excessive praises of these two readers).' Cf. *À la recherche du temps perdu*, vol. II, p. 881 (*Sodome et Gomorrhe*).

[2] 'And once the fatal outings are over, I shall "call on" you, as M. Cottard used to say.'

[3] 'As a rule, I am in favour of calling a spade a spade and not to seek originality and novelty by altering the names of things. For example, Reboux has written some pastiches. He called them: "After the manner of" (a title which, I admit, has made a hit). I too have often written *Pastiches* and have simply called them *Pastiches*. You will see that, if this is my "manner", it is not Mme Cottard's, or at least you will see it if you are good enough to read the next volumes of *Swann*, supposing that they ever come out.' Cf. *À la recherche du temps perdu*, vol. I, p. 256 (*Du Côté de chez Swann*).

dit en peinture"[1] (II, p. 181). In one of his last letters to Montesquiou, when relations between the two men were already strained because the Count had not failed to recognize himself in Charlus,[2] Proust protests against the term *singeries*, used in a recent work by Montesquiou: 'les "singeries" dont je ne peux pas ne pas m'appliquer un peu l'injuste blâme, puisque j'ai été le premier, si j'ai perdu depuis longtemps ce talent et cette habitude, à contrefaire—bien imparfaitement—le tour de votre langage et l'accent de votre voix'; and he adds significantly: 'Il y a bien dix années que je n'ai refait de ces imitations'[3] (I, p. 286). More specifically, he discusses, in two letters to Mme Straus, the use of proper names in a pastiche. Having decided to include the name of Mme Straus in a pastiche of Saint-Simon, he has qualms on purely aesthetic grounds: 'En principe je ne suis pas pour mettre dans un pastiche du dix-septième siècle des noms qui évoquent aussi puissamment que le vôtre toutes les grâces du vingtième. Cela fait dissonance, c'est-à-dire le contraire du pastiche'[4] (VI, p. 207). A few weeks later, he emphasizes once more the need to include a number of seventeenth-century names so as to give an air of authenticity to his pastiche (VI, p. 218).

In his correspondence with foreigners, Proust makes one or two references to his own lack of competence in other languages. In a letter to Mrs Sydney Schiff he confesses: 'je lis l'anglais très difficilement'[5] (III, p. 13). To Ernst Robert Curtius he writes:

---

[1] 'It is an easy and vulgar exercise. But after all I think all the same that I have put a certain breadth into it, that they are good "reproductions", as one would say in painting.'

[2] Cf. Painter, op. cit., vol. II, pp. 317ff.

[3] '"Apishness", an unjust charge which I am bound to apply a little to myself, for I was the first, even if I have long since lost the aptitude and the habit, to imitate—very imperfectly—your turn of phrase and the accent of your voice. . . For some ten years now, I have not done any imitations of this kind.'

[4] 'As a rule I am not in favour of putting in a pastiche of the seventeenth century names which evoke all the charms of the twentieth as powerfully as does yours. This produces a discordant note which is the very opposite of a pastiche.'   [5] 'I read English with great difficulty.'

'En voyant la magnifique connaissance que vous avez des lettres françaises et la façon si ingénieuse dont vous me citez en français, j'aurais voulu vous répondre en allemand. Hélas j'ai craint une trop grande disproportion entre votre français et mon allemand. J'ai une grande admiration pour la littérature et la philosophie allemandes mais votre langue ne m'est pas si familière (bien que je la mette à côté du grec parmi les langues les plus riches)'[1] (III, p. 311).

C. REMARKS ON THE STYLE OF OTHERS

Proust's remarks on the style of his friends are more often than not eulogistic and at times almost dithyrambic, whilst containing a number of shrewd and penetrating observations. He hails Montesquiou as a 'prince du verbe, si tant de titulaires sans grâce n'ont pas fait perdre à ce beau mot de prince son élégance dans le geste de la toute-puissance'[2] (I, p. 39). That his admiration for Montesquiou's style was quite genuine can be seen from the fact that even when he received an angry letter from the Count, he commented on the quality of the writing: 'dans sa folie . . . je crois qu'elle vous (viz. Jacques Boulenger) amusera, qu'elle vous paraîtra bien et pittoresquement écrite'[3] (III, p. 260). Mme Straus's style in her letters is said to compare favourably with that of Voltaire (VI, p. 182). While at work on an article for *La Renaissance latine*, 'je me disais tout le temps: Ah si je pouvais écrire comme Mme Straus! Et je me le disais bien profondément, . . . avec un regret intense de toute cette clarté, de ce bel équilibre

[1] 'Seeing that you have such a magnificent knowledge of French literature and that you quote me so ingeniously in French, I should have liked to reply to you in German. Alas, I was afraid of too great a disproportion between your French and my German. I have great admiration for German literature and philosophy but am not so familiar with your language (although I would rank it, with Greek, among the richest languages).'

[2] 'Prince of the word, if so many graceless holders of the title have not robbed this noble term, prince, of its elegance in the gesture of omnipotence.'

[3] 'In its very madness . . . I think that it will amuse you, that you will find it well written and picturesque.'

délicieux qui enchante dans vos phrases"[1] (VI, p. 35). Some of the letters to Mme de Noailles are even more wildly exaggerated in their praises which amount to what she herself has described as an 'undeserved apotheosis' (II, p. 9). Her style is 'inouï, sublime, à trois mille mètres d'altitude au-dessus de Goncourt . . . bien que n'étant pas César (ni rien) je pleure devant cette statue d'Alexandre'[2] (II, pp. 135–7). The term 'style' is hopelessly inadequate to describe her magic (II, p. 41); her words have become 'l'aphabet sacré de toute pensée'[3] (II, p. 123). More interestingly, he speaks of 'la pénétration de plus en plus organique (de votre génie) dans votre forme'[4] and finds an unusual image from biology to describe the process:[5] 'Il est admirable que ce phénomène de multiplication des cellules sonores par l'effet de l'infusion, de l'inoculation sous-jacente des mille richesses de la pensée ait pu se produire dans le langage, comme dans la musique. Ce même miracle de biologie spirituelle est bien émouvant'[6] (II, p. 202).

Some of the comments on Mme de Noailles's style are more specific, and occasionally a critical note is faintly audible. Hailing

[1] 'I told myself all the time: If only I could write like Mme Straus! And I said so with deep feeling, . . . with intense regret for all that clarity, that fine, delightful balance which charms one in your sentences.'

[2] 'Unheard of, sublime, at an altitude of three thousand yards above Goncourt (sic) . . . Though I am not Caesar (nor anything) I weep in front of this statue of Alexander.'

[3] 'The sacred alphabet of all thought.'

[4] 'The more and more organic penetration (of your genius) into your form.'

[5] On Proust's scientific images see esp. R. Virtanen, 'Proust's Metaphors from the Natural and the Exact Sciences', *Publications of the Modern Language Association of America*, lxix (1954), pp. 1038–59. Cf. also Mouton, op. cit., pp. 89ff.; my book, *The Image in the Modern French Novel*, pp. 140ff.; V. E. Graham, *The Imagery of Proust*, pp. 139ff. Cf. above, pp. 101f. and 111f.

[6] 'It is admirable that this phenomenon of the multiplication of sonorous cells through the infusion, the underlying inoculation of the manifold riches of thought should have been able to take place in language, as it does in music. This same miracle of spiritual biology is very moving.'

the appearance of a new book by her—'Grande date . . . pour nous tous. Pour la langue surtout'[1]—Proust confesses that he had feared that she would be unable to go on writing, 'tordant les mots pour les besoins de l'ineffable'.[2] Yet her style has continued to develop until it has reached 'la sécurité absolue de l'extrême audace. Un style qui, pour dire comme vous, promet plus que la beauté. Quoi? la vie, la mort? Une inquiétude pire que toutes deux. Et qui, je l'avoue, m'empêche de goûter au moment la beauté'[3] (II, p. 116). The criticism becomes more explicit in another letter where, referring to some poems Mme de Noailles had published in *La Revue des Deux Mondes*, Proust admits: 'j'y avais trouvé quelque chose d'un peu subjectif dans l'inspiration et parfois trop discontinu dans l'expression, malgré presque tout admirable'[4] (II, pp. 143f.). As Mme de Noailles herself points out in a footnote: 'On voit ici que l'infaillible sens critique de Marcel Proust lutte contre les forces de l'amitié qui refoulent et bâillonnent son libre jugement.'[5]

There are also several comments on the style of other friends, including a particularly interesting one on the syntax of Louis Martin-Chauffier, in connexion with an article which he had published in the *Nouvelle Revue Française*. 'Votre style,' writes Proust, 'style de vos lettres surtout et même de vos articles, me semblait courir, à force d'archaïsme et de préciosité abstraite, le risque de se dessécher, de se refroidir. Voilà mes craintes bien dissipées! Il n'y a pas une phrase qui ne vive, rendue nécessaire par une idée neuve et profonde. La phrase pousse, elle fleurit, et

[1] 'A great date . . . for us all. Especially for the language.'

[2] 'Twisting words in order to express the ineffable.'

[3] 'The absolute security of extreme boldness. A style which, to use your own words, promises more than beauty. What? Life, death? An anxiety worse than either. I must admit that this prevents me at the moment from enjoying the beauty.'

[4] 'I found in them something a little subjective in inspiration and occasionally too discontinuous in expression; nevertheless, nearly all of it is admirable.'

[5] 'One can see here how Marcel Proust's unerring critical sense is fighting against the forces of friendship which repress and gag his free judgement.'

elle a, comme vous dites si bien, . . . "les voiles des pétales et des feuilles".' In a postscript Proust also makes some specific suggestions: 'songez à éviter l'écueil des phrases trop longues (si drôles dans le pastiche que vous aviez fait de moi) si elles sont abstraites. Évitez la formule dix-septième siècle, ne gardez de cette admirable époque que sa réalité, le fond plein de vie, d'impressions senties et que l'apparente solennité ne doit jamais nous cacher'[1] (III, pp. 307f.).

Other remarks, though sometimes expressed in excessively flattering terms, also contain some valuable ideas. Commenting on an article by Jacques Boulenger, Proust writes: 'On a un peu honte d'avoir écrit de si gros volumes, comme j'ai fait, quand on voit quelqu'un en deux pages de revue . . . , tout en dessinant le portrait du modèle (moi), faire, grâce aux tons choisis, aux accents inconnus, son propre portrait'[2] (III, pp. 203f.). Boulenger's style also suggests an analogy which Proust had already used in his novel: 'Vous avez un style comme les téléphones prédits qui montreront en même temps le visage de la personne'[3] (III, p. 211). The style of Jacques-Émile Blanche is neatly summed up in another image from science: 'Votre style a

---

[1] 'It seemed to me that there was a danger that archaisms and a certain abstract preciosity might give your style, the style of your letters in particular and even that of your articles, a dry and cold quality. Now my fears have been completely dispelled! Every sentence is alive, made necessary by a new and deep idea. The sentence grows and flowers; it has, as you put it so well, . . . "the veils of petals and leaves." . . . Remember to avoid the danger of unduly long sentences (so funny in the pastiche you wrote of me) if the sentences are abstract. Avoid the seventeenth-century model; keep only the reality of that admirable period, the underlying richness of life, of impressions genuinely felt, which the apparent solemnity must never be allowed to conceal.'

[2] 'One is a little ashamed of having written such bulky volumes, as I have done, when one sees someone, in two pages of a journal, . . . drawing the portrait of the model (myself) and yet, at the same time, making a self-portrait, thanks to the tones chosen, to hitherto unknown accents.'

[3] 'You have a style like the telephones we have been promised for the future, which will show at the same time the face of the speaker.' Cf. À la recherche du temps perdu, vol. I, p. 930 (À l'ombre des jeunes filles en fleurs).

une tendance au centrifuge, un[1] sujet précis, roman ou portrait de peintre, le ramène à son centre'[2] (III, p. 173).

When discussing with his correspondents the style of other writers, Proust can give free rein to his critical verve. In a letter to Mme Straus from the end of 1907 there is a spirited attack on certain mannerisms: 'J'ai vu des gens de goût trouver le discours de D . . . charmant. Moi je n'ai jamais rien lu d'aussi bête et au fond d'aussi "académique".' He has no patience with academicians who pretend to be daring and modern in language whereas they are basically as conservative as the rest: 'pour trouver drôle, scandaleux, diabolique, d'"oser" dire à l'Académie "pousser une colle" etc., il faut être terriblement académique et avoir l'esprit imbu de ces mêmes préjugés qu'on consacre par cela même qu'on trouve extrêmement hardi et spirituel de rompre en visière avec eux. Bourget et lui avaient l'air de deux dévotes ravies de dire un mot un peu vif devant leur curé.' What he finds particularly irritating is the habit of using modern colloquialisms in an attempt to bring the past up to date: 'Au fond tout cet esprit dérive de la même idiotie qui fait écrire à des crétins comme R. . . "Je m'en fiche, comme dit Bossuet." C'est écœurant.'[3] In the *Temps perdu*, Proust was to pillory this affectation in the linguistic portrait of Professor Brichot who calls Blanche de Castille a 'vieille chipie',[4] speaks of the 'je m'enfichisme' of Talleyrand and

---

[1] The text has *au*, which is an obvious misprint.

[2] 'Your style has a centrifugal tendency; a precise subject, a novel or a portrait of a painter, brings it back to its centre.'

[3] 'I have met people of good taste who found D ...'s speech charming. I myself have never read anything so stupid and basically so "academic" ... To find it funny, scandalous, diabolical to "dare" say at the Academy: "Ask a sticky question" etc., one must be terribly academic and have a mind imbued with the very same prejudices which one confirms by the very fact of finding it extremely daring and witty to defy them. Bourget and he had the air of two pious women delighted to utter a somewhat lively word in front of the vicar.... Fundamentally, all this wit derives from the same stupidity which makes idiots like R ... write: "I couldn't care less, as Bossuet says." It is sickening.'

[4] 'An old cat' (vol. I, p. 252—*Du Côté de chez Swann*).

describes the Cardinal de Retz as 'ce struggle for lifer de Gondi'.[1]

The whole diatribe against academicians in the letter to Mme Straus ends on a despondent note: 'tout le discours était d'un toc comme style!... La vérité est qu'on croit que l'amour des lettres, de la peinture, de la musique s'est extrêmement répandu, et qu'il n'y a pas au fond une personne de plus qu'autrefois qui s'y connaisse et qui soit capable de distinguer le discours de D ... d'une page vraiment bien écrite'[2] (VI, pp. 91 f.).

Proust can even admire certain types of silence. Speaking of Mme de Pourtalès, he writes to Louis Gautier-Vignal: 'Je n'ai jamais causé avec elle. Mais ai écouté quelques silences très intelligents, ce qui est encore plus symptomatique et plus rare qu'une parole spirituelle'[3] (III, pp. 318 f.). In another letter to the same correspondent he says: 'Sans vous écrire je pensais à vous, mais perçoit-on à distance l'amical appel quotidien dont certains silences sont faits, plus qu'on ne perçoit l'harmonie des sphères?'[4] (III, p. 320).

D. IMAGERY

Among the various elements of style, imagery, and in particular metaphor, occupied a central position in Proust's aesthetics. In *Jean Santeuil* there are already, as we have seen, a number of

---

[1] 'The couldn't-care-less attitude of Talleyrand ... Gondi, that struggler for life' (vol. II, p. 876—*Sodome et Gomorrhe*).

[2] 'The whole speech was completely phoney as far as style is concerned ... The truth is that people think that the love of literature, painting, music is now extremely widespread, whereas basically there is not one more person than before who can judge these matters and is able to distinguish D ...'s speech from a really well-written page.'

[3] 'I have never had a conversation with her. But I have listened to some very intelligent silences, which is even more symptomatic and rarer than a witty word.'

[4] 'Without writing to you I have been thinking of you, but does one perceive at a distance the daily friendly call of which certain silences are made up, any more than one perceives the music of the spheres?'

remarks on the problem, and in *Contre Sainte-Beuve*, the out-lines of a coherent theory of imagery begin to emerge.[1] In *À la recherche du temps perdu* and in various other writings, Proust returned time and again to these matters. Towards the end of his life, his views on metaphor found their definitive expression in three well-known statements two of which have already been quoted:

Je crois que la métaphore seule peut donner une sorte d'éternité au style.[2]

Tous les à peu près d'images ne comptent pas. L'eau (dans des conditions données) bout à 100 degrés. À 98, à 99, le phénomène ne se produit pas. Alors mieux vaut pas d'images.[3]

La vérité ne commencera qu'au moment où l'écrivain prendra deux objets différents, posera leur rapport, analogue dans le monde de l'art à celui qu'est le rapport unique de la loi causale dans le monde de la science, et les enfermera dans les anneaux nécessaires d'un beau style; même, ainsi que la vie, quand, en rapprochant une qualité commune à deux sensations, il dégagera leur essence com-mune en les réunissant l'une et l'autre pour les soustraire aux contingences du temps, dans une métaphore.[4]

---

[1] On *Jean Santeuil*, see ch. 5. On *Contre Sainte-Beuve*, cf. my article, 'L'Esthétique de l'image dans *Contre Sainte-Beuve* de Marcel Proust', *Festschrift v. Wartburg*, vol. I, pp. 267–78.

[2] 'I believe that metaphor alone can give a kind of eternity to style' (in the article on Flaubert, referred to above, p. 122, n. 2; cf. also p. 44).

[3] 'Approximate images do not count. Water, under given conditions, boils at 100 degrees. At 98, at 99, the phenomenon does not occur. In that case it is better to have no images at all' (see above, ch. 5, p. 93, n. 2).

[4] 'Truth will start only at the moment when the writer takes two different objects, establishes their relationship, analogous in the world of art to the unique relationship of the law of cause and effect in the world of science, and encloses them in the necessary links of a beautiful style; or even, like life itself, when, by bringing together qualities common to two sensations, he isolates their common essence by joining them together in a metaphor, so as to preserve them from the contingencies of time' (*À la recherche du temps perdu*, vol. III, p. 889—*Le Temps retrouvé*). For a variant version of this crucial passage, see the note on pp. 1135f.

This last passage, from *Le Temps retrouvé*, shows that there is, in Proust's opinion, a fundamental affinity between metaphor and the rediscovery of the past through the process of involuntary memory. It is therefore not altogether surprising that, in an earlier part of the cycle, he should speak of the 'sacred use' for which certain images are reserved.[1]

In the correspondence we are concerned with, there are three passages of outstanding importance on the problem of imagery. One of them occurs in a letter to Jacques-Émile Blanche, written in May or June 1915:

je trouve les images nées d'une impression supérieures à celles qui servent seulement à illustrer un raisonnement . . . il y a un endroit où vous parlez . . . des cocardes qu'on s'épingle quand on a les pieds dans le sang. Je ne méprise pas ces images dont Taine faisait aussi un grand usage, mais j'aime mieux celles où, que vous parliez des hommes ou de la nature, vous délivrez de la vérité et de la poésie[2] (III, p. 109).

The same idea recurs in a letter from 1922 to Camille Vettard:

Quant au style, je me suis efforcé de rejeter tout ce que dicte l'intelligence pure, tout ce qui est rhétorique, enjolivement et à peu près, images voulues et cherchées (ces images que j'ai dénoncées dans la préface de Morand) pour exprimer mes impressions profondes et authentiques et respecter la marche naturelle de ma pensée[3] (III, p. 195).

---

[1] 'Des images si écrites et qui me semblaient réservées pour un autre usage plus sacré et que j'ignorais encore' ('Literary images which seemed to me reserved for another, more sacred use of which I was as yet unaware'—ibid., vol. III, p. 129—*La Prisonnière*).

[2] 'I find images derived from an impression superior to those which merely serve to illustrate an argument. . . There is a passage where you speak of . . . cockades one pins on when one's feet are wading in blood. I do not despise these images which Taine too used extensively, but I prefer those where you deliver truth and poetry, whether you are talking of men or of nature.'

[3] 'As regards style, I have tried to reject all that is dictated by pure intelligence, everything that is rhetoric, adornment and approximation, deliberate and artificial images (the kind of image I denounced in my

Spontaneity and authenticity were also among the qualities Proust had admired many years earlier in the imagery of Mme de Noailles. In the first of two letters from 1904, discussing the style of her volume, *Le Visage émerveillé*, he had suggested that there were two essential differences between this book and an earlier work of hers, *La Nouvelle Espérance*. Firstly, the language had changed: the violent and revolutionary innovations of the first book, 'la liberté et la révolte de langage de Saint-Simon',[1] had given way to a new harmony, to a kind of 'âge d'or de la langue reconquis', 'l'ordre et la pureté de l'Évangile'.[2] Secondly, poetry is omnipresent in *Le Visage émerveillé*, the whole book is impregnated with it, whereas in *La Nouvelle Espérance* it had appeared only in occasional flashes and had not formed an integral part of the style. The new volume is dominated by 'une espèce de vision géniale qui crée d'une façon constante'.[3] This is clearly seen from the imagery: 'Il y a peut-être dans *Atala* deux ou trois images parfaitement belles. Il y en a dans chacune de vos pages autant que de façons de dire.'[4] Even more important, Mme de Noailles has recaptured the freshness and spontaneity of biblical imagery: 'Depuis la Bible, la "singularité des images" est une chose qui m'exaspère parce que ce n'est pas le vrai génie et que cela ne sort pas directement de la langue et ne s'y fond pas. Or le miracle a eu lieu une seconde fois: dans le *Visage émerveillé*.'[5] And Proust takes a concrete example to show that it is 'absolument une image

preface to Morand), in order to express my deep and genuine impressions and to respect the natural progress of my thoughts.'

[1] 'The freedom and revolt in the language of Saint-Simon.'

[2] 'Golden age of language regained ... the order and purity of the Gospel.'

[3] 'A kind of inspired vision which is creative all the time.'

[4] 'In *Atala* there are perhaps two or three perfectly beautiful images. On every page of yours, there are as many of them as there are ways of saying things.'

[5] 'Since the Bible, the "singularity of images" is a thing that exasperates me, for it is not a sign of true genius, it does not spring directly from the language and does not blend into it. Now the miracle has happened a second time: in *Le Visage émerveillé*.'

de la Bible, aussi géniale, aussi antérieure à toute littérature, aussi supérieure à toutes'¹ (II, pp. 75–9).

The two letters on *Le Visage émerveillé* also contain several sensitive remarks on individual images. Some of the most interesting ones are concerned with Mme de Noailles's colour vision which, in Proust's opinion, makes her 'le plus grand des impressionnistes'. '"Je vois la vie bleu, jaune et violet"', he writes, 'me semble la phrase centrale, le "centre d'éclairage" de tout le livre'² (II, p. 85), and he also emphasizes the skilful way in which her colours are harmonized: 'vos hardiesses éteintes par l'harmonie de tout sont inouïes (je me rappelle le *vent bleu, l'allée rose*)'³ (ibid.).

Among Proust's comments on the metaphors and similes used by his correspondents, those on Montesquiou's imagery are couched in rather extravagant terms. One of his images reminds Proust of Ruskin who exercised a profound influence on Proust himself (I, p. 131). About another he says: 'Il y a là une comparaison des blessures du saint qui est d'une délicatesse, d'une invention, d'une grâce. Vous avez des yeux qui savent si bien voir qu'on se sent un peu aveugle et des mots qui savent si bien dire qu'on a envie de rester muet'⁴ (I, pp. 237f.). Proust's interest in synaesthetic correspondences between the senses, which is

¹ 'A purely biblical image, just as brilliant, just as anterior and superior to all literature.'

² 'The greatest of the impressionists... "I see life as blue, yellow and purple" seems to me the central sentence, the "focal point" of the whole book.' On Proust's colour vision, see N. Bailey, 'Le Rôle des couleurs dans la genèse de l'univers proustien', *Modern Language Review*, lx (1965), pp. 188–96. Cf. also G. Matoré, 'À propos du vocabulaire des couleurs", *Annales de l'Université de Paris*, xxviii (1958), pp. 137–50.

³ 'The boldness of some of your expressions fading into the general harmony is truly unparalleled (I recall "the blue wind, the pink path").'

⁴ 'There is here a comparison of the saint's wounds which shows such delicacy, imagination and charm. Your eyes can see so well that they make one feel slightly blind, and your words are so expressive that they make one inclined to remain silent.'

already noticeable in *Jean Santeuil* and becomes prominent in *Contre Sainte-Beuve* and the *Temps perdu*,[1] is seen from the postscript to another letter to Montesquiou where he writes, echoing Baudelaire: 'celui pour qui "les couleurs et les sons se répondent" c'est vous, et la transposition est au troisième degré. Car le peintre qui fait chanter ses barcarolles est . . . un pianiste!'[2] (I, p. 124). A letter to Jacques-Émile Blanche contains a salutary warning against ambiguous images: 'Un grand nombre de critiques ne s'occupent qu'à relever les fausses métaphores de ce genre. Il est inutile de leur prêter "le flanc"'[3] (III, p. 107).

In a number of letters, Proust comments on his own use of imagery. Louis Martin-Chauffier having written a pastiche of Proust, the latter congratulates him on some aspects of it: 'Vous avez distingué avec une justesse, parodié avec une drôlerie infinies, quelques particularités de syntaxe que je pense connues de nous deux seulement. Vous vous moquez de mes comparaisons d'une façon délicieuse'[4] (III, p. 297). Elsewhere, he stops in the middle of a letter—as he also does in his fictional works[5]—to comment on a simile or metaphor he had just used, suggesting a more apposite analogy (I, p. 84) or simply apologizing for 'une image informe'[6] (I, p. 82). To Jacques Boulenger he writes: 'Quel "coup droit" (mais les métaphores d'escrimeur doivent vous

---

[1] 'On synaesthetic images in Proust, see ch. 5 of my book, *Style in the French Novel*: 'Transposition of Sensations in Proust's Imagery.' Cf. also V. E. Graham, op. cit., pp. 232, 245 and *passim*. On *Jean Santeuil*, see above, ch. 5, p. 105.

[2] 'You are the man for whom "colours and sounds answer each other", and there is here a transposition of the third degree. For the painter who makes his barcarolles sing is . . . a pianist!'

[3] 'A large number of critics spend their whole time pointing out false metaphors of this type. It is unnecessary to give them "an opening".'

[4] 'You have discerned with infinite precision, and parodied with infinite humour, some peculiarities of syntax which I think only you and I know. You make fun of my similes in a delightful way.'

[5] Cf. my *Image in the Modern French Novel*, pp. 127f.

[6] 'A shapeless image' (in a letter addressed to Montesquiou's secretary, Gabriel d'Yturri).

paraître grotesques'[1] (III, pp. 256f.). In a letter to Camille Vettard, there is a striking passage comparing Proust's novel to a telescope trained on time. While developing the analogy, he inserts several brief asides commenting on the image itself: 'vous me comprendrez (vous trouverez certainement mieux vous-même) si je vous dis que l'image (très imparfaite) qui me paraît la meilleure[2] pour faire comprendre ce qu'est ce sens spécial c'est peut-être celle d'un télescope qui serait braqué sur le temps, car le télescope fait apparaître des étoiles qui sont invisibles à l'œil nu, et j'ai tâché (je ne tiens pas d'ailleurs du tout à mon image) de faire apparaître à la conscience des phénomènes inconscients qui, complètement oubliés, sont quelquefois situés très loin dans le passé'[3] (III, pp. 194f.). A letter to Gautier-Vignal refers to a simile Proust had used on a previous occasion: 'Je me rappelle même vous avoir dit cette comparaison stupide: C'est comme pour les lettres de souverains qu'il est plus convenable de ne livrer à la publicité que quand le destinataire les a reçues'[4] (III, p. 321). In another letter he even pretends to save up a successful comparison for future use. Having written to Mme de Noailles: 'il serait bien gentil . . . que gouvernât la France le seul poète, comme ce poète persan, auquel Gustave Moreau a donné le corps d'une femme et qui enflamme le peuple de sa robe, pourpre comme la vôtre, et de ses chants', he adds: 'Comparaison que je

[1] 'What a "lunge" (but fencing metaphors must seem grotesque to you).'

[2] Here Proust has added by pen, on the margin of the typewritten letter: 'Du moins actuellement' ('At least at present') (p. 194, n.2).

[3] 'You will understand me (you will certainly think of something better yourself) if I tell you that the (very inadequate) image which seems to me the best for making clear this special meaning is perhaps that of a telescope fixed on time, for the telescope enables us to see stars which are invisible to the naked eye, and I have tried (I am not, incidentally, in any way keen on my image) to make visible to our consciousness certain unconscious phenomena which, completely forgotten, are sometimes situated very far back in the past.'

[4] 'I even remember making a silly comparison when talking to you: It is like letters from sovereigns which it is more proper not to publish until after the addressee has received them.'

retiens pour si jamais un Calmette quelconque m'autorise à faire un article sur vous'[1] (II, pp. 35f.). Whether he is writing in a serious or in a jocular vein, he is keenly aware of, and sensitive to, imagery, other people's as well as his own.

E. OTHER ASPECTS OF LANGUAGE AND STYLE

The correspondence under discussion is full of remarks on specific points of language and style. The extraordinary precision and keenness of observation, the close and systematic study of individual and social features of speech, which underlie the innumerable linguistic portraits of the *Temps perdu*, are abundantly in evidence in the letters. The remarks cover all the various levels of language: pronunciation, spelling, punctuation, vocabulary, morphology and syntax.

I. PRONUNCIATION, SPELLING, PUNCTUATION

At the phonetic level, the interest which Proust shows, in the *Temps perdu*, in the quality and inflexions of the human voice and in the accent and intonation of his characters is clearly reflected in the letters. What Gide wrote about himself is even more applicable to Proust: 'Le mauvais romancier construit ses personnages; il les dirige et les fait parler. Le vrai romancier les écoute et les regarde agir . . . les moindres inflexions de leur voix, je les perçois avec la netteté la plus vive.'[2] In the correspondence,

---

[1] 'It would be very nice . . . if France were governed by her only poet, like the Persian poet to whom Gustave Moreau gave the body of a woman, and who inflames the people with her dress, purple like yours, and with her songs. . . This is a simile which I shall keep in case some Calmette or other should ever allow me to do an article on you.'

[2] 'The bad novelist constructs his characters: he controls them and makes them speak. The true novelist listens to them and watches them in action . . . the slightest inflexions of their voice, I perceive them with the most vivid clarity' (*Le Journal des Faux-Monnayeurs*, Paris, 1927 ed., pp. 97f.—27 May 1924).

Proust seems particularly fascinated by Montesquiou's voice and way of speaking. It is impossible not to think of Charlus when reading a passage in a letter to Mme de Noailles, which goes back to 1904, where he depicts the Count intoxicated with his own rhetoric, 'avec une exaltation presque maladive dans la voix suraiguë, soulignée de gestes qu'il faudrait imiter . . . électrisé par la violence du choc que lui causait cette phrase, il frappait le sol de ses pieds à se casser les talons, en se renversant en arrière'[1] (II, pp. 100 and 102). In the correspondence with Montesquiou himself, Proust's remarks are of course in an entirely different key. In a very early letter he assures the Count that his words 'résonnent encore pour moi dans la riche musique de votre voix'[2] (I, p. 8). A little later he speaks of Montesquiou's influence on himself, an influence which, he protests, may have led to unconscious imitation but never to caricature: 'par l'effet qui entraîne le corps à la suite de l'âme, la voix, l'accent se rythmaient sans doute sur l'allure de cette pensée empruntée'[3] (I, p. 20). In another early letter he writes: 'les "tout-puissants accords" de votre voix et de votre diction ont pour moi une vertu proprement magique (je dirais simplement "musicale", croyant dire infiniment, si cet adjectif n'avait à la longue perdu son sens)'[4] (I, p. 48). Incidental remarks on Montesquiou's voice and accent continue to appear in the later parts of the correspondence: 'Les vers ont gardé l'écho des surprises de votre voix'[5] (I, p. 105); 'Il y a là une

[1] 'With an almost morbid exaltation in his high-pitched voice, underlined by gestures which should be imitated . . . electrified by the violence of the shock which this sentence gave him, he stamped his feet so strongly that he nearly broke his heels, and leant backwards.'

[2] 'Are still reverberating for me in the rich music of your voice.'

[3] 'In accordance with the law which makes the body follow the mind, the rhythm of my voice and my accent was no doubt patterned upon the movement of the borrowed thought.'

[4] 'The "all-powerful notes" of your voice and diction have a truly magic property for me (I would simply say "musical", believing that I had said a very great deal, if this adjective had not lost its sense in course of time).'

[5] 'The lines have kept the echo of the surprises of your voice.'

fierté qui fait que dans la pièce votre profil se dessine et votre accent s'entend'[1] (I, p. 266).

Occasionally, Proust also comments on the speech of other friends. In a letter discussing Mme de Noailles's *Le Visage émerveillé*, he notes her fondness for the word *visage* and her peculiar way of pronouncing it: 'comme vous l'aimez ce mot visage, qui est si doux quand vous le prononcez, et qui sait retrouver à la fin de vos vers . . . la douceur de votre prononciation'[2] (II, p. 78). This letter was written in 1904, and there is a curious echo of it in *À l'ombre des jeunes filles en fleurs* where Bergotte has a predilection for the same word and pronounces it in rather an unusual way (I, pp. 552f.). In another early letter Proust reports to Mme Straus that his friend, Reynaldo Hahn, has great admiration for her husband, the lawyer Émile Straus,[3] and thinks he has 'la plus jolie prononciation qu'il ait jamais entendue'.[4] Proust confesses that he had not himself noticed this, but adds that this compliment from a singer will no doubt be welcome to a lawyer (VI, p. 14).

An amusing letter to M. Straus himself refers to a conversation the two men had about the correct pronunciation of *gu* in *Guise* and other words where it is followed by a front vowel. Proust cleverly works a number of relevant examples into the letter: 'Tout à l'heure quand vous m'avez cité l'exemple de *Guise* j'étais si fort intimidé par votre attitude qui semblait à tout le moins me menacer de la guillotine (et non gu-illotine) que je n'ai guère trouvé (et non gu-ère) à vous citer que Guiche'[5] (VI, p. 249).

---

[1] 'There is in this piece a proud quality through which your profile emerges and your accent can be heard.'

[2] 'How fond you are of this word *visage* ("face") which is so soft when you pronounce it, and which recovers at the end of the line . . . the softness of your pronunciation.'

[3] Émile Straus was actually her second husband. Mme. Straus, *née* Geneviève Halévy, and daughter of the composer Fromental Halévy, had previously been married to the composer Bizet who had died soon after the failure of *Carmen*; cf. Painter, op. cit., vol. I, p. 41 and *passim*.

[4] 'The most attractive pronunciation he has ever heard.'

[5] 'A few minutes ago, when you quoted to me the example of *Guise*, I

And he goes on in the same vein, citing a number of further examples. The little game is not without interest as it is symptomatic of the attitude of Proust and his circle—and of educated Frenchmen in general—to standards of correctness in language.

Proust was greatly intrigued by the effects of the disembodied human voice over the telephone and developed the theme at some length in a passage of *Le Côté de Guermantes* where the narrator speaks from Doncières to his grandmother in Paris and has a kind of premonition of her impending death.[1] The same theme is adumbrated in a letter from the end of 1904 to Mme Straus, following a telephone conversation in which her voice had sounded sad and tired and which had left him with a feeling of utter helplessness: 'cette voix qui évoque tout ce qui m'est le plus cher et le plus charmant, à portée de mon oreille mais émanant d'une femme que je ne peux ni voir, ni approcher, c'était vraiment trop Tantale, toutes les musiques d'Océanides de Paradis perdu que vous pouvez connaître ou imaginer'[2] (VI, pp. 18–20).

How sensitive Proust was to sound effects can be seen from a letter where he is referring to a preface he wrote to a book by Blanche: 'à cause des sonorités peu euphoniques, j'ai perpétuellement remplacé le mot être, par exister, ou des choses de ce genre'[3] (III, p. 152). Elsewhere he criticizes Boulenger for violating the rules of elision which he must have learnt at school.[4]

Even minute details of punctuation and spelling did not escape Proust's notice, such as for example the absence of quotation marks in a dialogue.[5] To Jacques Boulenger he writes: 'depuis

was so intimidated by your attitude, which seemed, to say the least, to threaten me with the *guillotine* (and not *gu-illotine*), that all I could think of quoting to you was *Guiche*.'

[1] *À la recherche du temps perdu*, vol. II, pp. 132ff.

[2] 'This voice which evokes all that is dearest and most charming to me, within reach of my ear but emanating from a woman whom I can neither see nor come close to, it was really too much like Tantalus, all the music of the Oceanids of Paradise lost that you can experience or imagine.'

[3] 'Because of the not very euphonious sound effects, I have constantly replaced the word *être* ("to be") by *exister* ("exist"), or other things of the same type.'   [4] III, p. 245.   [5] Ibid., p. 162.

huit jours, dès que je m'endors, je cherche l'orthographe que vous
donnez dans un de vos premiers livres au mot jockey'[1] (III, p.
208).

II. VOCABULARY

One of the most important and most persistent linguistic themes
in the writings of Proust is his interest in proper names.[2] The
development of this theme can be traced from *Les Plaisirs et les
jours*,[3] through *Jean Santeuil* and *Contre Sainte-Beuve*, to the
Temps perdu where it culminates in the famous 1.22 train to
Balbec, 'le beau train généreux . . . magnifiquement surchargé de
noms'.[4] In the cycle, proper names have become a major symbol

---

[1] 'For the last eight days, when going to sleep, I have been trying to
remember the way you spell the word *jockey* in one of your earliest books.'

[2] On the Proustian cult of proper names, see e.g. J. Vendryes, 'Marcel
Proust et les noms propres', in *Choix d'études linguistiques et celtiques*,
Paris, 1953, pp. 80–88; J. Pommier, *La Mystique de Marcel Proust*, Paris,
1939; V. E. Graham, op. cit., pp. 32f. and *passim*, and his article, 'Proust's
Alchemy', *Modern Language Review*, lx (1965), pp. 197–206; R. Barthes,
'Proust et les noms', in *To Honor Roman Jakobson*, pp. 150–8.

[3] This was already noticed by Gide; see his essay, 'En relisant *les
Plaisirs et les Jours*', in M. Proust, *Lettres à André Gide*, Neuchâtel–Paris,
1949, Appendix II, p. 116. Cf. above, p. 105.

[4] 'The beautiful, generous train . . . magnificently overloaded with
names' (vol. I, pp. 385f.—*Du Côté de chez Swann*). It may be noted that
this section of the novel is entitled *Noms de pays: le nom* ('Country names:
the name'), and has its counterpart in section II of *À l'ombre des jeunes
filles en fleurs: Noms de pays: le pays* ('Country names: the country'). As
far back as May 1914, Proust had emphasized the structural relationship
between these two sections, in one of the first letters he wrote to Jacques
Rivière (*Marcel Proust et Jacques Rivière: Correspondance (1914–1922)*,
ed. P. Kolb, Paris, 1955, p. 4). As Professor Kolb points out in a footnote,
'on voit l'importance qu'avaient ces sous-titres, dans le plan primitif du
roman, pour en faire ressortir la symétrie structurale. Au chapitre de *Swann*
où le narrateur évoque ses rêves de voyages et de personnes, devaient faire
contraste les chapitres où il ferait la découverte de Balbec et de ces
personnes dans la réalité'. ('One can see the importance which these sub-
titles had in the original plan of the novel, in order to bring out its
structural symmetry. The chapter in *Swann* where the narrator evokes his
dreams about travel and people was to contrast with the chapters where he
would discover Balbec and these people in reality.')

of a fundamental Proustian notion: the tragic gap between imagination and reality. It is not surprising that such a central theme should have left some traces in his correspondence. In a letter to M. Émile Straus, the evocative power of proper names is interlinked with another, even more fundamental theme, that of time and memory, and inspires a precise and elegant image taken from natural science: 'Il y a des noms que notre passé a fini par aimanter. Ils traînent après eux comme de la limaille de fer, mille souvenirs inséparables et attirés'[1] (VI, p. 252). In other passages, proper names evoke historical and literary associations. That of Mme de Noailles has a distinctly seventeenth-century aura (II, p. 44), whereas the syllables which make up the name Montesquiou 'pour toute oreille bien née ou toute imagination bien élevée, sont si riches de passé, de présent et d'avenir'[2] (I, p. 100). In the same letter Proust asks for the Count's permission to dedicate to him one of his short stories. The whole passage—like many others in the correspondence with Montesquiou—is rather artificial and has a hollow ring: 'Vous jugerez si cette voie n'est pas trop mal construite ou trop mal fréquentée pour inscrire au mur un nom si glorieux et si cher aux lettres. Ainsi souvent dans des rues obscures où les maisons n'ont pas de style et les carrefours pas de perspective, le passant rêve au nom lu à l'entrée'.[3]

There are also several references to the use of proper names in literature. Speaking of an article by Montesquiou, where real people appear under fictitious names, Proust writes: 'Le lecteur littéraire s'en tiendra aux noms que vous donnez et d'ailleurs

[1] 'There are names which have become magnetized by our past. They drag after them, like iron filings, a thousand memories which are inseparably attracted to them.' On images of time and memory in Proust, see chapter 5 of this book.

[2] 'For any well-born ear or any well-bred imagination, [the syllables of Montesquiou's name] are so full of past, present and future.'

[3] 'You will have to decide whether this road is not too badly built or too little frequented for inscribing on the wall such a glorious name so dear to literature. Thus it often happens that in obscure streets where the houses have no style and the cross-roads no perspective, the passer-by muses about the name read at the entrance.'

jamais les vrais noms ne seront aussi beaux. Qui s'est jamais appelé d'un plus beau nom que Beaufin de Saint-Lunaire!'[1] (I, p. 71). He congratulates Mme de Noailles on the very effective way in which she uses proper names in her poetry: 'Tous ces noms clairs font mourir et déjà on défaille à Palma, "point le plus doux des Baléares". Mais quand on arrive à *Sainte-Sarah, Saint-Alcibiade,* c'est presque trop fort. Vous n'avez employé que des mots lumineux et doux, "clairs comme un vase" '[2] (II, pp. 158f.) This letter is probably from 1906, and in the following year Proust published an article in *Le Figaro* on Mme de Noailles's volume, *Les Éblouissements,* in which he praised the same aspect of her style, in particular her skill in putting proper names 'à la place d'honneur du vers, à la rime, à la rime qui les fait chanter, accompagnés par la musique assortie de la rime voisine'.[3] At the same time, Proust is also aware of the danger of accumulating too many names in a literary text. He tells Montesquiou that in an article he wrote for *Le Figaro,* he would have liked to refer to a work by the Count but 'je n'ai pu arriver à trouver le joint, sans que cela eût l'air, surtout ajouté à la quantité de noms propres qu'il y a déjà dans l'article, d'une pure carte de visite'[4] (I, p. 184).

The magic of proper names is also touched upon in a letter to Louis Martin-Chauffier: 'par la logique naturelle après avoir affronté à la poésie du nom de lieu Balbec la banalité du pays

[1] 'The literary reader will stick to the names you have given, and anyway real names will never be as beautiful. Who has ever had a more beautiful name than Beaufin de Saint-Lunaire!'

[2] 'All these limpid names are unbearably beautiful, and one already feels faint when one reads about Palma, "the gentlest spot in the Balearic Islands". But when one comes to *Sainte-Sarah, Saint-Alcibiade,* it is almost too much for one. You have only used brilliant and soft words, "limpid like a vase".'

[3] 'At the place of honour in the line, in the rhyme, in the rhyme which makes them sing, to the accompaniment of the well-matched music of the neighbouring rhyme.' This article has been reprinted in *Chroniques* and also as an appendix to vol. II of the *Correspondance générale.*

[4] 'I did not manage to find a way without it giving the impression—especially when added to the large number of proper names already included in the article—of a mere visiting-card.'

Balbec, il me fallait procéder de même pour le nom de personne de Guermantes"[1] (III, pp. 305f.). In a letter to Boulenger, Proust comments on the name Martin-Chauffier itself, describing it as a 'nom boylesvien'[2] (III, p. 258).

Other comments are concerned with the psychological and social implications of proper names. 'Je sais que rien qu'un nom peut faire du mal comme il peut faire du bien',[3] Proust writes to Montesquiou, quoting some lines from Sully Prudhomme ('démodés, mais que je m'obstine à trouver délicieux')[4] in support (I, pp. 173f.). There is, he claims, a great deal of vanity associated with proper names: even with the wisest of men, those single-mindedly dedicated to the pursuit of truth, 'malgré tout, l'amour-propre, le vain bruit du nom propre, tiennent encore tant de place'[5] (I, p. 122). The mere mention of a name in a literary work may preserve the memory of an unimportant person for posterity, as in the case of some people cited by Montesquiou, albeit ironically, in the preface to his collection of poems, *Les Hortensias bleus*; as Proust puts it in an image worthy of Charlus: 'Je regrette seulement tel nom cité dans la préface qui, de par votre ironie, survivra, petit ver qui reste pris dans le piédestal de marbre, bestiole indigne pourtant de devenir fossile'[6] (I, p. 41).

Proust's interest in etymology, and more particularly in the derivation of proper names, which led to the long dissertations on these subjects by the vicar of Combray and Professor Brichot in the *Temps perdu*, is reflected in several letters. They show how seriously he took this side of his work. Only a few months before

---

[1] 'It was only natural and logical that, having confronted the poetry of the place-name Balbec with the banality of the actual Balbec country, I should do the same for the surname Guermantes.'

[2] 'A name worthy of Boylesve.'

[3] 'I know that a mere name can do harm just as it can do good.'

[4] 'Old-fashioned, but which I persist in finding delightful.'

[5] 'In spite of all, vanity, the vain noise of a proper name, still occupy such an important place.'

[6] 'I only regret that such and such a name mentioned in the preface will survive, thanks to your irony, a small worm caught in the marble pedestal, a tiny beast unworthy of becoming a fossil.'

his death, he wrote to Louis Martin-Chauffier: 'Soyez rassuré pour les terribles étymologies que je devais vous demander. Je m'en suis tiré tout seul de mon mieux, ou plutôt fort mal. On mettra ce qu'elles ont de fantaisiste ou d'erroné sur le compte de mes ignorants personnages. Il y a pourtant plus d'un an que je dois écrire à François de P...[1] pour lui demander celles des Guermantes et Cambremer'[2] (III, p. 304). A few years earlier, he had been in touch with some experts on place-names: 'J'avais demandé [un conseil pour les étymologies] à M. Dimier (que je ne connais d'ailleurs pas), lequel m'avait gentiment répondu en m'offrant de me mettre en rapport avec M. Longnon. Du reste, je ne manque pas de gens pouvant m'apprendre toutes les étymologies'[3] (III, p. 298). He also mentions such consultations elsewhere in the correspondence (III, pp. 266 and 279). A casual remark to Mme Straus is also symptomatic of his interest in these matters: 'le Manoir de la Cour brûlée (que j'aimerais savoir le sens de ce nom!)'[4] (VI, p. 205).

The correspondence abounds in remarks on various other aspects of vocabulary. It is perhaps worth pointing out that, in a letter to Mme Straus from 1908, there is a passing reference to Michel Bréal, the founder of modern semantics, whose book, *Essai de sémantique. Science des significations*, had appeared eleven years earlier and had been enthusiastically reviewed by

[1] The Marquis François de Pâris; cf. Painter, op. cit., vol. II, p. 357. On the etymology of the name *Guermantes*, see Graham, *The Imagery of Proust*, pp. 70 and 244f.

[2] 'You can set your mind at rest regarding the terrible etymologies which I was going to ask you about. I have managed on my own as best I could, or rather very badly. Whatever is fanciful or wrong in them will be attributed to my ignorant characters. And yet for more than a year I have been intending to write to François de P . . . to ask him about the etymology of Guermantes and Cambremer.'

[3] 'I had asked M. Dimier (whom I do not actually know) [for some advice about etymologies], and he kindly answered by offering to put me in touch with M. Longnon. Besides, there is no lack of people who could teach me all about etymologies.'

[4] 'The Manor of the Burnt Court (how I should like to know the meaning of this name!)'

Paul Valéry in the *Mercure de France*.[1] Proust mentions Bréal—
to whom his own family was indirectly related[2]—among a number
of illustrious scholars who have strong claims to be elected to the
Academy: Boutroux, Bergson, Maspéro, Alfred Croiset (VI, p. 100).

From the point of view of Proust's aesthetic theories, the most
significant discussion of lexical problems is that contained in the
second letter to Mme de Noailles about *Le Visage émerveillé*. In
this letter Proust makes several important statements on the
stylistic functions of words and raises some wider issues. What he
admires most in the volume is the unity of the style: 'tout y est
baigné dans une atmosphère enchantée où baigne déjà le premier
mot et qui enveloppe encore le dernier.' Everything is in its right
place and fits into the ensemble: 'il n'y a pas un ton à changer,
pas un mot qu'on ne (*sic*) pourrait retirer sans faire crier toute
cette vie et faire fuir aussitôt tous les reflets brisés, comme quand
on ferme une fenêtre dans un magasin au soleil, sur une place.'
Mme de Noailles, he suggests, has this in common with Molière
and La Fontaine that the outstanding feature of her art is not its
depth or any other particular quality, but rather 'une espèce de
fondu, d'unité transparente, où toutes les choses, perdant leur
premier aspect de choses, sont venues se ranger les unes à côté des
autres dans une espèce l'ordre, pénétrées de la même lumière,
vues les unes dans les autres, sans un seul mot qui reste en dehors,
qui soit resté réfractaire à cette assimilation... Je suppose que
c'est ce qu'on appelle le Vernis des Maîtres'[3] (II, pp. 86f.). On
reading this passage one is reminded, amongst other things, of the

---

[1] See F. Scarfe, *The Art of Paul Valéry*, London, 1954, pp. 56f.

[2] See Marcel Proust, *Correspondance avec sa mère*, ed. P. Kolb, Paris,
1953, p. 40, n.3.

[3] 'Everything in it is steeped in an enchanted atmosphere; the first word
is already steeped in it and the last is still enveloped in it... There is not
a single tone to change, not a word that could be removed without making
this whole living world cry out and immediately putting to flight all the
broken reflections, like closing a window in a shop in the sunshine, on a
square... A kind of blending, of transparent unity, where all objects,
having lost their primary appearance as objects, have lined up next to each
other in a kind of order, impregnated with the same light, seen reflected
in each other, without a single word remaining outside and resisting this

famous analysis of Bergotte's style in *À l'ombre des jeunes filles fleurs*.[1]

In another letter to the same correspondent we have one more example of that 'undeserved apotheosis' to which Mme de Noailles refers in the preface: 'il me semble que j'ai le désir et la vénération des choses quand vous les avez nommées, comme Dieu qui créa en nommant'[2] (II, p. 136). In the *Temps perdu*, this idea will be further developed when the narrator discusses the technique of 'metaphorical' transposition in Elstir's paintings.[3]

Proust's constant awareness of time and its workings was bound to arouse his interest in changes in the meanings of words. In *Jean Santeuil* there is already a character who is a mine of information on 'le sens qu'avait autrefois un mot, l'usage d'où ce mot dérivait, les raisons de fait pour lesquelles on ne pouvait croire que ce fût dans tel sens que l'eût entendu tel écrivain'[4] (p. 479). In *Du Côté de chez Swann*, the narrator's grandmother is equally fond of old furniture and of 'les vieilles manières de dire où nous voyons une métaphore, effacée, dans notre moderne langage, par l'usure de l'habitude. Or, justement, les romans champêtres de George Sand qu'elle me donnait pour ma fête, étaient pleins, ainsi qu'un mobilier ancien, d'expressions tombées en désuétude et redevenues imagées, comme on n'en trouve plus qu'à la campagne'[5] (I, p. 41). In the correspondence, several remarks

assimilation. . . I suppose this is what is known as the Varnish of the Masters.'

[1] *À la recherche du temps perdu*, vol. I, pp. 549ff.

[2] 'It seems to me that I desire and venerate things when you have named them, like God who created by naming.'

[3] Vol. I, p. 835 (*À l'ombre des jeunes filles en fleurs*).

[4] 'The sense which a word had in the past, the usage from which this word was derived, the factual reasons for not believing that a given writer meant it in such and such a sense.'

[5] 'The old forms of speech where we see metaphors obliterated, in our modern language, by the wear and tear of habit. Now, precisely, the rustic novels of George Sand which she gave me for my name-day, were, like old furniture, full of expressions which had fallen into disuse and had regained their metaphorical quality, such as one finds now only in the country.' Cf. above, p. 96.

on words and idioms are concerned with the usage of earlier periods or writers. Thus Proust ends a letter to Boulenger by assuring him: 'je suis à votre entière disposition pour Rivière, Martin-Chauffier, Boylesve, Bergson, tout l'univers comme on disait au dix-septième siècle'[1] (III, p. 251). In a letter to Souday he states: 'M. de Charlus . . . est une vieille Tante (je peux dire le mot puisqu'il est dans Balzac)'[2] (III, p. 76). In another letter to the same critic, Proust amuses himself by writing a pastiche of an article by Souday, which includes the following passage: 'Une moitié de la dernière colonne prend la défense des gens du monde que M. Proust fait parler d'une façon trop grossière, mais plus vivante, on l'avouera, que M. de Goncourt quand il fait dire au cimetière à l'aristocratique Mme de Varandeuil: "O Paris! fichue cochonne de grande ville qui n'as pas de terre pour tes morts sans le sou" '[3] (III, pp. 100f.).

There are also some interesting notes on contemporary changes in vocabulary. Some of these changes show the impact of the First World War on the French language. Writing to Mme Straus at the end of 1917, Proust points out—as Thucydides had done in the history of the Peloponnesian War—that words are apt to change their meaning in war-time: 'La vie change le sens des mots, enlève tout sens aux usages, et la Guerre autant que la vie'[4] (VI, pp. 188f.). As early in the war as April 1915, when commenting on a series of letters which Jacques-Émile Blanche had published in the *Revue de Paris*, Proust had pointed out a small but

---

[1] 'I am entirely at your disposal for Rivière, Martin–Chauffier, Boylesve, Bergson, the whole universe, as people used to say in the XVIIth century.'

[2] 'M. de Charlus . . . is an old Aunt (I may use the word since it occurs in Balzac).' In popular French, *tante* can also mean 'homosexual' (*Petit Robert*).

[3] 'Half the last column is in defence of society people whom M. Proust makes speak in too coarse a way, but one which, it must be admitted, is more lifelike than M. de Goncourt when he makes the aristocratic Mme de Varandeuil say in the cemetery: "Oh Paris, you dirty swine of a big town who have no earth for your penniless dead." '

[4] 'Life changes the meaning of words, deprives customs of all sense—and war does so just as much as life.' Cf. above, p. 2.

significant anachronism: 'Dans la lettre du 14 août, vous dites que votre ami Cacan croit le 9 août qu'il relèvera de vos amis dans les *tranchées*. Il n'a été question de tranchées qu'après la bataille de la Marne, en septembre. Il se peut donc que ce soit prophétique... Mais alors pour une prophétie ce n'est pas assez appuyé.' And Proust goes on to discuss the implications of the mistake: 'Avec ou sans tranchées, les gens diront certainement que ce sont de fausses lettres, écrites après coup... Or "tranchées" leur fournira un argument merveilleux, tranchées laissera "passer le bout de l'oreille". Mais même si le genre épistolaire était ici un simple artifice de composition (et fort légitime), alors il serait encore plus nécessaire de supprimer tranchées, de respecter, dans une œuvre toute littéraire et composée, la vérité de l'époque, ne pas faire tenir à un Français d'avant la Marne le langage... d'un Français d'après'[1] (III, pp. 105f.). It would seem that Blanche was impressed by these arguments since he replaced *tranchées* by *fosses* when the letter was republished as part of a book.[2]

Elsewhere Proust complains about the banality and inadequacy of clichés. In a letter to Montesquiou, part of which has already

[1] 'In the letter of 14th August, you say that your friend Cacan thinks on 9th August that he will replace some of your friends in the *trenches*. There had been no question of trenches until after the battle of the Marne, in September. It may be a prophetic statement... But then, if it is a prophecy, it is not sufficiently emphasized... With or without *trenches*, people will certainly say that these letters are not genuine but were written after the event... Well, *trenches* will provide them with a marvellous argument, *trenches* will "show the cloven hoof". But even if the letter form were no more than an artifice of composition (and a very legitimate one), then it would be even more necessary to delete *trenches*, to respect, in an entirely literary and fictitious work, the truth of the period, not to make a Frenchman before the Marne speak the language ... of a Frenchman after that event.'

[2] See Kolb, *La Correspondance de Marcel Proust*, p. 101. The word *tranchée* itself is very old (Bloch–Wartburg date it from the XIIIth century); '*guerre de tranchées (opposé à* guerre de mouvement) s'est dit *spécialement* de la guerre de 1914–18, après la bataille de la Marne' ('*trench warfare* (as opposed to *war of movement*) was used to refer in particular to the war of 1914–18, after the battle of the Marne'—*Petit Robert*).

been quoted, he says: 'je dirais simplement "musicale" . . . si cet adjectif n'avait à la longue perdu son sens, pour avoir été appliqué à la voix banale de tant de prétendues Circés qui l'ont assurément "changé en bête" '[1] (I, p. 48). Writing to Mme de Noailles, he refers elliptically to a mutual acquaintance who delights in clichés, and Mme de Noailles provides a footnote which reminds one of certain manias of Dr Cottard: 'Marcel Proust évoque ici un jeune étranger dont la conversation, souvent agréable, glissait parfois vers la banalité; nous remarquions aussi chez lui une facilité auditive dans l'association des idées. Le mot "vent" amenait "vent alizé", le mot "décadence" "décadence des Romains" '[2] (II, p. 131).

In view of the extreme care shown by Proust in portraying his characters through their vocabulary and their favourite expressions, it is not surprising to find in the correspondence a number of observations on particular words. His sensitivity to lexical nuances is seen from a passage in a letter to Mme de Noailles; 'Je pense que c'est fait à peu près au moment des vers de la *Revue des Deux Mondes*, à cause du goût pour le mot *gosier*, pour le mot *évident* et d'autres signes encore, les tu et vous du printemps et encore bien d'autres choses, mais il se peut aussi qu'à une certaine distance de temps ce soient les mêmes choses qui vous aient donné envie des mêmes expressions'[3] (II, p. 146).

[1] 'I would simply say "musical" . . . if this adjective had not lost its sense in course of time because of being applied to the banal voice of so many alleged Circes who have certainly "turned it into a beast".'

[2] 'Marcel Proust is referring here to a young foreigner whose conversation, often agreeable, sometimes had a tendency towards banality; we also noticed in him a certain auditory facility in the association of ideas. The word *wind* would call forth *trade-wind*, the word *decline*, *decline of the Roman Empire*.'

[3] 'I think this must have been written approximately at the same time as the poems in the *Revue des Deux Mondes*, because of your fondness for the word *throat* (*gosier*), for the word *évident* and other signs as well, the *thou*-s and *you*-s of spring and many other things, but it is also possible that at a certain distance in time, the same things suggested to you the same expressions.'

He teases Montesquiou for saying *aubépin* instead of *aubépine*, 'par le même souci de décence que cette fleuriste dont Mme Straus disait: "Elle est si convenable qu'elle s'appelle Cambron"'[1] (I, p. 237). In a more serious passage, he admires Montesquiou's skill in throwing words into relief by placing them at the very end of a sentence: 'l'opposition qui se résume, à la fin de la période, par "l'aristocratie et l'industrie" qui se trouvent, l'un et l'autre mot, remplis et retentissants dans tous les sens que vous leur avez infusés'[2] (I, p. 203).

Some of the passages in which Proust objects to certain words and expressions show how strongly he felt on these matters: 'recevoir le livre avant sa "parution" comme on dit affreusement'[3] (III, p. 157); 'l'affreux et vulgaire mot "crasse"'[4] (III, p. 189). He warns Blanche: 'Il y a encore des mots dont je trouve que vous abusez: "hurler", "tocsin"'[5] (III, p. 116). In a letter to Sydney Schiff he cavils at this sentence in *Le Figaro*: 'avait donné un *thé* en l'honneur du shah de Perse et un *goûter* en l'honneur du prince de Grèce'.[6] Proust comments: 'J'ai inutilement rêvé à la différence qu'il y avait entre un thé et un goûter. Faut-il penser qu'il y a eu un petit four au thé . . ., ou qu'au goûter on ne peut pas avoir de thé?'[7] (III, p. 55). He is critical of certain adjectives:

[1] 'Because of the same concern for decency as the florist of whom Mme Straus used to say: "She is so proper that she is called Cambron"'— an oblique reference to General Cambronne who is associated with a well known taboo word. Cf. a similar pun on the name *Cambremer* in *À la recherche du temps perdu*, vol. I, p. 341 (*Du Côté de chez Swann*).

[2] 'The opposition which is summed up, at the end of the period, by *aristocracy and industry*, both of them filled and resonant with all the meanings you have instilled into them.'

[3] 'To receive the book before its publication (*parution*), as people say in horrible French.'

[4] 'The awful and vulgar word *crass*.'

[5] 'There are still words which I think you use too much: *roar* (*hurler*), *tocsin*.'

[6] 'Had given a *tea-party* in honour of the Shah of Persia and a *goûter* in honour of the Prince of Greece.'

[7] 'I have been musing in vain on the difference there is between a tea-party and a *goûter*. Is it perhaps that there were petits fours at the tea-party . . . or that one cannot have tea at a *goûter*?'

'Je n'aime pas beaucoup *sale typhoïde*'[1] (III, p. 110); 'je n'ai pas compris votre adjectif "*évitante*" '[2] (III, p. 24); on the other hand he notes that it is symptomatic of his relations with Montesquiou that 'je ne finis jamais une lettre à lui sans l'adjectif "respectueux" que je ne mettrais pas à quelqu'un ayant la même différence d'âge, mais que j'aurais connu plus tard, et non, comme lui, quand il venait chez mes parents'[3] (III, p. 254). His interest in idioms, which play such an important part in the linguistic portrait of Dr Cottard, is shown in this passage from a letter to Boulenger: 'je ne peux pas dire un mot sans que vous ayez l'épée toute prête (je tâche d'éviter les fausses locutions mettre en garde, etc.)'[4] (III, p. 248).

As can be seen from Proust's correspondence with Reynaldo Hahn, he occasionally amused himself by coining comic neologisms. There are a few examples of this in the letters under discussion: 'l'état de ma moribonderie'[5] (III, p. 239); 'il sera absent ces jours-ci, mais dans quelques jours re-libre'[6] (III, p. 246); 'Rivière partait le jour même en re-vacances'[7] (III, p. 264); 'j'aime les deux frères (pas charlusiennement!)'[8] (III, p. 262). He also compliments Montesquiou on having coined a new adjective: 'Peut-être je ferais mieux d'employer ici l'heureux adjectif, aux profondeurs mélancoliques et certaines, que vous avez élu français en l'appliquant à Mme Desbordes "doux-amer" '[9] (I, p. 10). Proust also likes another of the Count's inventions which sets his

---

[1] 'I do not care much for *foul typhoid*.'

[2] 'I did not understand your adjective *avoiding*.'

[3] 'I never finish a letter to him without the adjective *respectful* which I would not use when writing to someone with the same difference in age, but whom I had met later and not, like him, when he used to visit my parents.'

[4] 'I cannot say a word without our being at daggers drawn (I am trying to avoid wrong idioms such as *to put someone on his guard*, etc.).'

[5] 'My state of *moribundity*.'

[6] 'He will be away during the next few days, but will be free again in a few days' time.' [7] 'Rivière left that very day on a second holiday.'

[8] 'I love the two brothers (not in the Charlus way!).'

[9] 'Perhaps it would be better if I used here the happy adjective, with melancholy and unquestionable depths, which you have made French by applying it to Mme Desbordes: *bitter-sweet*.'

own verbal fancy in motion: 'Stullifère "est admirablement formé!" Mais *Albufère* [the Duc d'Albufera] n'est pas, croyez-le, un stullifère . . . il n'en est pas moins un sauvageon très fructifère'[1] (I, pp. 201f.).

In a letter to Mme Straus, Proust protests: 'je n'ai pas l'art du calembour'[2] (VI, p. 176); he also criticizes Bourget for the puns he made in the course of a speech (VI, p. 91), and is not very happy about book-titles based on word-play. Writing to Jacques-Émile Blanche about the proposed title *Impressions and réimpressions*, he points out: 'Le titre est spirituel et joli mais . . . je ne suis pas très partisan de ce genre de titre car sur une couverture, une allitération, une gracieuse plaisanterie fait comme ces photographies plaisantes où un monsieur a pour toujours une mine spirituelle qui eût pu être agréable, fugace'[3] (III, p. 122). Nevertheless he did not, in his correspondence, spurn this form of witticism which is one of the distinctive features of the style of Dr Cottard. Most of the puns are uninteresting, whether they bring together two homophones (*cœur* and *chœur*: II, p. 207) or two meanings of the same word (*grippe* in the sense of 'dislike' and of 'influenza': VI, p. 199). The cleverest example of word-play occurs in a letter to Montesquiou: 'je vous remercie de distinguer mon dessein et mon dessin dans ces pastiches'[4] (I, p. 210). There is also a witty pun on the name of Sydney Schiff: 'Je pensais à vous tout le temps et à force de dire Schiff, Schiff, ma plainte prenait un peu de celle de Tristan attendant la Nef'[5]

---

[1] '*Stulliferous* is "admirably formed"! But *Albufera* is not, believe me, *stulliferous* . . . he is none the less a very fructiferous seedling.'

[2] 'I do not possess the art of punning.'

[3] 'The title is nice and witty, but . . . I am not very much in favour of this kind of title, for, on the cover of a book, an alliteration, a graceful joke has the same effect as those funny photographs where a gentleman has for ever a witty look which, if fleeting, might have been agreeable.'

[4] 'I am grateful to you for distinguishing between my intention (*dessein*) and my design (*dessin*) in these pastiches.'

[5] 'I was thinking of you all the time, and, as I was saying Schiff, Schiff, my lament was a little like that of Tristan waiting for the ship.' (A pun on the German word for 'ship', *Schiff*).

(III, p. 26). A similar witticism involving a proper name, Mme de Guermantes's joke about *taquin* and *Tarquin* le Superbe, recurs, as already noted (see above, p. 135), in the correspondence.

III. GRAMMAR

The many observations Proust makes in the *Temps perdu* on the grammar of his characters and of the social sets to which they belong have their counterparts in various passages of the correspondence. In one of these, Proust analyses a syntactical peculiarity of Montesquiou's style with great precision and sensitivity as well as with a touch of malice. Speaking of the Count's admiration for certain sentences in d'Annunzio, he points out that 'vous aussi avez atteint, dans le rendu de certaines choses et de certaines pensées, une perfection qui déconcerte'.[1] He goes on to suggest that the characteristic form of Montesquiou's syntax is a kind of 'litany'. Such sentences 'donnent l'agrément au lecteur qu'elles ont dû vous donner à vous-même et qui n'a pas dû être mince. Car quelle réussite que ces chapelets de noms, et votre "spécialité" est surtout (c'est votre phrase type) quand le verbe est différent, les substantifs aussi, et que le tout est pourtant absolument symétrique dans l'extrême variété'[2] (I, p. 214). In another letter to Montesquiou, there is also a passing reference to 'ces belles et pathétiques énumérations où vous excellez'[3] (I, p. 231).

The pastiche of an article by Souday, which was mentioned above, contains a reference to Proust's own essay on the style of Flaubert and some searching comments on the syntax of tenses in

---

[1] 'You too have achieved, in the rendering of certain objects and certain thoughts, a disconcerting perfection.'

[2] 'Give the reader the same pleasure which you yourself must have derived from them and which cannot have been slight. What a success these strings of names are, and your main "speciality" (your typical sentence) is the contruction where the verbs are different, the nouns too, and yet the whole structure is perfectly symmetrical as well as being extremely varied.'

[3] 'Those beautiful and moving enumerations at which you excel.'

M

that writer. Proust starts with a quotation from Flaubert: 'Les modes, les temps des verbes, tout cela, ce sont des blagues, on peut écrire ce qu'on veut, du moment que c'est bien.'[1] Though Proust refuses to go as far as Flaubert, he points out: 'c'est précisément M. Proust qui a montré que Flaubert, en violant les lois de concordance, a produit ses plus beaux effets non de littérale correction, mais de vivante beauté grammaticale.'[2] He goes on to quote from memory this sentence from Flaubert: 'Ils habitaient maintenant en Bretagne un jardin et montaient tous les jours sur une colline d'où l'on *découvre* la mer.'[3] The unexpectedness of the present tense is here, Proust argues, of great expressive value: 'Comme le présent de l'indicatif quand on attendait l'impar-fait . . ., n'éclaire-t-il pas d'un rayon la pérennité de cette colline "d'où l'on découvre la mer" en contraste avec la fugitive existence de ceux qui la gravissaient? Montesquieu, La Fontaine, sont pleins de ces sauts brusques qui, grâce à l'inobservance d'une loi grammaticale, donnent au tour une variété délicieuse'[4] (III, pp. 99f.).

A letter to Mme de Noailles refers to a somewhat similar feature in her syntax. In the style of her novel, *La Domination*, Proust detects a possible influence of Barrès on the use of tenses: 'j'y vois quelque chose qui pourrait être barrésiste. Et si cela l'est, vous devriez ne pas vous y adonner, si au contraire cela est en vous et dicté par vous-même, n'y pas résister. C'est le brusque

---

[1] 'Moods and tenses of verbs, that's all bunkum, one can write what one likes as long as it is good.'

[2] 'It is precisely M. Proust who has shown that Flaubert, by violating the laws of the sequence of tenses, produced his finest effects, not of literal correctness but of living grammatical beauty.'

[3] 'They were now living in a garden in Brittany and every day they climbed on a hill from where one *can see* the sea.'

[4] 'How the Present Indicative, when one was expecting the Imperfect . . . illumines the perennial character of the hill "from where one can see the sea", contrasting it with the fleeting existence of those who climbed on it. Montesquieu, La Fontaine are full of these sudden changes which, through the non-observance of some grammatical law, give the construction a delightful variety.'

emploi du présent de l'indicatif, là où on met généralement l'imparfait et le parfait'[1] (II, p. 121). Mme de Noailles adds in a footnote: 'Je donnai raison à l'impeccable et scrupuleux raisonnement de Marcel Proust. Que de fois il fut un conseiller lucide!'[2]

Another passage in the pastiche of Souday discusses some aspects of negation in French. In his review of *Sodome et Gomorrhe II*, Souday had criticized Proust's comments on some words spoken by the lift-boy of the Balbec hotel: 'J'ai pas pour bien longtemps, disait le lift qui, poussant à l'extrême la règle édictée par Bélise d'éviter la récidive du *pas* avec le *ne*, se contentait toujours d'une seule négative.'[3] 'Bélise s'est gardée d'édicter une règle si fausse,' Souday had objected, 'et à Martine disant: *Ne servent pas de rien*, ce n'est pas le *ne* qu'elle déconseille:

> De 'pas' mis avec 'rien' tu fais la récidive,
> Et c'est, comme on t'a dit, trop d'une négative.'[4]

Proust first of all points out that he had stated that the lift-boy had gone beyond the 'Bélise rule'. He then makes some further points, three of which are interesting. Firstly, he feels that the rule had been badly formulated by Molière. 'L'analyse logique et la

[1] 'I can see something which may be due to the influence of Barrès. If so, you should not yield to it; if, however, it comes from you and is dictated by yourself, you should not resist it. It is the sudden use of the Present Indicative where one would generally put the Imperfect and the Perfect.'

[2] 'I agreed with Marcel Proust's flawless and scrupulous reasoning. How often he has been a lucid adviser!' On relations between Barrès and Mme de Noailles, see Painter, op. cit., vol. II, pp. 19f.

[3] '"I haven't got much time off", said the lift-boy who, carrying to extremes the rule laid down by Bélise for avoiding the redundant use of *pas* with *ne*, was always satisfied with a single negative' (*À la recherche du temps perdu*, vol. II, p. 793). Bélise is one of the characters in Molière's *Les Femmes savantes*.

[4] 'Bélise took care not to lay down such a wrong rule, and when Martine said: "Are of *no* use for *nothing*" ("*Ne* servent *pas* de *rien*"), it was not to the *ne* that she objected: "You are repeating yourself by putting *no* (*pas*) with *nothing* (*rien*); it is, as you have been told, one negative too many!"' (*Correspondance générale*, vol. III, p. 98, n.1).

grammaticale voudraient la révision entière, la refonte de ces deux vers incorrects. Ils ne sont pas moins merveilleux, et dans la verve de l'ensemble qui s'arrêterait à la gaucherie du tour? Preuve qu'il ne faut pas être trop grammairien quand on juge.'[1] Secondly, he wonders whether *rien*, derived from the Latin *res*, is really negative here. Thirdly, he argues that 'le liftier du roman n'est pas plus fautif qu'Assuérus: "Que craignez-vous, Esther? Suis-je pas votre frère?" Et le dix-septième siècle parlait souvent ainsi "sans licence poétique". M. Benda, qui se pique d'en écrire, quand il lui plaît, la langue, imprime couramment, dans les articles de journaux: "A-t-on pas vu l'Europe?", etc. "Est-il pas étrange que?", etc.'[2] (III, pp. 98f.).

Another syntactic construction singled out for comment is the verbless sentence. In a letter to Jacques-Émile Blanche, Proust writes: 'Votre habitude excellente puisque personnelle et caractéristique, de faire perpétuellement des phrases sans verbe (ce que grammaticalement je ne conseillerais pas d'imiter mais que j'aime chez vous) vous induit plus que tout à cette tentation de notation pour la notation. C'est presque la forme grammaticale où la pure notation se loge naturellement (et à bon droit du reste puisque qui se borne à constater n'a que faire de verbes). Mais surtout cela abrège tant, qu'un détail insignifiant . . . que vous hésiteriez peut-être à rapporter dans une phrase plus construite vous semble acceptable sous cette forme rapide, comme ces objets peu nécessaires qu'on hésitait à mettre dans sa malle mais qu'on finit par

[1] 'Logical and grammatical analysis would require a complete revision, a recasting of these two inaccurate lines. They are wonderful all the same, and given the verve of the whole passage, who would pay attention to the clumsiness of the phrasing? It only goes to show that one should not be too much of a grammarian when one is passing judgment.'

[2] 'The lift-boy of the novel is no more incorrect than Assuérus [in Racine's *Esther*]: "What are you afraid of, Esther? Am I not your brother?" [instead of "*Ne* suis-je *pas*?"]. And people in the XVIIth century often spoke like that "without any poetic licence". M. Benda, who prides himself on writing in the language of that century when he feels like it, frequently prints in newspaper articles sentences like: "Has one not seen Europe?", etc. "Is it not strange that . . . ?", etc.'

emporter parce qu'ils ne tiennent pas grande place"[1] (III, p. 113). Elsewhere, Proust protests against the vogue of certain other elliptical constructions. He writes to Souday: 'je ne peux trouver les derniers "luxe" (puisqu'on emploie maintenant, même pour les livres, cette manière abrégée et barbare de parler qui fait dire un verre de champagne ou un pneu, et qui est plus offensante étendue aux choses littéraires)'[2] (III, p. 90). *Pneu* is also mentioned in a letter to Boulenger: 'm'envoyer ce qu'on appelle un "pneu" (hélas!)'[3] (III, p. 222). Elsewhere, Proust remarks briefly on a characteristic feature of the style of the same friend: 'j'ai compris que le côté brusque, le "Voyons", le "Bonne santé" était plus Jacques Boulenger, je veux dire plus une particularité de style, qu'une marque de sécheresse'[4] (III, p. 207).

In *Jean Santeuil*, Proust had already noted that the poetess Mme Gaspard de Réveillon, modelled on Mme de Noailles,[5] used adjectives in a striking way: 'le choix exquis et involontaire de ces

---

[1] 'Your habit, excellent because it is personal and characteristic, constantly to write sentences without a verb (a habit which I would not, from a grammatical point of view, recommend others to imitate, but which I like in your style), leads you more than anything into the temptation of notation for notation's sake. It is almost the grammatical form which pure notation naturally assumes (and with good reason for whoever wants merely to note things has no use for verbs). But above all, this abridges things to such an extent that an unimportant detail, . . . which you might hesitate to report in a more grammatical sentence, seems acceptable to you in this rapid form, like those not very necessary objects which one hesitates to put into one's trunk but which one takes in the end because they do not occupy much space.'

[2] 'I cannot find the latest *de luxe (editions)* [*luxe*, short for *éditions de luxe*] (since people use nowadays, even when talking of books, this abridged and barbarous way of speaking which makes us say a *glass of champagne* or a *pneu* [short for *pneumatique*], and which is more offensive when applied to literary matters).'

[3] 'To send me what, alas, is called a *pneu* ["express letter transmitted by pneumatic tube"].'

[4] 'I have come to realize that the abrupt side, the *Come now! (Voyons)*, the *Good health! (Bonne santé)*, were a typical Jacques Boulenger feature, that is to say a peculiarity of style, rather than a sign of dryness.'

[5] See Painter, op. cit., vol. I, p. 205.

adjectifs qui lui arrivent tous plus beaux les uns que les autres
tandis qu'elle parle, comme ces figures de cotillon qu'une personne
placée dans la coulisse passe au conducteur'[1] (pp. 525f.). It is
interesting to find him, in a letter from 1905, complimenting
Mme de Noailles on her choice of adjectives: 'Parfois c'était sur
un adjectif incroyable que je restais suspendu, comme "la place
favorisée"'[2] (II, p. 113). He also praises Montesquiou's skill in
placing an adjective in the position where it can play its part
most effectively (I, p. 33).

Proust's interest in language is so all-pervasive that even the
minutest grammatical details do not escape his notice. He blames
himself for aligning two 'genitives' in succession ('la publicité de
l'expression de cette ferveur':[3] I, p. 118), and criticizes another
writer for treating *chrysanthème* as a feminine noun (VI, p. 65).
He also remarks on the social register to which certain expressions
belong: 'Vous "ne doutez pas", comme disent les gens du
monde'[4] (I, p. 213); '*qu'il ait la bonté de faire vendre "au
mieux"* comme on dit en matière de Bourse'[5] (VI, p. 219). Well
versed as he is in the French classics, he is able to comment on
various aspects of their usage. He explains to Mme Straus that
the phrase *à la fin* does not have in Saint-Simon the same meaning
as today (VI, p. 229). Another point where syntax has changed
since the days of Saint-Simon is the use of *dont* where we should
now write *ce dont*. Referring to Mme de Noailles's statement:
'Un volume de vers qui ne ressemble pas à mes deux premiers,
dont je suis confuse',[6] Proust points out that this may mean one
of two things: 'Cela peut vouloir dire (c'est très Saint-Simon) que
vous êtes confuse que votre nouveau volume soit si dissemblable

[1] 'The exquisite and involuntary choice of these adjectives that come to
her, one more beautiful than the other, while she is speaking, like those
figures in a cotillon whom a person in the wings passes on to the leader.'

[2] 'At times I would linger over an incredible adjective like "the
favoured place".'   [3] 'The publicity *of* the expression *of* this fervour.'

[4] 'You *can have no doubt*, as society people would say.'

[5] 'Would he kindly sell *at best*, as people say when referring to the
Stock Exchange.'

[6] 'A volume of poems which is unlike my first two, *of which* I am
ashamed.'

des deux premiers. Dans ce cas les personnes qui écrivent moins bien diraient: "Ce dont je suis confuse".'[1] On the other hand the Countess may have meant to say—though Proust hopes she did not—that she was ashamed of her two previous volumes (II, p. 157). In another letter to Mme de Noailles, there is a brief reference to the language of Balzac: he never says 'admiration *pour* votre génie', but '*de* votre génie' (II, p. 89).

When drawing attention to specific mistakes, Proust sometimes apologizes for being so pedantic in matters of grammar. 'J'ai oublié de vous signaler,' he writes to Blanche, '(ce qui est du reste de ma part purisme un peu exagéré) un "en" qui n'est peut-être pas tout à fait correct'[2] (III, p. 126). Writing on another occasion to the same correspondent, he discusses at length the syntax of the noun *souvenir*, adding: 'surtout pardonnez-moi de faire ainsi le pion de sixième . . . Et je vous supplie de ne pas vous méprendre sur ma pensée quand je fais des objections à "souvenir", elles sont purement de grammaire, de logique, de symétrie, de clarté'[3] (III, p. 149). This does not, however, prevent him from going into minor details of phrasing, such as the ambiguity of a sentence (III, p. 106), the use of *lamenter* without a reflexive pronoun (III, p. 168), or a clumsy construction 'où deux "dont" se "commandent"'[4] (III, p. 121).

In a lighter vein, Proust repeatedly refers, in two letters to Schiff, to the passage from *vous* to *tu* in their relationship. Like Voltaire who had written a poem on "Les *Vous* et les *Tu*",[5] Proust is intrigued by the problem of *tutoiement*; pretending that he is

[1] 'It could mean (this is very much in the Saint-Simon manner) that you are ashamed because your new volume is so different from the first two. In that case, people who write less well would say: "*a fact of which* I am ashamed".'

[2] 'I forgot to point out to you (what is anyway a somewhat exaggerated kind of purism on my part) an *en* which is not perhaps entirely correct.'

[3] 'Above all, forgive me if I act as a first form master . . . And I implore you not to misunderstand me when I object to *souvenir*: the objections are purely grammatical and logical, related to symmetry and clarity.'

[4] 'Where two *whose*-s (*dont*) "govern" each other.'

[5] See L. Spitzer, *A Method of Interpreting Literature*, Northampton, Mass., 1949, ch. II: '*Explication de Texte* Applied to Voltaire'.

not sure of his ground, he combines the two forms of address: 'J'ose à peine vous (ou t') écrire . . . la diffusion de vos (ou tes) livres',[1] etc. (III, p. 48). He also notes some hesitation on this point in the letters of his friend, and reminds him of Mallarmé's lines:

J'ai souvent rêvé d'être, ô duchesse, l'Hébé
Qui vit sur *votre* tasse du baiser de *tes* lèvres[2]
(III, p. 54)

In a letter to Montesquiou, there is a brief reference to the social implications of *tutoiement*: a gaffe committed in society reminds Proust of a character in Molière 'qui tutoie en parlant ceux de plus haut parage'[3] (I, p. 142).

This chapter has been confined to only a small section of Proust's correspondence; yet even this limited sample has given some idea of the richness, diversity and intensity of his linguistic interests. His remarks, often important in themselves, gain in significance by being set against the wider background of his literary works. As Professor Cocking has pointed out, 'the proper appreciation of Proust's attitude to what he is putting before the reader depends not only on a minutely adjusted awareness of local style but on bringing to bear on particular instances impressions derived from the book as a whole, on the cross-reference of attitudes';[4] and this applies not only to the *Temps perdu* but to his life-work viewed as a unity. What emerges in this case from the complex and intricate system of cross-references is the extraordinary range and persistence of his linguistic interests. Some of these he shared with other educated Frenchmen or with the social circle in which he moved; other major themes, such as his ideas about metaphor and proper names, were deeply rooted in his

[1] 'I dare hardly write to *you* (or *thee*) . . . the diffusion of *your* (or *thy*) books.'

[2] 'Duchess, I have often dreamt about being another Hebe who lives on the kiss of *thy* lips on *your* cup.'

[3] 'Who says *thou* when speaking to persons of higher rank.'

[4] J. M. Cocking, *Proust*, p. 74.

philosophical and psychological theories; others again were intimately connected with his conception of style as an individual mode of vision. Proust's own vision was so completely novel and original that—to use a famous simile of his own[1]—it has the same effect on the reader as the trying on of new lenses: it may be painful at first until one becomes accustomed to it, and then one begins to see the world in an entirely different light. But since the style of a writer is the linguistic expression of his vision,[2] this meant that Proust had to bend the language, without violating it, to fresh and unusual tasks. The uniqueness of his vision, and of the idiom through which it is expressed, is one of the main reasons for his deep and abiding interest in what T. S. Eliot once called 'the intolerable wrestle with words and meanings'.[3]

[1] *À la recherche du temps perdu*, vol. II, p. 327 (*Le Côté de Guermantes*).

[2] See above, p. 128, n. 3. There is one passage in the correspondence which seemingly contradicts this conception and the organic unity of matter and manner which it implies. In a letter to Jacques-Émile Blanche, Proust says: 'J'ai . . . quelques éloges à ajouter sur votre forme dont je n'ai pas assez parlé. J'ai tellement pris l'habitude de distinguer chez un écrivain "le fond et la forme" ' ('I have . . . some praises to add concerning your form of which I have not said enough. I have so much acquired the habit of distinguishing between "form and substance" in a writer'—vol. III, pp. 139f.). J. Mouton comments on this passage: 'C'est ici simple politesse à l'égard de son correspondant dont il se reproche de n'avoir pas assez loué la "forme". En fait, toutes les idées de Proust sur le style écartent ce dédoublement qui, en tant que méthode d'analyse, aide souvent à une meilleure compréhension des textes, mais demeure absolument inintelligible au créateur' ('This is mere politeness towards his correspondent; he blames himself for not having sufficiently praised his "form". In actual fact, all of Proust's ideas on style rule out this dichotomy which, as a method of analysis, often helps us to a better understanding of the texts, but remains completely incomprehensible to the creative writer'—op. cit., p. 35). Cf. above, p. 92.   [3] See above, p. 48.